The New York Giants Base Ball Club

THE NEW YORK GIANTS BASE BALL CLUB

The Growth of a Team and a Sport, 1870 to 1900

by JAMES D. HARDY, JR.

McFarland & Company, Inc., Publishers
Jefferson, North Carolina, and London

The present work is a reprint of the library bound edition of The New York Giants Base Ball Club: The Growth of a Team and a Sport, 1870 to 1900, *first published in 1996 by McFarland.*

LIBRARY OF CONGRESS CATALOGUING-IN-PUBLICATION DATA

Hardy, James D. (James Daniel), 1934–
　　The New York Giants base ball club : the growth of a team and a sport, 1870 to 1900 / by James D. Hardy, Jr.
　　　　p.　cm.
　　Includes bibliographical references and index.

　　ISBN-13: 978-0-7864-2728-4
　　ISBN-10: 0-7864-2728-0 (softcover : 50# alk. paper) ∞

　　1. New York Giants (Baseball team)—History—19th century.
I. Title.
GV875.N42H37　　2006
796.357'09747'1—dc20　　　　　　　　　　　　　　　　96-23281

British Library cataloguing data are available

©1996 James D. Hardy, Jr. All rights reserved

No part of this book may be reproduced or transmitted in any form or by any means, electronic or mechanical, including photocopying or recording, or by any information storage and retrieval system, without permission in writing from the publisher.

Cover art: John Montgomery Ward from an Allen & Ginter baseball card, 1887 (Library of Congress)

Manufactured in the United States of America

McFarland & Company, Inc., Publishers
　Box 611, Jefferson, North Carolina 28640
　　www.mcfarlandpub.com

To my mother and Uncle George,
who passed down their love of baseball to me,
and to my wife,
who has lovingly put up with a lot of baseball

TABLE OF CONTENTS

Preface		1
CHAPTER ONE	The American Game	5
CHAPTER TWO	The New Base-Ball Club	35
CHAPTER THREE	The Building Years	48
CHAPTER FOUR	"We Are the People"	74
CHAPTER FIVE	The Brotherhood War	92
CHAPTER SIX	An Attempt to Recover	134
CHAPTER SEVEN	Andrew Freedman	154
CHAPTER EIGHT	The Baseball Trust	171
CHAPTER NINE	Under New Management	192
Notes		199
Index		235

Baseball is the very symbol, the outward and visible expression of the drive and push and rush and struggle of the raging, tearing, booming nineteenth century.
					MARK TWAIN

PREFACE

Baseball is no longer essential to the psychic life of the nation. It was once, from 1900 into the 1950s, but that was then and this is now. We are in the 1990s five decades from World War II, long enough to recognize and regret the present marginality of baseball, long enough to know that the former centrality of baseball will be forgotten if not recorded. It has also been long enough to know that ritual reassurances about the beauty or importance of baseball, whether in print or on film, are essentially elegiac. While this fact is the cause of profound regret to many, myself among them, it is still a fact.

The essential reason for the modern marginality of baseball is that the game no longer exemplifies the moral characteristics that we, as a people, use to define ourselves. Baseball has always been a game of character as much as talent. Virtues such as courage, resolve, steadfastness, work, a willingness to sacrifice for the team, and self-discipline were all advertised by baseball as required to play the game and were also held up as the proper virtues for all Americans. Baseball once reflected what we thought we ought to be. Character was once what we thought defined an American. But cultural self-definitions have changed and baseball has not. Entitlements are more the modern definition of an American, while resolve and steadfastness seem to have faded. Self-discipline gives way to understanding and forgiveness. Baseball lacks the cultural resonance it once had.

The sometime national pastime is also unfortunate in its style and pace. Baseball is an elegant and graceful game, with precise movement and a measured tempo. It is a subtle game, the only one where the defense has the ball. It places, above all, a premium upon order and efficiency. But it lacks the macho emphasis on sheer force and power that characterizes football, which is currently so popular. Baseball also does not feature, though it does not totally lack, the virtuoso athletic performances of exquisite balletic skill that are the heart of basketball and are so justly admired.

Further, as interest in baseball slowly wanes, baseball loses its most important function: its connection to personal time. With its volumes of statistics, its encyclopedias and its books of history, baseball preserves its past and, in that process, the past of the fans as well. The fan measures his life by, among other things, his connection to baseball. I have seen Mel Ott and Joe DiMaggio play, Willie Mays as a rookie, Sal Maglie throw at Carl Furillo, Warren Spahn and Robin Roberts pitch, and Ryne Sandberg play at Wrigley. I remember Larry Jansen, Big Jawn Mize, Whitey Lockman and Dave Koslo better than I do high school (and with a great deal more affection). I listened on the radio as Enos Slaughter scored the winning run from first in the 1946 World Series, and a year later I heard Cookie Lavagetto double off Bill Bevens, breaking up the no-hitter and winning the game. I remember Russ Hodges describe Bobby Thomson's home run in 1951. Lord, was baseball exciting!

Every fan has such memories of some team and some time, and they are signposts on the journey. Often the journey is even larger than life. I inherited my love for baseball from my mother and her brother, my Uncle George, both of whom learned baseball from their father. He took them to watch the Atlanta Crackers, taught them to keep score, and told them stories about seeing Ty Cobb as a busher. After moving to New York in the thirties, my mother rooted for the Giants, while Uncle George, who lived in Brooklyn, followed the Dodgers. I became a third-generation baseball fan, inheriting a past older than myself and extending close to the beginning of the game as the National Pastime. The historical dimension to baseball is personal, and the diminution of fandom, both in size and intensity, can only lead to a weakening of baseball as an American cultural benchmark.

However, there was a time…. This time, from Honus Wagner to Van Lingle Mungo, is sufficiently long ago that it has become the stuff of myth as well as history, both cultural and personal. This Edenic past is cherished as well as remembered. It is part of the personal history of some, the cultural myth of all, and is also an exemplum of the general golden age now long past but once unquestionably real. In those days the game was good and the players were great, the Black Sox and institutionalized racism notwithstanding. You could get into the game for a buck, less for the bleachers. The players lived near the park and were working stiffs like the rest of us. In New York, the players took the subway home after the game and discussed the game with the fans. The teams stayed put, so municipal memory merged with personal memory. Nostalgia is the faculty that invests the past with simplicity and virtue, and those who seek to debunk it only whisper in a vacuum. Nostalgia, after all, grows out of love.

In American baseball, unlike Greek myth, the golden age was not coexistent with the beginning of time. There was baseball before 1900, before the good years. There was baseball developing, before it had become part of what it meant to be an American. What was baseball like in those days, when veterans of the Civil War marched on July 4 and people remembered Andrew Jackson, slavery and the potato famine? In general, baseball in that Paleozoic era was much like baseball today. During the eighties there were major rule changes almost every year, but after 1890 only the pitcher's rubber (1893) and the infield fly rule (1895) changed the basic geometry of the game. The players wore knickers in the first National League game and they wear them now. Even labor and management issues and conduct were about the same. The reserve clause (1879 to 1975) and arguments about its legality were part of baseball rhetoric in the 1880s and the 1980s. There was a strike in 1890 as well as in 1994, and the issues, money and control of the game, were the same then and now. Only the numbers are different. Five thousand dollars a year was a good salary in 1890; five million dollars is a good one now. In 1890 players making ten times the average family income claimed they were wage slaves oppressed under the heel of capital; today players making 100 times the average family income are saying the same thing. In 1890 wealthy owners claimed the poor clubs were going broke, and today the same thing is heard. Both sides appealed to the public, went to court, held press conferences, told implausible and outrageous lies. The fans were disgusted and sportswriters called for less wrangling, less news from the owners, and more attention to the game itself. Only the numbers have changed.

So baseball has been remarkably stable. America has changed, from regarding baseball as a lower-class urban amusement, to seeing baseball as a reflection of the national character, to leaving the baseball ethos for a different self-image. But the game has remained almost unchanged. This resemblance to the past is what makes the voluminous baseball statistics so important; the current game can reasonably and validly be compared to yesterday. It is this stability embodied in statistics that gives baseball its temporal depth. Indeed, baseball may realistically be viewed as the only functioning remnant of Victorian America left to us. In a society obsessed with youth and afflicted with neophilia, the survival of baseball is remarkable. But nothing lasts forever, and baseball is no longer essential to the psychic life of the nation.

This book deals with the early years of baseball, before 1900, and a single team, the New York Giants. The Giants before McGraw were occasionally very good and frequently very fashionable. But they had not yet become the trademark team of the National League, the team that mastered the fundamentals and exemplified "inside baseball." Even when they were good, they were still outshone by Chicago, Boston and Baltimore. Yet the Giants were one of the premier franchises in the National League because New York was the premier city in the country. The National League was healthier when the Giants were good, and it was at its sickest when the Giants were at their worst. So this book is also about the city of New York as it grew from a large and essentially unmanageable Victorian city into a huge and essentially unmanageable modern metropolis. Much of the focus is on what made New York what it was: the immigration, the political machine, the failure of city services, the crime and corruption, the garish and exotic excitement of it all. New York was a gaudy goulash of religions and nationalities kept in marginal order by an Irish machine that governed outside of and often in opposition to the formal law. Babylon on the Hudson was what H. L. Mencken called New York, and the Giants were a part of that stupendous and theatrical city. Baseball did not evolve in isolation; it was part of the mix of urban as well as small-town America in the Gilded Age.

Part of the function of a preface is to acknowledge the help and encouragement received, and I have received a lot. The chairman of the Louisiana State University history department John L. Loos consistently supported this project. My colleague in the Honors College, Professor Gale H. Carrithers, Jr., has read the manuscript and has made valuable suggestions. The dean of the Honors College, Billy M. Seay, has encouraged me throughout the completion of this project, and has provided the clerical and editorial help needed. Arthur Schott, the eminent baseball historian from New Orleans, has graciously allowed me to use his extensive personal library on baseball history. Two honors students, Rebecca Powell Lartigue and her sister Karen Powell, have typed the book and helped with editorial suggestions. My teenage son, James J. Hardy, has been drafted to help with the index, and I am very grateful for his assistance and computer skills. And my wife put up with it all, a not-inconsiderable indulgence in view of the papers and books cluttering up our kitchen table. Now and then she would remark that it was time to finish this project, as, of course, it was. So this book has been finished, and, like all books, contains errors. For this sad fact I accept responsibility, only hoping that the errors are few and unimportant.

Chapter One

THE AMERICAN GAME

On April 8, 1889, New York welcomed a squad of baseball players who had just returned from a tour around the world. The festivities took traditional form: a Victorian champagne banquet at Delmonico's, complete with toasts and speeches. Ball players in full dress mingled with such luminaries as Mark Twain, Theodore Roosevelt, and Chauncey Depew and were introduced to the 250 guests in a manner befitting returning heroes. A local hero, John Montgomery Ward, shortstop for the world champion New York Giants, responded gravely to the applause of the assembled gentlemen. Abraham G. Mills, formerly president of the National League, delivered an address in which he stated that

> ...we all willingly pay tribute to one particular game, which our guests have succeeded in stamping as the National — the great American game of baseball.[1]

Great applause greeted this remark. His toast, while it lacked grandeur, had the ring and character of simple truth.[2]

The American stamp to the game depended on more than the development of the rules and customs of play, though by 1889 there were those who could remember a generation of baseball history.[3] The same and more might be said of other American sports, such as horse racing, boxing, or cheating Indians. Baseball's national character came from the extraordinary way the game fit into an America that was becoming increasingly industrialized, increasingly urban, increasingly immigrant, and increasingly in need of organized spectator diversions. Theater was one example; baseball was another.

Moreover, baseball reflected to an amazing degree the prevailing trends and notions of Gilded Age America. Baseball, as well as society at large, embraced the entrepreneurial ethic, used all kinds of schemes to restrict competition and reduce costs, and broke labor unions. Baseball drew the color line.[4] Baseball men also shared the Victorian's aversion to vice and liquor, along with his addiction to uplift.

Those in baseball generally mirrored the prevailing American types. Andrew Freedman, owner of the New York Giants during the nineties, was a corrupt Tammany politician, and Albert Spalding, owner of a sporting goods business and the Chicago White Stockings, was indistinguishable from any other rising Midwestern businessman. Chris von der Ahe, who owned a grocery, a huge beer garden, and the St. Louis Browns, was almost a caricature of an immigrant German saloon keeper. John Montgomery Ward, the Giants' shortstop, did as thousands of his contemporaries and chose the law as his path to place and eminence. Bill Sunday, an outfielder for the Chicago White Stockings, underwent an adult conversion to religion at the hands of mission people who ministered to the boozy. Hundreds of thousands of other Americans of his generation had the same experience, frequently more than once. There was no one in baseball who could not be found in quantity all over America. It tied the game to the nation.

I

> As every team was composed of drunks, they were evenly matched in this regard.[5]

That was certainly how most of the club owners, and much of the public, saw the players. The fans tended to view the players' drinking with indulgence and amusement and seldom criticized a player unless he was drunk on duty or too hung over to play. But the owners had a sterner ethic. They saw baseball as a business and their players in terms of capital investment. Owning their players' contracts, they made the short mental jump, natural in an age of contract labor and company towns, to assuming they owned the players' persons as well. The baseball magnates devoutly believed that sober men played better ball than drunks. Thus, the owners took a variety of measures to curb "the great elbow act."

The acknowledged leader in this line was Albert G. Spalding, the owner of the Chicago White Stockings. A former player himself, Spalding was perfect proof of the French proverb that the best gamekeepers are reformed poachers. Over and over he repeated the owners' official position:

> ...drunkenness ... is the most conspicuous evil connected with professional ball playing.... This trouble has proved to be not only destructive to the morale of every club ... in which it exists, but it is a powerful barrier to the financial success of the club....
>
> The hundreds of thousands of dollars invested as capital in base ball stock companies can no longer be placed in jeopardy by the continued trifling with this growing evil. Every base ball city in the land suffered from it ... and it undoubtedly bankrupted a third of the clubs which encountered failure last season.[6]

Spalding attempted to safeguard his capital investment by a variety of means. He exacted temperance pledges from his players, only to find them falling off the water wagon after a predictably brief and disagreeable experience with Puritan morality. Spalding also set detectives on his players, who were inevitably trailed into some low dive.[7] He supported the efforts of his manager, Adrian "Cap" Anson, to restrain the players' resort to Demon Rum. And Spalding preached, endlessly. His baseball Guides during the eighties were filled with lamentations about the wicked effect of booze. In 1889 Spalding uttered his direst warning yet:

> The two great obstacles in the way of success of the majority of professional ball players are wine and women. The saloon and the brothel are the evils of the base ball world at the present day.[8]

In spite of Spalding's best efforts, however, these "evils" continued to thrive.

Not all of the baseball magnates were as aroused as Spalding by the thought of players enjoying themselves. Neither the owner of the New York Giants, John B. Day, nor his manager, James Mutrie, felt that alcohol was the overriding evil of the game. Indeed, Day put a bar in the Polo Grounds in 1884, in open defiance of the league rule against booze in the ball park, and he even had waiters circulating through the stands taking orders. The Giants sold their fans all the popular liquors of the day, feeling that this service was essential to gracious living and a full enjoyment of the game.[9]

The Giants were not immune to the effects of incautious guzzling, of course. In 1883 outfielder Mike Dorgan had to be sent home, felled by heat and liquor. The effects of this combination were not lethal. Dorgan recovered, returned to the team, and played, more or less as a regular, through 1887.[10] In 1888 the problem seemed to have returned. The Giants opened the season in Washington, where they unexpectedly lost a game, and then dropped the home opener to Philadelphia, looking particularly inept while doing it. Gossip circulated to the effect that the Giants' bad performance was due to orgies and dissipation in Washington. Club management felt it necessary to issue a denial.[11] But the Giants did not start winning until mid-season, and the rumors continued:

> ...two of the New York players most relied upon had been out enjoying themselves in the lower part of the city last Tuesday evening long after hours. Manager Mutrie, when approached in the matter, denied any knowledge of the escapade and did not seem to be overanxious to get at the details.[12]

Mutrie further claimed that several of his players never touched strong drink, and most of those who did drank "...in such moderation that he could not say anything against it."[13] Finally, Mutrie announced that when it became necessary for the manager to sit up in the lobby all night to make certain the players were in bed, then he would send in his resignation. Mutrie evidently believed that if he trusted his men they would be worthy of that trust, a view common to advanced thinkers in penology.

In spite of Mutrie's theories, most of the New York players caroused and frequented brothels, sometimes in the grand manner. During the 1888 season a Giant player accompanied umpire "Honest John" Kelly, a professional gambler, and a saloon keeper on an epic toot in Detroit. They began at Kit Howards' house of horizontal refreshment, where they enjoyed themselves until a late hour. Their stay at Kit's ended on a sour note when Honest John Kelly assaulted one Emma Gordon, an inmate of the house, kicking her, punching her, and knocking out two of her teeth. The boys then went to Kit Fleming's, another house of ill repute, where their stay ended when they broke up the parlor furniture. They had better luck in their third brothel, where they remained until Honest John was arrested for assault and battery on Emma Gordon. His friends compromised the case out of court for $25, and Kelly was sobered up sufficiently to umpire the game that afternoon. There is no record as to whether or not the anonymous New York Giant was able to play.[14]

Although neither Spalding's preaching nor Mutrie's tolerance was able to end boozing, the problem seemed to diminish in importance in the magnates' minds after 1890. Slow recovery from the Players' League war of 1890 and the depression of the nineties turned attention from morality to profits. Moreover, the aggressive and abusive style of play developed by the Baltimore Orioles gave baseball reformers a new cause: the abolition of cheating, rowdyism, and "kicking" against the umpire's decisions. Finally, many players began to follow the advice of Harry Wright, who had organized the Cincinnati Red Stockings, baseball's first professional team, and who remained in the game as a manager until 1893. Stay in shape, Harry cautioned. Develop regular habits, eat well, avoid tobacco and whiskey. Treat baseball as a profession. Otherwise, Harry Wright warned, your career will be shorter than it should. It was sound advice from one of the game's leading figures.

The temperance movement in baseball was much wider than the common sense of Harry Wright, Mutrie's acceptance of reality, or Spalding's commercial Puritanism. There was also the church, and it had an impact on baseball, notably in the genuine Christian conversion that overcame Chicago outfielder Billy Sunday. Billy Sunday was born on a poor farm about a mile from Ames, Iowa. He had a rather modest boyhood, consisting mostly of poverty, isolation, and lots of hard, dull work. He survived it, however, and at twenty was the star of the Marshalltown, Iowa, baseball team. The most famous graduate of that institution was Cap Anson, the manager of the Chicago White Stockings (now Cubs), and the home folks bragged to him about their new star. Impressed, Anson signed Sunday for the Chicago team, and in 1883, Billy left Iowa for the first time and came to Chicago as a major league baseball player.[15]

Billy was joining the strongest team in baseball, and he was good enough to stick. Playing was less of a problem than adjusting to urban life, a spacious existence replete with saloons, sporting women, gambling, ethnic diversity, and the hard-drinking ball players whom Anson and Spalding tried to control. Eventually the contrast with rural mores became too much. One Sunday afternoon in 1886, Billy and a group of players were sitting on a curb after having left a saloon. A group across the street was singing the old country gospel hymns. Billy began to cry, and one of the gospel singers came over to the ball players.

> "We are going down to the Pacific Garden Mission. Won't you come down to the mission? I am sure you will enjoy it. You can hear drunkards tell how they have been saved and girls tell how they have been saved from the red light district." I arose and said to the boys: "I'm through. We've come to the parting of the ways," and I turned my back on them.[16]

This was a dramatic way to cure boozing, and it was normally only a temporary aberration. But Billy stayed converted. It did not affect his playing, for he remained in the National League, but it did change his life, permanently. Upon leaving baseball in 1891, Billy Sunday went into YMCA work.[17] After a tour in these religious sweatshops, Billy began to work as an evangelist, and by 1900 he had become the foremost itinerant Christian in America.

Few ball players of the Gilded Age were so ripe for conversion as was Billy Sunday. He was a rural, native-born Protestant brought up in a society where good and evil were sharply etched and irrevocable. The greatest cultural force in his life was a Biblical religion in which men were either saved or damned. Though morally rigorous, American rural religion of the last century was not exclusively predestinarian. Plenty of folks believed that a man determined his own salvation. He took his stand for the Lord, or he went to hell. That's what they taught Billy, and that is what he believed. He might go to the city, earn a huge salary, wear store-bought clothes, booze with the boys and fall into sin, but he never forgot his faith nor thought he was doing right. And in due course he was converted — not into something new, but into what he had always been.

Billy Sunday's hostility to booze, a central feature of his conversion, was certainly enhanced by his profession as a ball player. It was not merely that players drank whiskey; every small American town had its drunk or two. But ball players belonged to a social class popularly believed to be most susceptible to drunkenness and most in need of reform. In substantial numbers, the players of the Gilded Age were born into urban, immigrant, working class families. Protestant, small town, Americans like Billy Sunday, or Cap Anson, or Albert Spalding thought they knew what that meant. Since the fifties, native-born Americans had been accustomed to thinking of urban immigrants as low, ignorant, boozy rowdies, allergic to work and addicted to violence, totally under the heavy thumb of the priest or ward politician. Political cartoons, newspaper stories and journal articles reinforced this unflattering view of newer Americans. It also found expression in political parties, from the Know-Nothings before the war to the Populists in the nineties.[18] Many imagined that working class immigrant ball players were peculiarly addicted to the "unholy Trinity of Whiskey, Tobacco, and Loafing." They were liable to bribes by gamblers. They would honor their contracts only under threats of doom and ruin. A blacklist was needed to keep order and discipline among such unworthy charges. Both the owners and the general public were sure the players drank more, patronized more bawdy houses, squandered more, caroused more, and paid less attention to their wives and children than they would have if they had earned less. They were going to end up dead broke and dead drunk. Certainly Billy Sunday thought this was true. He ended his conversion story by recounting the fate of three of his teammates who had finished in the gutter.[19]

So hostile was the baseball establishment to the urban aspect of the game that the leading magnates made a serious and official attempt to expunge baseball's urban heritage from the record. In 1904 a "blue ribbon" committee began to collect evidence on the origins of baseball and in December, 1907, created the myth that it had been invented in 1839 by General Abner Doubleday in a cow pasture near Cooperstown, New York.[20] This bucolic image was reinforced in numerous ways. Pictures of kids playing baseball in a pasture became quite popular, and Spalding used one for the frontispiece of his memoirs. Men like Cap Anson, Billy Sunday, or Spalding himself, all born in the country, were presented to the public as the typical major league player, an untruth in almost every respect. Nicknames added to the rural flavor. Clyde "Pea Ridge" Day (Pea Ridge, Arkansas, where else?) was the champion hog caller of the majors and pitched ineffectively for three teams in the twenties. It was an amiable practice, designed to amuse urban readers and make the game seem more American. Urban living, with its ethnic diversity and reputation for sin and crime, seemed an improper birthplace for the National Game and its players.[21]

Urban living was not the only cause of the unorthodox and charming lifestyle that the public assumed the ball players enjoyed. It was equally important that large numbers of the players were Irish Roman Catholics. As Catholics, the players had presumably escaped the rigorous moralism and self-righteousness that characterized native Calvinism. To many an American Puritan, Catholicism, with its doctrines of forgiveness, seemed mighty soft on sin. Even worse than a foreign faith was being Irish. Before the influx of Italians, Greeks, and Slavs in the eighties, the Irish had been the focus of much of American nativism. With the Irish, drinking was considered an ethnic character deformity. If Germans were poor, the Irish were thought to be squalid; if the English were unemployed, the Irish were considered lazy. A few players, such as John Ward, Tim Keefe, Roger Connor, or James O'Rourke of the Giants, rose above these invidious stereotypes to the rank of hero and gentleman. Most players did not.

Like so many ethnic generalizations, the unflattering comments about Irish players bore no resemblance to the truth. But the urban character of baseball was certainly clear. Most of the Irish lived in the large cities, and baseball and theater were the outstanding popular entertainments of the late nineteenth century. Bear baiting, lynching, and setting stray dogs afire, the depraved amusements of rural America, were liable to draw police attention in New York or Boston. And, in any case, baseball — with its strong institutional and psychological ties to politics, the saloon and music hall — fit the urban life-style perfectly.

Many of the New York players came from cities at a time when most Americans did not. Some were from New York itself. Infielders John Troy, Tom Esterbrook and Frank Hankinson, and pitcher Mickey Welch were all native New Yorkers. Tim Keefe and Mike Slattery came from Boston, Mike Tiernan from Trenton, while several players, including James O'Rourke, Roger Conner, Pat Gillespie, and Mike Dorgan were born in Connecticut industrial towns. A few, of course, were from small farming communities. George "Piano Legs" Gore, an outfielder acquired from the Chicago White Stockings, was born in Saccarappa, Maine, and John M. Ward came from Bellefonte, Pennsylvania. At the time of the Civil War, neither place was a major industrial or urban center.

The Giants also boasted a substantial number of Irish players. By 1885 the Giant outfield consisted of O'Rourke, Dorgan, and Gillespie, and, when the latter two faded, they were replaced by Tiernan and Slattery. The team's best pitchers were Tim Keefe and Mickey Welch, while Roger Connor and John Ward were the stars of the infield. The Giants did not, however, acquire the player considered by Gilded Age kranks (fans) to be the quintessential Irishman, Michael Joseph "King" Kelly, until the very end of his career. Not only was Mike Kelly the leading catcher of his time, he was also an outfielder, an infielder, and now and then, a pitcher. An exceptionally intelligent player, King Kelly was a student of the game. He not only played it, he also improved it. He was one of the first outfielders to back up throws to second base. Through study and practice he became one of the best base runners in the National League, though he was by no means the fastest. He stole bases by guile and skill. To compensate for a relative lack of speed, Kelly invented the hook slide, whereby the fielder had only the runner's toe to tag. So adept did he become at base running that he wrote books about it and was immortalized in a popular song, "Slide, Kelly, Slide!," which was sung in music halls and shouted from the stands.[22] The King, always a spectacular player, obliged as often as he could.

Mike Kelly began playing sandlot baseball in Paterson, New Jersey, and by 1878, he entered the National League. In 1880, he was signed by the Chicago White Stockings and the glory years began. He played for five pennant winners in Chicago, and led the league in hitting in 1884 and 1886. In 1887 Kelly

Mike "King" Kelly: 1888. The idol of the sporting public in the '80s, though he lacked the formal social approval enjoyed by John Ward.

was sold to the Boston Red Stockings for the unheard of price of $10,000, an event that stunned the baseball world and caused newspaper editorials on the moral (?) and financial implications of the size of the deal. In Boston he promptly became a popular hero of the very first magnitude, rivaling even John L. Sullivan, then at the height of his fame. Little boys followed him through the streets. Men crowded around him in saloons to shake his hand. Fans hollered "Slide, Kelly, Slide!" whenever he got on base. During the off-season Kelly went on the music hall stage, where he was an enormous success. It was not that he could sing and dance, but he did have one vital talent: he loved people and he had the knack of making everyone around him feel happy.

Off the field Kelly was an immaculate dresser. He was expansive, generous, and cheerful. He liked to be around people, and he spent most of his time in music halls and saloons. He drank heavily and constantly, frequently to excess and often to stupor. But he was usually a happy drunk, and he had no enemies. He never refused anyone a loan and routinely bought drinks for the house. When he went to Boston in 1887 he received a $5000 annual salary, plus the proceeds of benefits organized for him. He spent it all, and much more, and was always in hock to the club. Even in his last days, when he was through as a major league player and his debts were much greater than his salary, the King never turned a friend away nor begrudged a stranger.

This generosity came more from the spirit than the purse. When Billy Sunday experienced his conversion to Christianity, Mike Kelly was the first teammate to offer him encouragement and support.[23] His ability to keep the faith was demonstrated most poignantly during the bitter Players' League dispute in 1890. Already over the hill and sadly in need of cash, the King was approached by Albert Spalding, owner of the Chicago team and head of the National League committee. Knowing Kelly's immense popularity, Spalding offered him a deal. Ten thousand dollars, right now, and a three-year contract for any figure the King might name. It was a fortune, more money than Mike had ever seen before.

> "Does it mean that I'm to join the League? Quit the Brotherhood? Go back on the boys?"
> "That's just what it means. It means that you go to Boston tonight."

But Mike Kelly stayed with the boys. He passed the money up. And it was his last chance. Age, booze, and the growing difficulties of staying in shape were terrifying reminders that the golden days were nearly over.

King Kelly's death in November, 1894, came suddenly, surprisingly. He took the boat from New York to Boston to join the London Gaiety Girls Theatrical Company in which he had a minor comedy part. While on the boat the King gave his dress suit as security for a man who boarded the ship without ticket or funds. It was his last public act. He caught pneumonia on the trip and died the next day.[24] The shock of his passing was followed immediately

John Montgomery Ward: 1888. As well as being a proper social role model for Victorian young men the elegant and fashionable Ward symbolized the social and artistic success of the Giants.

by his promotion to sainthood. His body lay in state in the Boston Elks Hall, and thousands of mourners passed by to do him homage.

Baseball was more than leisure entertainment for the urban Irish; it was also identification and advancement. By the Gilded Age the Irish were moving out of penury and the slums in substantial numbers. Baseball, like theater, police, church, or politics, was a form of social mobility. Baseball players were highly visible and became a source of social inspiration, a model for upward mobility.

John Montgomery Ward probably came as close as anyone to setting the proper example. Born in Bellefonte, Pennsylvania, he went to Pennsylvania State College in 1877. At the end of his freshman year, however, his guardian informed him that the money had run out. Ward left school and got a job as a pitcher on the Renovo, Pennsylvania, town team, largely as the result of his college reputation. That summer he pitched in such diverse spots as Renovo, Williamsport, Philadelphia, Buffalo, and Janesville, Wisconsin. The next year Ward pitched for Binghampton until the club collapsed and then was picked up by Providence in the National League. In 1879, he pitched Providence to the pennant, and in 1880 he threw a perfect game. When his arm faded he was sold to the Giants, where he was an infielder, outfielder, captain, manager, and the leading base stealer in the National League.[25]

Ward's activities off the diamond were as spectacular as his playing. He received a law degree from Columbia in 1885 and a prize for work in political science there the next year. In 1887, after a whirlwind courtship, he married the actress Helen Dauvray. He became the author of a book on how to play baseball.[26] In 1885 Ward founded the Brotherhood of Professional Base Ball Players, and tried by negotiation with the owners to reform such practices as blacklisting, indiscriminate fines, the reserve rule and selling contracts. The letters and articles he wrote on baseball law were models of clear prose and cogent argument and are still used in sports litigation.

When the baseball magnates refused to deal with his Brotherhood, Ward organized the rival Players' League in 1890 and went into competition with Organized Ball. The Players' League collapsed after a single season in a wallow of debts and default, and the players themselves drifted back to the National League and the American Association. It was Ward's greatest failure, but he recovered nicely to manage both Brooklyn and New York before retiring in 1894 to practice law. After leaving baseball Ward became one of America's leading amateur golfers, part owner of the Boston Braves, and one of New York's more important society lawyers. His clients included both sports and theatrical figures, among them a man he had played against, John McGraw. When Ward died suddenly during the winter of 1925, he had become a wealthy and respected man, a pillar of the New York establishment.

Ward was essentially a serious man, dignified, reserved, aloof, and somewhat aristocratic. Even when a player, his friends had been in the law, business, and the professions, or the more serious branches of the theater. He did not drink heavily or frequent saloons. He saved his money and invested it wisely. Nonetheless, this handsome, complex and fashionable man held the respect of his fellow players. Few understood him or were among his friends, but most trusted him, and they followed him in overwhelming numbers into the Players' League when he asked them to. In spite of his tastes and social position, he was unswervingly loyal to the player's cause. After the Brotherhood collapsed, the players followed his orders when he managed in Brooklyn and New York. When he retired after the 1894 season, the team was genuinely sorry to see him go.

Ward was immensely popular with the fans as well. He was removed as the Giants' captain on July 13, 1887, but the fans cheered louder than ever in his next game.[27] In 1888 Ward was a holdout asking for a substantial raise. When he finally signed and appeared in a New York uniform, the crowd cheered him and booed the others, even though the Giants lost the game and Ward himself made three damaging errors.[28] In 1890, when he moved to the Brooklyn club in the Players' League, many of the Giants' fans followed him. When he began to practice law he had as many fashionable clients as he could handle, many of them fans and friends from his baseball days. Ward had a career as notable and distinguished as that of King Kelly, or the Tammany politician, George Washington Plunkitt.[29]

II

> The only American on a certain block on the upper East Side is a tall, gaunt, bespectacled old man.... The block is occupied by Germans, Czechs, Hungarians and Italians and, barring the children, the old man is the only person who can speak English.
> The neighbors speak of him as the "Yankee gentleman," or "that American."
> As to the old man, he feels like a foreigner on the block.... he (was) a mere stranger who could not speak the language of the place.[30]

Was that how it was to be? Would the tide of immigrants grow so great that English itself would be lost in the large cities? Many a nervous native thought it might, and the agitation for restrictive immigration, which began as early as the Know-Nothings, became more focused after 1875 when the Supreme Court struck down existing state regulations on immigration. In 1882, Congress passed an immigration law, and exclusionary pressure, from that starting point, continued to build in fits and starts.[31] And the numbers seemed to confirm cause for alarm. Between 1850 and 1919, 23,492,630 people came to America, and 17,097,640 came through New York.[32] To the nativists, America seemed to have become a "nation of immigrants," though that term had not been coined.[33]

For the nativists, immigration was a national problem, because the nature of the nation was at stake. It was not merely the problem of New York and the smaller seaboard cities; everything American was at risk. Those frightened by the immigrants had several complementary definitions of the specific danger inherent in the newer Americans. For some it was race, as in Chinese Exclusion, or a "gentlemen's agreement" with Japan and whole phantasm of the "Yellow Peril." For others it was ethnicity; the peoples of southern and eastern Europe were inferior to the "Anglo-Saxon" stock that had originally composed America. In 1899 William Z. Ripley published *The Races of Europe*, which he divided into three groups in descending order of soundness: the Nordic from the north, Anglo-Saxons all, the Alpines from a central zone, and the Mediterranean from the south.[34] For Gilded Age racists, the current immigration consisted of the last two relatively degraded types, who would spoil American purity by a reversion to primitive genetic characteristics. Or again, religion was seen as crucial. A Protestant nation could not remain unchanged amidst an influx of Catholics and Jews. More, the political institutions of freedom were incompatible with the absolutist and degenerate political culture of southern and eastern Europe, which fit so naturally into the corrupt urban machines. Still more, the new immigrants depressed wages through the sweatshops and caused ruinous municipal expenditures because of their poverty. Wherever one turned the immigrants meant danger, especially since their numbers were so great. The nativists called for restriction.[35]

In a general way, nativist arguments fell into two contradictory categories. On the one hand, the immigrants were supposed to be a serious economic threat to American labor. They were willing to work for the lowest possible wages in sweatshops, unsafe factories, and in mines that were virtually a death sentence. The immigrant depressed wages, inhibited the growth of unions, and made safety inspection, even when on the books, a dead letter. The United States Industrial Commission *Reports* stated these social fears. But there was another hand. The immigrants were also considered to be ignorant, impoverished, alien, unused to the ways of representative government. It was argued they knew no English, had outlandish names and religions and customs, and in all of these ways were inferior social stock, which, one suspected, was also inferior breeding stock that bred like crazy. Nativists never explained how such inferior persons could present such ferocious economic competition, but never mind. Nativism, *au fond*, was not about logic or economics; it was about comfort and memory. The nativists were *unbehagen*; that is uneasy, uncomfortable, nervous about immigration, since the immigrants seemed so genuinely alien and so overwhelmingly numerous that they never could, perhaps would never have to, become "American." Older Americans were comfortable with the America they grew up with, and which they controlled. Nostalgia combined with anxiety to convince nativists that the immigrants were a cultural threat to all that older Americans thought of as good and homelike.

It was not necessary to be consumed by the phantoms and spectres of nativism to view the wave of immigrants as a force driving America toward immense social change. The United States Industrial Commission and the United States Immigration Commission documented the magnitude of change and reflected concern over its economic and social impact. Equally concerned about the magnitude of change involved in immigration, though sympathetic to the immigrant and interested in helping the new Americans make the adjustment, were people like Lilian Wald who founded settlement houses, the labor leader Joseph Barondess, and the newspaper editor and writer Abraham Cahan.[36] The men and women who administered immigrant aid societies and associations were all eager for the immigrants to succeed economically, learn English, fit into America, and they were anxious over the prospect and penalties of failure.[37] Less concerned over the changes that might come to America than over the change that must transform the individual immigrant in his journey toward Americanization, the immigrant leaders still, like the nativists, saw immigration in terms of change.

That change was chronicled in many ways, from police reports to social workers, but probably the best impression came from the press. The Gilded Age was the heyday of the daily paper, a time when adult literacy had become almost normal (at least in town) and when papers sold for less than a nickel. Most towns had one or two, while New York had eight morning and seven evening dailies, to say nothing of weeklies and foreign language journals. Competition was ferocious, and also underhanded, corrupt and devious as papers intrigued endlessly with municipal police and politicians for favors. The "news" reported was frequently a lie, occasionally invented *ex nihilo*, and sometimes "synthesized" with interesting and imaginative detail to give "verisimilitude to an otherwise bald and unconvincing narrative." H. L. Mencken's story of beat reporting around 1900 probably came close to the truth. He described reporters for the three major Baltimore dailies meeting in a saloon and making up the name and family details of a Polish worker killed in an industrial accident.

> "Why in hell ... should we walk our legs off trying to find out the name of a stevedore kicked overboard by a mule? ...The fact that another poor man has given his life to engorge the Interests is not news.... I move ... that the name of the deceased be Ignaz Karpinski, that the name of his widow be Marie, and his age was thirty-six ... and that he leaves eleven minor children.[38]

As it was said, so was it done.

Mencken also described the method he and Frank Kent of the *Sun* used to bring Walter Alexander, the vastly more experienced municipal reporter for the *American*, into an information pooling arrangement. Mencken and Kent simply invented municipal news, including some spectacular "whoppers," thus disturbing Alexander's editor, who thought his guy must be missing some of the dirt at City Hall. After all, any municipal corruption, no matter how implausible, could hardly be dismissed as false, and Alexander, who had been on the beat for a dozen years, should be getting the best stuff.[39] Such practices would not be tolerated today, I suppose.

Imaginative and inventive journalism extended beyond local events. It included the international sphere, as the Spanish-American War illustrated. Here the furious competition between the two sensational and scandalous "yellow" penny papers, the *New York Journal*, owned by William Randolph Hearst, and the *New York World*, owned by Joseph Pulitzer, reached its mendacious nadir. The *Journal* and the *World* went far beyond "synthesizing" the news, beyond making it up out of whole cloth, and entered the existential realm of creating the news and then lying about their creation. Hearst described this "New Journalism" with the slogan: "While others Talk, the *Journal* Acts." What he meant, of course, was that the *Journal* carried rumor, publicity stunt and invention beyond anything anyone had ever previously dreamed of or imagined.

The *ne plus ultra* of the new journalism came on February 12, 1898, when two *Journal* stars, the reporter Richard Harding Davis[40] and the artist Frederic Remington, turned in a smasheroo of a story. Davis, who believed in showing respect for women, was outraged at stories of women being brutalized. He dispatched a story about a Cuban woman aboard an American ship being strip-searched by Spanish officers. Remington contributed a delicate line drawing of a naked woman, seen from behind, standing before Spanish officers who were searching her clothing. Davis had not seen this, of course. He had heard about women being stripped and searched, but what he heard was considerably less spectacular than what he reported. And, indeed the story was not completely false. There were both women and Spanish officers in Cuba. When this got to New York, the *Journal* outdid itself. Huge headlines of patriotic and chivalric outrage proclaimed Davis's story, and Remington's picture was printed five columns wide. The *World*, not surprisingly scooped on this invention, interviewed the ship passengers when they got to Key West, found the *Journal* story not absolutely accurate in all details, and published an exposé claiming that its rival was (horrors) lying.[41] But the *Journal* was lucky. On the evening of February 15, the *Maine* blew up, and by the 17th the two yellow papers were putting out extras on the *Maine* complete with art work, and everyone forgot everything that had happened earlier.[42]

War correspondents and their editors at home were not the only ones addicted to the purple prose in wartime literature. There was purple poetry as well, and the newspapers published a lot of it. A favorite theme was the reunion of north and south under one battle flag, a view of the war which left recent immigrants out. The Baltimore *News* published one such effort, entitled "Chickamauga":

> They are camped on Chickamauga!
> Once again the white tents gleam
> On that field where vanished heroes
> Sleep the sleep that knows no dream.
> There are shadows all about them
> Of the ghostly troops today
> But they light the common campfire —
> Those who wore the blue and gray.⁴³

There were plenty of poems on the *Maine*, of course, and quite a few on Dewey and Manila Bay.

> O Dewey was the morning
> Upon the first of May;
> and Dewey was the Admiral
> Down in Manila Bay;
> And Dewey were the regent's eyes,
> Them orbs of Royal blue;
> And Dewey feel discouraged?
> I Dew not think we Dew.⁴⁴

There was a poem ("Exordium") by Theodore Dreiser, another by James Whitcomb Riley, one by Thomas Nelson Page and another by Michigan governor Hazen S. Pingree. There was even a poem on newspaper coverage of the war, "The Roarersville Bazoo":

> I want to tell you, people if you're hankerin after news
> Just git the Roarersville "Bazoo", and then that same peruse
> It ain't no yaller junnel, but it's strictly up-to-date
> An' when thar's statements to be made it starts right in to state
> An' war news! gosh all hemlocks! its a hummer you can bet!
> It's told of lots of battles which the same ain't fought as yet.⁴⁵

That about covered it.

The war was hard on the participants; war always is. But it was good for the press, good for the reporters, good for the Republican party, good for business and good for Teddy Roosevelt. The colonel published a book on the war so full of his own exploits that Mr. Dooley thought it should be entitled "Alone in Cuba." But Mr. Dooley was a cynical man, and a Democrat.⁴⁶ Most people thought Teddy was a genuine hero and a great American. And the war was also good for the immigrants. As confidence soared and business expanded there was more work. But there were also psychological benefits. Through the newspapers the immigrant could participate in the war fully, just like everyone else. Having an opinion on the *Maine* was part of being an American. Finally, a country that felt better about itself also felt better about its newest arrivals.

War coverage and yellow journalism were not the only genres of newspaper work on tap in the years around the turn of the new century. There was also a second kind of "new journalism" practiced mainly under the direction of Lincoln Steffens in the *New York Commercial Advertiser*. Steffens acquired the *Commercial Advertiser* in 1897 and quickly turned it into a journal of opinion, literature, and what would be called today with barbaric stodginess "indepth reporting."[47] One of the things Steffens did was to engage Abraham Cahan as a reporter. Cahan, who had been in America since 1882, was already the author of a novella, *Yekl* (1896), which had been a critical though not a commercial success. Cahan was set to reporting of the Jewish ghetto on the Lower East Side, and he responded with a series of memorable articles on various aspects of life in the ghetto. His articles reflected not a "new journalism," but an older form, the *feuilleton* of French literature and journalism of the previous generation. Cahan was the Jewish/American equivalent of Balzac or the later prose-poems of Charles Baudelaire.[48] All wrote about small slices of life and character, cut from the whole garment of the city, and presented as interesting, or typical, or odd, or amusing, or instructive. The writer of *feuilletons* sought to find the whole in the part, the macrocosm in the microcosm, a view of life given its most complete redaction in the *Confessions* of St. Augustine. Authors of *feuilletons* could not, of course, examine the entire city detail by detail, character by character or incident by incident. So the single glimpse must complement a more general description. And even the general description is only a part. Nicolai Gogol's *Nevsky Prospekt* could not, certainly, include the remarkable events encountered in *The Nose*.[49]

Cahan thus entered a genre of high journalism indeed, but one beautifully suited for his description of the ghetto, of Jewish customs and religion, and of immigration in general. So grand a story could not be reduced to an epitome of laws, regulations, government administration, or statistics, the *Reports* of the United States Immigration Commission notwithstanding. But the *feuilletons* could tell it, not only in part but also in tone and tint and memory. The themes of Cahan's *feuilletons* for the *Commercial Advertiser* were descriptions of the chasm between the old ways and the new, the efforts made by immigrants to adjust, and the pain and joy of the old religion, the old customs, the old rituals, the old priorities.

Among the new ways was an increasing concern with American politics, as opposed to those of Russia, Germany or Italy. The Spanish-American war provided a significant, and even exhilarating, topic of conversation in which immigrants could participate along with the native-born. Cahan described an immigrant claiming that the

> ...Americans are a lot of braggarts and bluffers, and that's all. They can fight the whole world — with their tongues.
> "Why do you live in America, then, if you don't like the country?" asked two voices in duet.
> "I didn't say I disliked America, did I?" ...The country is not the Yankee's property. He has no title deed for it. Columbus discovered it for all."

The final word in this cafe belonged, not to the intellectuals or the bilious, but to an enraged Italian grocer.

> Spanish people bad people. A Spaniard lived in the house, owed me $4, ran away, never paid me. All Spain bad.[50]

For the immigrants, the Spanish-American war was essentially the work of a moment. The work of a lifetime was adjustment. Although sheltered by ethnic ghettos, the immigrant struggled always to adjust to America, and that usually involved repudiation of much that was cherished of the old. Such was the reception that awaited the renowned rabbi Jacob Joseph, who came from Vilna to be chief rabbi of New York. At home he was a wonder of scholarship and interpretation; in America

> the learned Talmudist was satirized as a "greenhorn," "a back number," "a man who makes funny speeches."[51]

It was unsettling, disturbing, ultimately inexplicable, and it made the chief rabbi ill. In the end he became an invalid and a symbol of the problem of adjustment.

There were other symbols of adjustment, ones more economic, and the pushcart was foremost among them. Retail merchants of whatever nationality, and many manufacturers as well, started with the pushcart. It was the first step. From rag-picker or fish monger, one might hope for anything. But here, too, the specific vagaries of the new world required an adjustment. When threatened with a close election against the dreaded reformers in the person of the austere and honorable Seth Low, Tammany decided on unusual tactics. The police rounded up pushcart peddlers, charging them with blocking the streets and sidewalks. The "illustration method in politics" was designed to show the poor that they needed to vote and vote right, or constant arrest would become "the kind of life you will get if you vote them reformers into power."[52] Alas, Low won, but Tammany, down but never out, would come back.

The acculturation process went both ways, of course, with America learning from the immigrants. This happened often enough in the realms of cooking, language, and literature but only rarely in law. But sometimes the new world understood the old. A case came before Magistrate Olmstead of the Essex Market Court. It involved a chicken that the Jewish butcher said was *kosher* but the customer, Mary Bloom, swore was *treife* (unkosher). The butcher insisted on the magistrate rather than having a rabbi decide. Magistrate Olmstead looked carefully at the chicken and decided for Mary Bloom.

> "I have many cases of this kind," said his Honor. "This practice of substituting *treife* chickens for *kosher* ones must be stopped." "Long live America!" said Mary. "Even the Gentiles are fond of *kosher*. May his Honor be enrolled in the Book of Life!"[53]

One can hardly doubt that he was.

Cahan's interest extended to whatever was part of the Americanization of the immigrant, and this was reflected in his first novel *Yekl*, published with the assistance and recommendation of William Dean Howells in 1896. The novel opened with Yekl, not Jake, using sports to prove to his fellow sweatshop inmates that he was no greenhorn. Jake understood America, "you can betch" and he proved it with baseball: "Alla right ... But what will you say to baseball? All college boys and tony peoplesh play it."[54] Never mind that his cultural wisdom was delivered mainly in Yiddish; it was convincing to all who heard. After all, what was more American than baseball?

Seen from the distance of three or four generations, two world wars and the invention of television, striking ironies appear in the story of immigration in the Gilded Age. While the nativists were fearful that all America was being irrevocably changed (and diminished), one notices the irregular settlement pattern of immigrants in America. In the south, New Orleans became a city of immigrants and experienced the tensions standard in New York, Philadelphia or Chicago.[55] But most of the south remained a rural and smalltown society composed of those who had survived slavery and the war. Psychologically the south was paralyzed by race and frozen by nostalgia for the world of Colonel Sartoris and Diddie, Dumps and Tot. Economically impoverished, living among the weed-clad ruins of a former day, the south had little place for the energetic and future-oriented immigrants whose very lives and doctrine embodied change and improvement. And the immigrants themselves could find only a marginal place in a society that venerated the past, possessing deep cultural feelings by which the immigrant could not be moved.[56]

Even in the northeast and the middle border, immigration left as many counties untouched as transformed. Except for mining, it was the cities that were remade by Gilded Age immigration.[57] The urbanization of America and immigration are virtually the same thing, as migration from abroad equalled or exceeded in many cities migration from the countryside. During the years from 1870 to 1900, the center point of American population continued to move west through southern Indiana, an indication that the great out-migration from small town America had not yet begun.[58] Thus it was possible, in many parts of this vast republic, to live and work without really being aware of immigration, except in the abstract, without seeing a newer American except as an exotic oddity that came through on the train now and then. It was also possible to write and joke about an America where immigration was incidental. Willa Cather might not be able to, but Booth Tarkington and Josh Billings were, and they portrayed a genuine slice of Americana. Even the baseball anthem, "Casey at the Bat," had a small-town setting.

But the mining, industrial and commercial cities and counties were changing dramatically, both in size and culture. So rapidly were the cities changing that they had less and less in common with non-immigrant America.

The "Roarersville Bazoo" may have been recognizable to the reader of the *World* and the *Journal*, but not to those of the *Jewish Daily Forward* or even the *Commercial Advertiser*. Urban America felt this difference. Rural Americans after the war increasingly were thought of as rubes and hicks, fit purchasers of the Brooklyn Bridge. After all, the play is "Aaron Slick from Punkin Crick," not David Levinsky from Vilna. David might be green, but he was urban. The theatre reflected this growing cultural division in other ways as well. As Uncle Tom plays and minstrel shows continued as tank-town favorites, their place in cities was being taken by vaudeville, and, in the new century, kinescopes and moving pictures, mostly made in New York. Differences in dress, in slang, and food between city and small town complemented the divergence in theatre. Attitudes on social issues reinforced the growing sense of cultural difference, The Anti-Saloon League, the Women's Christian Temperance Union and revivals all enjoyed small-town support, but the city was skeptical. Elections reflected these cultural differences. In 1896 William Jennings Bryan set the south and the prairies aflame, if Vachel Lindsay can be believed, but the immigrant areas were cool. In New York, where the Democrat Bryan got plenty of votes, Tammany turned the troops out to save congressional, state and local candidates. A Tammany leader, asked about the coinage of silver, replied that Tammany favored more money, of all descriptions, for everyone. For the cynical Tammany Tigers, the silver crusade was crazy and Bryan was a rube.[59]

If the immigrant came to a country where his arrival was a major part of immense cultural change, the immigrants still felt that they were not fully American and that they must remedy this defect. Hyman Kaplan, the Jewish immigrant going to night school to become more American, is both funny and painful. He thought he knew who the real Americans, the average Americans, were. They were the small-town Yankee of the middle border or the New England states, whose humor was that of Josh Billings, who understood the immense resonance of the Uncle Tom's Cabin plays, and who were so expertly described by Booth Tarkington.

> His English is the United States language as spoken by the average citizen to be met on a day coach anywhere in the Central States. He is clean-shaven ... his apparel is neither new or old.[60]

Such an average American was a far cry from the new immigrant, the "greenhorn," and the immigrant strove to imitate it. There was no need for the outside culture to impress on the newcomer the desire to adapt. Americanism was internal. The newcomers wished ardently if sometimes despairingly, and always with the sadness of lost worlds, to become Americans, and that seemed to mean self-fashioning upon the Yankee or Hoosier model. The immigrant was a 100 percent American before that dreadful concept was articulated. No nativist critic viewed "foreignness" with more distress than did Yekl and even

Gitl. "Dot'sh a kin a man I am!" Yekl/Jake always said about his embrace of English and of American customs, and an entire immigrant generation followed his example. Those who looked back to the old country too much often went back. For those who stayed, they did not think about the ways they had changed America or might change her still. They thought instead about how they might change themselves.

As with so much else, Abraham Cahan caught the nuances of ongoing Americanization better than anyone else. In "Katie and Leah" from the *Commercial Advertiser* of December 30, 1899, Cahan described the pain and anguish of the transition:

> "Your mother was a Pious woman," said Leah. "I know her; she was a blessing in Israel.... To think of her daughter fixing up a Christmas tree like a Gentile!"
>
> ...Katie retorted with heat. "...all you say comes from being green in America, Leah. Wait till you have learned the ways of this country. It is not Russia. It's America, my dear," she added, with some venom.
>
> The other was shocked. "America? America? Is that reason enough why we should celebrate the Christian holidays and become Christians?"[61]

It was like that for everyone, of course. Jewish, Italian, Polish, it made no difference.[62] All made the same psychological journey, willingly or reluctantly. Even if one lived in a neighborhood where only the old language was heard, the children still went to school. And, anyway, the adults had to work, and no one wished to be a greenhorn forever.

Again, ironically, in their drift and eddy toward "Americanization," the immigrant intellectuals were well behind their people. Priests and rabbis encouraged the use of the old customs and the old language and the old forms of religion and culture. Journalists and writers ran newspapers and periodicals in Polish, Italian, Yiddish, and many another European language.[63] Immigrants were encouraged to send back to the old country for brides, or even to go in person. Joseph Gernsbacher, a Jewish immigrant to New Orleans, left shortly after the war for Germany, where he found a suitable bride and on October 23, 1867, married her in New York. It was all in a good cause, of course — the effort to preserve the community, the richness, the learning, the art, the language of the old culture. But it was also in vain, looking back instead of forward. The America of the Gilded Age was a powerful magnet, else few would have come, and the immigrants themselves preponderantly looked to the future not the past. Reb Sender might tell young David Levinsky that America was a place where "one become a Gentile."[64] Perhaps it was. Perhaps it was not. But it was a place where one became an American.

And baseball, like the theatre, was part of the process of becoming an American. The two differed in that the theatre was a more active field of the immigrant endeavor; the Marx brothers, George Burns, Rudolph Valentino,

Irving Berlin or Louis B. Mayer all illustrate that. Baseball was more passive. It was not something one did. It was, instead, something one learned about. This included the columns of the *Jewish Daily Forward*, which in 1909 carried a long article on baseball and included a diagram of the Polo Grounds.[65] To know something about baseball seemed to be a part of learning about America, about its mysterious and polyglot spirit. And, of course, when the "worthy editor" of the *Jewish Daily Forward* approved of baseball — not necessarily the game itself, mind you, but of knowing about the game — then it was clear to the entire community that baseball was important.[66]

And so the game that was so American became part of the immigrant's self-identification as an American. The spare, elegant game of line and angle and form transcended language and culture. It also transcended social milieu. The game that was so American grew and prospered in the most exotic and "foreign" cultural environment that America could offer: the large urban centers filled with recent immigrants. Largely the result of a convergence of circumstances, baseball thriving in large entertainment markets and immigrants settling where there was work and kin, baseball grew in an immigrant environment and came to be, for new generations arriving, a possible occupation and a path to identification with America. This was implicit in the years before FDR and became explicit with Joe DiMaggio. A player of incomparable elegance and grace and class and character, Joltin Joe DiMaggio made it much harder to maintain the vile but still common ethnic prejudices against Italians. Gian Carlo Menotti could not achieve the same effect; America does not care about opera. Lucky Luciano and Al Capone could not; Americans admire crime only in the abstract. But Americans knew the importance of baseball, and Joe DiMaggio became an authentic American hero. Yekl would have understood that.

III

There were psychological as well as social reasons for the success of baseball in Gilded Age America. Not the least of these was skill. Baseball was, and is, a game requiring exceptional physical abilities. This sharply separated the player from the fan. In this, baseball was not unlike the circus, also an entertainment favorite in the decades before the Great War. Moreover, baseball's peculiar combination of individual and team play gave the game an additional dimension of skill beyond the single player. Baseball was not a succession of unrelated virtuoso performances. A player could do well, performing brilliantly in an individual role, but the success of one player did not always lead to victory for the team. None of this was either rare or unusual. All of it happened every day. And the fans understood it completely.

These skills, both team and individual, were advancing. From the sixties into the eighties players got steadily better at their trade. Before the Civil War, any reasonable fit and agile young man could learn the game and catch on with one of the many teams in the New York area, where baseball was born. By the eighties this was impossible. Only a tiny fraction of the men playing ball, far less than a single percent, even obtained a trial with a major league team, much less made the team. The nation was full of hopeful young "phenoms," the stars of their town, college or company teams, who hoped for a shot at a major league job. But the odds against success increased yearly. Almost all of the kids were sent home. They were strong and willing, but they were just not good enough. In the entire country, only one or two men a decade possessed the extraordinary physical abilities and baseball skills of a King Kelly. And the marginal major league players, the ones who stayed only a couple of years, were themselves excellent athletes, far superior to the boys who starred for town or college teams.

The team skills improved just as dramatically. By the eighties newspaper stories abounded with descriptions of sacrifice bunts or hit-and-run plays. Sportswriters encouraged this trend, constantly urging the advantages of "team play" and praising the player who "sacrificed himself for his team." In 1888 a columnist wrote of the Giants:

> The desire for personal records is at last cast aside, and now any one of the players will sacrifice his chances to help along another player. That is the proper spirit and always walks hand in hand with a championship nine.[67]

And the press was right. It was the proper combination of individual and team skills that produced victory, and the most successful teams, such as the Chicago White Stockings, St. Louis Browns, the Baltimore Orioles, and the Boston Red Stockings, excelled in this difficult art. The others, envious of victory, struggled to copy and catch up. In time, they did.

The heightened levels of skill made the game more interesting and exciting, far more fun to watch. But there were levels of drama behind physical skill, whether team or individual. The player must compete with himself, and with time. A key to the game, both then and now, was character. It was not always the man with the greatest raw talent who became a star in the majors. It was also a question of discipline, of hard and continuous work. There was an enormous amount to learn about baseball, and it took years of dedicated, almost ruthless, determination to learn it. King Kelly, no matter how much of a bon vivant he was as a civilian, was a disciplined and dedicated player. He worked for years on his hook slide, which he had developed to compensate for his lack of speed. He practiced throwing at a second base until he had one of the most accurate arms in baseball. Learning baseball was a task that never ended.

On occasion, all of the practice and learning was summed up in a single moment. John Ward became a major leaguer in one play. In 1877 he was given a trial with the Philadelphia Athletics. The day he reported, he was put into the box.

> In the first inning there was a very high fly hit up to me.... I have since then seen baseballs do strange things, but I don't remember ever to have seen one make so many eccentric moves as that one. At one time it seemed to be falling ten feet to my right, and the next instant it had jumped ten feet to my left. I grew light-headed and faint. To make matters pleasanter, a couple of demons stood there, yelling in my ears. "Run hard! He'll never get it!" I realized my "nerve" could be judged by that catch. I made one last desperate effort to collect myself, the ball came within reach, I clutched at it, and it stuck fast in my hands. That gave me confidence....[68]

It also kept him on the team.

Superb skills and a steady nerve were enough to get a man to the majors, but it was not always enough to keep him there. A player needed luck, an appealing commodity in the superstitious environment of Gilded Age America. Injuries were the dreaded demons, and they were common. In 1891 John Sharrott, a promising young New York pitcher, broke his shoulder sliding into a base, and it ruined his career. Buck Ewing, one of the greatest of the New York players, developed a mysterious sore arm in 1890, and he was finished as a catcher. Larry Corcoran, who pitched Chicago to three pennants, developed a sore arm in 1884, and he was through for good. In the days before gloves everyone suffered from sore hands and broken fingers. It was a harsh era, simply described by George Ellard:

> We used no mattress on our hands,
> No cage upon our face,
> We stood right up and caught the ball,
> With courage and with grace.[69]

And perhaps, with a little bit of luck as well.

Desperate to avoid injuries and ailments, major league players clung to intense superstitions, trying to develop a kind of sympathetic magic to protect them. Many adopted black waifs as mascots, and kept them in change and root beer as long as the team and the player did well. Buck Ewing, the Giants' catcher, and Cap Anson of Chicago had this habit. The most extravagant instance of a major league mascot occurred between 1911 and 1914. A man names Charles Victory Faust came to John McGraw, the Giants' manager, and said that a fortune teller had predicted that the Giants would win the pennant if Faust were on the team. Faust was the worst player ever seen or heard of, but the superstitious McGraw kept him around for luck. And the Giants won. Faust was back in 1912 and the Giants won again. In 1913 it was the same thing. Charles Victory Faust warmed up before every game and the Giants won the pennant again. But the next year Charles Faust died before the spring training began and the Giants came in second.[70] Everyone in baseball knew why.

There was one demon that no superstition or magic could defeat. It was time. Year by year, as the fans watched and cheered, their favorites grew older, slower, less steady and less able to play. It was a continuing parable of mortality — for the older player whose career moved inexorably toward its end and for the fan watching the new men play and remembering when Cap Anson broke in and how Chicago won the pennant in '76. For the veteran, struggling to substitute guile and experience for the strength of youth, the battle was hopeless; there was always a new man to take his place, if not now, then soon. But that's how baseball was, how it must always be.

> There's always someone sitting on the bench, just itching to get in there in your place. Thinks he can do better. Wants your job in the worst way: back to the coal mines for you, pal!
> The pressure never lets up. Doesn't matter what you did yesterday. That's history. It's tomorrow that counts. So you worry all the time. It never ends. Lord, baseball is a worrying thing.[71]

IV

The organizational framework of major league baseball was still evolving in the early eighties.[72] The first permanent step had come with the formation of the National Association of Professional Base Ball Players on St. Patrick's Day in 1871 at Collier's Cafe, a saloon on Broadway at 13th Street in New York. The National Association was founded on the realistic assumption that all of the better players were professionals, whether they admitted it or not, whether they were paid under the table or openly, whether they played for "amateur" or professional teams. The founders of the National Association further assumed that it was better to proclaim publicly their professional status than to hide it and lie about it, a notion that college football has steadfastly refused to accept.

Beyond an open admission of professionalism, the National Association made little headway in dealing with the problems of baseball. Players were a rowdy and undisciplined lot. They frequently broke their contracts and moved from one team to another, sometimes in mid-season. This practice, known as revolving, tended to reduce public confidence in the honesty of the game. So did open betting on games by players, and conversations with gamblers followed by errors on the field could only sustain the suspicion that the fix was in. These evils were all well known and frequently criticized, but the National Association lacked the authority to stamp them out.

That authority came with the formation of the National League on February 2, 1876, at the Grand Central Hotel in New York. The new league was the invention of William A. Hulbert, owner of the Chicago franchise in the National Association. The league was formed primarily because Hulbert signed (revolved) four players from the champion Boston team and Cap Anson from Philadelphia, and he was afraid that the rest of the Association would vote to bar his five new players from competition. So he moved to forestall this by setting up his own league, and he persuaded seven other club owners to go along with him. Yet this sleazy beginning produced a new day for baseball.

Hulbert's basic idea was the sharp division between the "club" and the "team." The club was to be a business like any other. There were shareholders who bought stock and were responsible for the club's operation and solvency. They met the expenses of playing. They paid for the grounds, the costs of travel, and the salaries of the players. If gate receipts exceeded these costs, the owners kept the remainder as a profit. If the club lost money, as most did in the early years of the National League, then the owners paid the difference out of their own pockets.

On the other hand, the "team," that is, the players, became essentially employees of the club. They signed a contract with the club agreeing to play for a season at a specified salary. In addition, the players agreed to refrain from excessive boozing, disorderly conduct, and dishonesty, and promised to stay in shape and follow their manager's orders. The arrangement was very precise and quite workable, and it was to be backed by the full power of the new league.

The full implications of the difference between the club and the team emerged with the establishment of the reserve rule on September 30, 1879. On that date the National League magnates passed a rule which bound the reserved player to his present club and which also bound the clubs in the league to refuse to sign players reserved by others. It was the most important addition to baseball law since the establishment of the National League itself. It decreased the freedom of players to sell their skills, and it substantially increased the authority of both the club and the league. The reserve clause was adopted for two reasons. It was designed to stabilize the personnel of the teams, thus increasing fan interest, and to reduce salaries, which had risen beyond the abilities of the clubs to pay. It succeeded in both objectives.

All of this meant that baseball developed a unique mixture of competition and monopoly. On one level it was all competition. The teams, playing on the field, fought to win. No quarter was given here, and the players used and abused the rules in every way they could. Two of the most famous and successful managers in baseball, Cap Anson of Chicago and Ned Hanlon of the Baltimore Orioles, demanded that their players bend the rules in a ceaseless search for victory. Club owners supported their managers in the press and league meetings and praised the brutal diamond competition as showing the proper American will to win. The clubs competed as well as the players. Club owners tried to find the best players they could, in part, of course, because bad teams drew enormous and unrelenting criticism from fans and the press. But the magnates were also caught up in the spirit of competition. Most of them believed that winning the pennant was a very important achievement, and not a few spent themselves into bankruptcy trying to do it.

On another level, however, baseball was all monopoly. The clubs, having gained control over their teams, were themselves bound by the rules of the league. Each club owner had to observe the reserve list, no matter how much he wanted a player on it. All player contracts must be approved by the league president. Clubs must fulfil their playing schedules, whether they were losing money or not. Each club received a territorial monopoly of its city, which no other club could invade. The clubs must use umpires from the list approved by the league. The rules of the league, not the whims and business decisions of the club owners, were the laws of baseball. Transgression of the league rules meant expulsion from the league. Moreover, it also meant expulsion from Organized Baseball, the agreement which tied all of the professional leagues into a national monopoly. The club owners either joined the monopoly and conformed to the rules, or were ruined.

Hulbert, a hard and autocratic man, made this system stick. In 1876 the New York and Philadelphia clubs refused to send their teams west for the last road trip of the season, alleging the excessive costs involved. Hulbert heaved them out of the league. The next year he barred four Louisville players from baseball for life when they were caught throwing games. He also enforced his decrees on "morality." No Sunday baseball, Hulbert said, and no sales of beer and whiskey on the grounds. The admission charge would be fifty cents.[73] Both Cincinnati and St. Louis opposed all three policies, and evaded them. Hulbert eased both clubs out of the league — St. Louis in 1877 and Cincinnati in 1880.

These displays of leadership, coupled with Hulbert's efforts at keeping the game honest, meant that the new system would succeed. Between 1876 and 1885 most of the clubs in the National League turned the corner from red ink to black, and Organized Baseball moved from an idea into reality. Baseball had become the prototype that professional sports have followed ever since.

V

In December of 1882, the National League magnates, meeting in plenary session, decided that the league needed to be strengthened. Several of the clubs had lost money the previous season, and they looked like they were going to do it again. The worst offenders were Troy and Worcester, which had finished seventh and eighth in the pennant race.[74] Even worse, a new major league, the American Association, had completed its first season and was clearly going to survive. The new league was a definite threat, particularly in economic terms. While the National League charged fifty cents, the Association demanded only a quarter. Moreover, the new Association sold beer and whiskey in the ball park and did not try to mix business with morality. To complete the somber prospects, the league president, William Hulbert, died in 1882, and the club owners needed a strong man to take his place.

The crisis was so severe that the magnates temporarily buried their animosities and jealousies. They elected Abraham G. Mills the league president, and he moved decisively to meet the problems. Like everyone else, Mills had been impressed with the success of the American Association, and he decided that peace with the new league was better than war. Mills wrote out the National Agreement, still the basic charter of Organized Baseball, in which the rival leagues agreed to respect each other's contracts and territories.[75] Mills also moved to strengthen the National League itself. In spite of considerable opposition, Mills successfully sustained the fifty-cent admission and the ban on booze. Like Hulbert, he felt this was necessary if baseball were to become profitable and respectable. But some of the weaker franchises would have to go. Troy and Worcester were the immediate casualties. The Worcester club was moved to Philadelphia, and Troy lost its franchise to New York.[76]

The Troy club was purchased by the Metropolitan Exhibition Company, which consisted primarily of John B. Day and his brother-in-law, Joseph Gordon. Day was a cigar manufacturer and a Tammany politician in good standing, which was essential for success in this type of business. The company had two teams. Gordon placed the independent Metropolitans in the American Association, and Day put the Giants, or New-Yorks as they were first called, in the National League.

Day had gotten a weak team when he purchased Troy. The club had entered the National League in 1879, but it never had a winning season. In 1879 Troy had been last. The team had struggled up to fourth in 1880, but had fallen back to seventh by 1882. The franchise had consistently lost money, which is always discouraging. But Day was hopeful. He knew he was going to do better. After all, this was New York.

The initial task facing the new management was to form a team. An old catcher, John Clapp, was hired as manager. Clapp had entered the National League in 1876 after four years in the National Association, and he had managed before. His last command, Cincinnati in 1880, had finished dead last.[77] The nucleus of the team had to be players inherited from Troy. Some of these were outstanding athletes, then at the start of their careers. A superb young catcher, William "Buck" Ewing was among them. He had entered the National League in 1880 and was just beginning to reach his prime, which was good enough to place him in the Baseball Hall of Fame.[78] Another Troy star who came to New York, and was also elected to the Hall of Fame, was the pitcher, Michael Welch.[79] "Smiling Mickey" was a small man with a constant grin, whose pitching career spanned the years of change from underhand to overhand throwing. He was effective both ways. Cheerful and uncomplicated,

Smiling Mickey charmed everyone he met. Long after his pitching career was over Mickey worked the gate at the Polo Grounds, where he greeted the regulars by name. He was an enormous consumer of beer, and was fond of saying: "Pure elixir of malt and hops, Beats all the drugs and all the drops."[80] Given the state of nineteenth-century medicine, only a hardened moralist could argue with that.

Ewing and Welch were joined by two other players from Troy. Roger Connor was a big, slugging first baseman who also broke into the game in 1880. He lasted eighteen years in the majors and was the home-run champion until Babe Ruth broke his record of 136. Like Buck Ewing and Smiling Mickey Welch, Connor became a great favorite of the New York fans and a member of the Hall of Fame.[81] The fourth Troy player to go to the Giants was Pat Gillespie, a journeyman outfielder who lasted eight years in the National League.[82]

Players whom Day and Gordon thought were good enough to keep but not good enough to play with the Giants were sent to the Metropolitans in the American Association. Once such a decision turned out to be a horrible blunder. Tim Keefe, a pitcher also elected to the Hall of Fame, had had a poor year in 1882, winning only 17 games while losing 26. So Day shunted him off to the Metropolitans, where he quickly became the best pitcher in the American Association.[83]

Day and Clapp added to the roster of Troy players by purchase. They obtained John "Dasher" Troy and John Montgomery Ward from Providence. Troy was an infielder of modest abilities, who became a bartender at the Polo Grounds after he was finished playing. Ward, however, was a star performer who was later elected to the Hall of Fame. He had pitched Providence to the pennant in 1879, but now it was obvious that his arm was about gone. The inexperienced Giants management might not notice this fact, and, even if they did, would be glad to acquire an established star to help draw the fans. Ward, who was no fool, realized that his pitching days were over and switched to the infield where he ultimately became a great star at shortstop.

Free agents rounded out the Giants' roster. Mike Dorgan, an outfielder who had been released by Detroit in 1881, was signed by New York. So were Ed Caskin and Frank Hankinson, infielders of such modest ability that they had been released by Troy. James "Tip" O'Neill was picked up from the amateur ranks as a reserve pitcher, and John Humphries, a left-handed catcher, came from Cornell University. Finally, the Giants purchased Grayson Pearce, a marginal outfielder, from Columbus in the American Association. Pearce was to be used only when no one else could play.[84] A dispassionate observer looking over this collection of players could only conclude that it was a mixed and generally uninspiring roster.

In baseball, in the spring, there are few dispassionate observers. Everyone is wildly optimistic. All the players are going to have a great year. Everything is going to turn out right. This fever is even worse with an expansion franchise, and with the Giants in 1883 it approached a state of delirium. The Giants engaged in a series of spring exhibition games as a warmup for the season, and they won most all of them. They beat Yale University, which was nice but not unexpected. The most glittering promises for the season appeared in the Giants' victory over the Metropolitans, New York's American Association club. The spring series began on April 13 before 5500 people, and the Giants won handily, 8 to 3.[85] The Giants continued to win, taking seven of the eight games played.[86] Expectations rose accordingly. Fans abandoned all reason and began to think that the Giants really were a good team. Sportswriters, not yet bred to cynicism, reflected this mood:

> The patrons of base-ball are elated over the New-York Club's chances of taking a good place in the race for the championship of the league. Since the opening of the season, this team has displayed very good form. The members are handling the bat in capital style and the game played in the field has fulfilled the expectations of its projectors.[87]

Could mortal man say more?

Chapter Two

THE NEW BASE-BALL CLUB

May 1, 1883. It was moving day again, when all oral and customary leases ended, and when much of the city moved. The civil justices were kept busy issuing warrants in dispossess proceedings, which gave tenants two hours to clear out. From early in the morning the crush of horse-drawn wagons clogged the streets, particularly in the narrow and crooked streets below Houston. On ordinary days New York had an ample supply of horse residue on the streets, but on May Day that amount was materially increased. The noise level rose as well. Multilingual shrieks of rage and regret mingled with the professional curses of the teamsters and the sobs of confused and frightened children. The authorities, of course, were helpless. No one could control the traffic nor stop the fights nor mitigate the abuse loaded on movers and beasts. It was chaos, leavened with angst and bellows and threats and despair, and a pungent potpourri of sweat and manure. Thank God it didn't rain. The papers reported no murders of consequence attending the annual ritual of agony and dislocation, one of the many penalties for being poor in the Gilded Age. But the more than 500 dispossess warrants issued were certainly one of the reasons "New-York continues to be the worst governed city in the republic."[1]

Meanwhile, far uptown from the reeking chaos of relocation, all the hopes of spring were put to the test. The New York Giants opened their first National League season amidst all the excitement and ceremony appropriate to so stupendous an event. Thousands of fans pushed far uptown to the Polo Grounds at 110th Street and 5th Avenue. Here Day had put up some wooden stands and had stretched a canvas fence, creating two playing fields, one for each of his teams. The game put a considerable strain on New York's public transportation. The Second, Third, and Sixth Avenue Elevated lines ran special trains, but the cars were still overcrowded. By four o'clock, when the game began, about 15,000 people had crowded into the Giants' half of the Polo Grounds, including some ladies who sat decorously in the grandstand out of the crush, and General U.S. Grant, already dying, and trying desperately to finish his memoirs to leave his family a legacy. So great was the mob that most simply milled around in foul territory and hardly saw the players, let alone the game. The Seventh Regiment Band played music, and a large amount of betting completed the sporting scene. New York was the favorite over Boston, 10 to 8.

When the game began the Giants hit first, and Buck Ewing was the opening batter of the opening inning in the first game. Alas, Buck struck out, but the next hitter, Roger Connor, tripled to right field. John Montgomery Ward followed with a sharp ground ball to the Boston shortstop, who booted it and Connor scored. Then Pat Gillespie got a hit and both he and Ward scored on Mike Dorgan's single. Three to nothing. The huge crowd cheered, and word of these stirring events was relayed to adjacent saloons, and the betting odds changed 3 to 1 on the Giants. The few who stuck with Boston in spite of the grim news were destined to lose their money. New York added a run in the second and two more in the third, and won the game easily, 7 to 5. The fans were delighted.

> As the last man was put out, the crowd began to pour cheer after cheer upon the victors. The Band played "See the Conquering Heroes Come," and, after no end of hand shaking, the New York men retired to their quarters among the leaders in the championship race.[2]

The only blot on an otherwise perfect day was New York's fielding. The Giants made six errors, which would be about average for the rest of the season. The shortstop, Dasher Troy, made five of them, and, as a result, all of Boston's runs were unearned. But, on May 1, no one worried about this. The boys had won, and it looked to John B. Day as if he were going to make money on his new team.

Opening Day has a magic that is not recaptured until the World Series, so the second game against Boston lacked the crowds, the band, the celebrities and the excitement of the first. Fewer than 3,000 fans came to the Polo Grounds to see if the Giants could do it again. They watched a superb game, with the Giants winning it, 3 to 2, on Ward's home run in the bottom of the ninth. Ward also pitched, demonstrating a necessary versatility in an era when teams carried about a dozen players.[3]

This gratifying, and somewhat unexpected victory was followed by another. The Giants beat Boston for the third time and swept the series. Again, the local boys won it in the bottom of the ninth. Ward pitched for the second straight day but not very well. Boston pounded him and the Giants made their usual quota of errors in the field. By the end of the third inning, Boston led, 5 to 1, but the Giants caught up and tied the score at nine runs apiece at the end of eight innings. In the last of the ninth John Clapp singled Ward home with the winning run "amid deafening applause."[4]

The attendance at the third game was recorded as 4,218, more than enough to fill the small wooden stands Day had erected. It was an exceptional turnout by the standards of the times, and even the Giants' attendance for the second game, a bit under 3,000, was well above average for the National League. The New York crowds caused surprise as well as pleasure. One paper commented:

> ...it was asserted last winter ... when the admission fee to the Polo Grounds was doubled, the attendance ... would fall off greatly. Such has not been the case so far this season....[5]

Of course, there would be days when only a few hundred patrons would straggle in to see the Giants, but the team usually drew exceptionally well. It amply justified Mills' decision to put a franchise in New York.

Three games, no matter how well played or well attended, do not set the tone for an entire season. For the Giants and their fans, the bubble burst the very next game. Providence came into the Polo Grounds, bringing their great pitcher, Charles "Old Hoss" Radbourne. In 1882, when he was just warming up, the Old Hoss had won 31 games. In 1883 he was going to win 49, about three years work for a modern super-star.[6] Radbourne had no trouble with the Giants. He was the winning pitcher as Providence pounded New York in the opening game of the series, 11 to 3. The next day it happened again. The local heroes could not hit Radbourne and the Old Hoss set them down, 3 to 1. Following their usual custom, the Giants gave the game away with eight errors. After a Sunday rest to observe the Sabbath, Radbourne won the last game of the series, 14 to 2.[7] After the game, the Providence manager, Harry Wright, who had been in professional baseball since the Cincinnati Red Stockings in 1869, said that he had a pretty strong team with an excellent chance to win the pennant.[8] No one in New York had any reason to doubt that, unless Radbourne's arm fell off.

After the Providence series the Giants departed on their first western swing. Even though the Giants had left town, New York was not bereft of novelty and excitement. On May 24, 1883 the Brooklyn Bridge was formally opened. The official orgies included President Arthur, the mayors of both cities, assorted dignitaries, designated orators, and a huge crowd of people. Beneath the canopy of flags, Abram S. Hewitt, the principal orator, read a long speech on the meaning of the Bridge. His themes were progress and unity. The bridge was a symbol of physical, economic and moral progress. America could now do what had previously been impossible, and New York could cleanse itself from the dank corruption of the Tweed era. Virtue, technology, and social organization had triumphed over graft and blind obstruction. The country was unified from coast to coast; the two cities had been brought together. The nation itself was symbolically reunited after the War by the Bridge.

> ...who can venture to predict the limits of our future wealth and glory? Beyond all the legends of oriental treasure, beyond all dreams of the Golden

Brooklyn Bridge 1894. Regarded by contemporaries as a wonder of the world and a moral symbol of national purpose, it became the foremost landmark of New York before the skyscrapers (collection of the New York Historical Society).

>   Age, will be the splendor, and majesty, and happiness of the free people dwelling upon this fair domain.[9]

The Bridge was simultaneously the "Eighth Wonder of the World," a roadway to wealth, and an act of moral regeneration.

The last was certainly not the least important to Hewitt. An industrialist, the son-in-law of Peter Cooper, and a supporter of labor unions, Abram Hewitt believed in a moral and prosperous America. He could not accept the notion that America was, either in politics or business, irredeemably corrupt. Out of evil, out of Tweed's reign, out of the influence-peddling and sub-standard materials that had plagued the Bridge's construction must come a new sign of hope and redemption. "And we know that all things work together for good to those that love God and to those who are called according to his purpose."[10] The words of St. Paul might be used here in a secular cause, but they well expressed the spirit of the occasion. Abram S. Hewitt believed them, and so did his audience. Few people contemplating the majesty of the Brooklyn Bridge could suppose that America was not once again on the right path.[11]

The right path, however, seemed to elude the Giants. If the Bridge meant hope and progress, then the Giants rapidly came to mean ineptitude and disappointment. They played very bad baseball on their western tour. The nadir came in Chicago, where the Giants got their first look at Cap Anson's National League champions. The strongest team in the league, both financially and professionally, the White Stockings had won the pennant for the past three years and were the general favorite to do so again. Chicago had some marvelous players, beginning with Anson himself, one of the best first-basemen to play the game. There was also the stupendous King Kelly and an excellent pitching staff, Larry Corcoran and Fred Goldsmith. Pitchers still threw with an underhand motion, and a two-man rotation was all that most teams used. Finally, the White Stockings were well managed. Anson ran a taut ship, expected plenty of hustle, and got the most out of his men.

Not only did Chicago have exceptional players, the team also played a more sophisticated game than did its rivals. Chicago routinely backed up throws to any base. The team used bunts and hit-and-run plays. The infielders played in approximately the modern positions instead of close to the base, which was then the style in most of the rest of baseball. Chicago also used the stolen base as a major offensive weapon. These improvements were not all widely copied throughout the National League; the hit-and-run play, for instance, was so little used that the Baltimore Orioles of the nineties could legitimately claim that they reinvented it. But the other innovations of the "Chicago game" were quickly absorbed into the pattern of baseball, and they transformed it completely.[12]

The fledgling Giants were out of their class against this potent bunch and promptly lost three straight games. Only in the first did they have much of a chance to win. Behind 8 to 3 at the end of seven innings, the Giants put on a rally and scored four runs in the eighth and ninth to fall only one run short. Other than that flurry Chicago won easily. Not even Smiling Mickey Welch could defeat the league champions.[13]

After dying in Chicago the Giants moved on to Buffalo and Cleveland, where New York defeats were interrupted only by rain. By the time the Giants returned to New York from their trip, they had lost eight games and had won just once. They had also slipped to seventh place in the league standings. It was a disappointment to the hopeful New York fans and press.

Once back in New York the Giants started to play better baseball to the intense relief of John B. Day. The Giants began their home stand by winning three out of four games from Detroit. One of these victories was particularly pleasing. John Ward, already a decided crowd favorite, beat Detroit, 4 to 1, and for a couple of hours he looked like the pitcher he once had been. The Giants also won the last game of the series, 13 to 7, though not without difficulty. The boys ran up a quick lead of 8 to 0, but then Detroit began to hit Welch hard. They scored three runs in the third inning and three more in the fourth. At this point New York captain Buck Ewing had had enough. Feeling that Smiling Mickey had lost his stuff, Ewing called Ward in from center field to see what he could do. Relief pitchers were almost unknown in 1883, and Ewing's move was applauded by kranks and press alike as an exceptional example of fine baseball judgment.[14]

Chicago followed Detroit into town, giving the New York kranks their first opportunity to see the famous champions. Almost 6,000 people turned out for the first game. They were rewarded with an incredible spectacle. The White Stockings used their best pitcher, Larry Corcoran, "...regarded as one of the foremost manipulators of the ball...." But Corcoran, good as he was, had a bad day, and his team had an even worse one. Chicago made the appalling total of 20 errors, give or take a couple, and lost the game to the resurgent Giants by the score of 22 to 7. Compared to the White Stockings that day, the Giants looked like a pretty good team. They made a mere 10 errors; Smiling Mickey pitched fairly well; and Buck Ewing hit two home runs, then a single game record.[15] The kranks went home happy. They may not have seen a good game, but they had seen a spectacular one.

The next day things returned to normal. Chicago played "...in its usual form...," clipping the Giants, 5 to 2. The New Yorks, however, surprised everyone by winning the next two games. The series finale was a replay of the opening game. New York won, 16 to 8, and the White Stockings made 15 errors. Larry Corcoran was again pounded hard. The weather added to the Chicago woes. A drizzling rain fell all afternoon, and even though there were about 2,000 fans at the park, the New York management was resigned to calling the game and giving everyone his half a buck back. But Cap Anson, who thought that the Giants were a pretty sad squad and did not want to miss a chance to beat them, insisted that the game be played. It was, and Chicago lost.[16] The champion White Stockings left New York having lost three of the four games played. It was a distant early warning that the White Stockings were not going to repeat.

Buffalo followed Chicago into the Polo Grounds, and the main attraction changed from the game to the umpire. As the Giants began to play in their "usual form," the disappointed kranks became convinced that the umpire was stealing the game.

> Mr. Decker, who was the umpire yesterday ... made several decisions that greatly incensed the spectators. He was loudly hissed during the greater part of the game. When the contest was completed, Decker started toward the dressing room, but before he reached the gate ... a considerable number of people had gathered directly in the path. A policeman evidently noticed the surly looks of the spectators, and ... succeeded in getting Decker safely in the dressing room before anyone could attack him.[17]

The Giants lost the game by the convincing margin of 11 to 4, and made their usual quota of errors in so doing. It is hard to see how Decker's decisions were any worse than the Giants' baseball.

But the fans were unwilling to accept that. No explanations of the difficulties of umpiring were really satisfactory. There was only one umpire, who had to make all the decisions and interpret hazy and confusing rules. No matter

"The Bleaching Boards." Probably the 1888 world series. Personal comfort seems to have taken a back seat to love of baseball. The informality of dress seen in the bleachers at Wrigley Field had not yet become part of baseball.

how capable or conscientious he was, he could not do it well all the time. There were always going to be plays that the fans could see better than he could. Every game would bring close calls where the umpire's decision could only be an intelligent guess. Whichever way those decisions went, they provoked the loud and abusive wrath of one of the teams. If the offended players were on the home team, berating the umpire could lead to a riot.

That impressed no one, from the league president to the players or the kranks on the "bleaching boards." Gilded Age America was a society with a rather high tolerance for violence. Gang wars were frequent in the urban centers; Baltimore, for instance, boasted of its nickname of "Mob Town." In New York, such massive municipal disturbances as the Dead Rabbit Riot of 1857 and the Draft Riot of 1863 were still remembered. Richard Croker, the Grand Sachem of Tammany Hall in the nineties, got his start in politics as the chief brawler of the Fourth Avenue Tunnel Gang during the fifties. The scale of disorder had declined somewhat since those balmy days, but not its ferocity. Life in urban slums was decidedly unsafe, as the under-manned police forces concentrated on protecting property and overlooked such youthful exuberance as stabbing and mugging, particularly when the victim was obscure.

This acceptance of violence was a characteristic of more fashionable classes as well, where it was called manliness. Middle class values dictated a sharp delineation between male and female roles, and masculinity included physical recreation, particularly when it had the added attraction of a touch of danger. Getting hurt, and "bearing it like a man," was a solid part of the male psychology of the late nineteenth century. Theodore Roosevelt symbolized this, as he did so many of the values of the Gilded Age. Although Teddy's addiction to the strenuous life was almost pathological, it was only an exaggeration of the common view. Sports were held in high esteem, particularly the more rugged ones, and it was during the eighties and nineties that the college football hero was born.

All of this carried over to the spectator role, as the enormous popularity of boxing indicated. It also applied to baseball. Proper fan conduct included vigorous rooting and occasional outbreaks of limited violence in loyal support of the "boys." The true, red-blooded American male could do no less. He was bound in honor and custom to view the umpire as a poltroon, who would, if not carefully watched, rob the boys of the victory that was rightfully theirs. These feelings were echoed in a popular song of the day:

> Mother, may I slug the umpire,
> May I slug him right away,
> So he cannot be here, mother
> When the clubs begin to play?
> Let me clasp his throat, dear mother,
> In a dear, delightful grip,
> With one hand, and with the other,
> Bat him several in the lip.[18]

These homicidal sentiments were not pure poetic fancy; umpires were frequently assaulted, as often by the players as by the kranks. The players bullied umpires because they knew the kranks approved of such conduct, and hoped it would increase their popularity and extend their careers. The owners accepted it because they knew the prospect of a brawl would increase kranks' loyalty and lure customers to the game.

And that is just the way it worked. Several thousand New Yorkers turned out for the next game, attracted to the Polo Grounds by such gaudy goings-on as a possible lynching. The fans were doubly disappointed. Decker was not lynched, or even seriously threatened, though he was booed freely enough. And the Giants lost again.[19] By the middle of June the Giants were mired firmly in seventh place. Only the wretched Phillies were beneath them. Newspaper comment on this was severe.

The New-York nine are not doing the work their friends expected of them and what in reality they ought to do considering the salaries the players receive.[20]

The judgments of doom and censure, although ultimately correct, were still a bit premature. The Giants were not dead yet. They began to revive by sweeping four games from the horrible Phillies and came into the Independence Day doubleheader with a modest winning streak. In the morning a crowd of about 3,000 fans saw Boston and the Giants play an exciting game. Tip O'Neill started for the Giants, but as was all too often the case, he didn't have it. In the third inning Mickey Welch came in from center field in relief. The Giants remained behind until the eighth inning. Then, down by four runs, they staged a seven run rally and won the game, 10 to 7. The afternoon affair was even better. Providence used Old Hoss Radbourne, who had already beaten the Giants five times. But the Giants won anyway. Smiling Mickey Welch pitched a two-hitter and won the game, 1 to 0. Eight thousand kranks, the largest crowd since opening day, cheered with joy.[21] And well they might. The Giants were moving up. They were now in fifth place. They had won six games in a row and were playing .500 baseball for the first time since the opening week of the season.

But that double victory on the fourth of July was the high point of the season for the Giants. Providence won the next day, 18 to 1, as the local boys made 19 errors and Tip O'Neill gave up 11 runs in the first inning. Thereafter, although the team had spurts of good baseball, the Giants never got back to .500. Injuries were part of the reason. Clapp was out with a broken finger, as was the third baseman, Frank Hankinson. Buck Ewing was frequently out with a swollen hand, an injury endemic to catchers in the days before mitts. Two of the regular outfielders, Pat Gillespie and Mike Dorgan, were sick; Dorgan, a victim of "heat and liquor," was in such bad shape that the club had to send him home. Clapp was forced to improvise a lineup. He used pitchers O'Neill and Welch in the outfield, and moved Ward from outfield to third base, although Ward was unfamiliar with infield play and made lots of errors. J. H. Humphries, the left-handed catcher from Cornell University, played while Ewing was hurt. Toward the end of the season the Giants were seldom playing their best lineup.[22]

Just as serious was the decline of the pitching staff. O'Neill had never won consistently, and during the last part of the season he could hardly win at all. Ward had just about lost his stuff. He won games now and then, but his arm hurt, and he could not be part of the regular rotation. This left it up to Welch. Smiling Mickey was one of the best pitchers in the league, but he could not do it all. He needed help, and it was to be a couple of years before he got it. Meanwhile, when Welch could not pitch, the Giants' chances of winning were mighty poor.

The Giants' slide toward the bottom of the league, which had been gentle while the boys played at home, accelerated rapidly on the road. The team started its second western trip on July 9th. New York fans and sportswriters feared the worst. One reporter commented that if the Giants

> ... win half the games in which they play they will accomplish much better results than many expect of them. An old baseball enthusiast predicted yesterday that they would meet an uninterrupted series of defeats.[23]

Things never got quite that bad, but they came close. After the Giants lost four games in Buffalo, the situation was deemed serious enough for John Day to drop his tobacco business and join his team. Everyone applauded the move in the hope that Day could get more out of the players than Clapp had. The custom of blaming the manager for the team's defeat was already well established.

If Day's presence inspired the players, it was probably only marginal. Ewing's return to the lineup helped more, but even that was not enough. When the Giants finally returned home after a month on the road, they had lost thirteen games and won only six, and dropped to sixth place in the league standings.[24] They had played terrible baseball. The team had made dozens of errors. When the pitching had been good, which was not often, the team could not hit. Tip O'Neill had pitched four games on the trip and had lost them all; in fact, he would win only one more game all year, against Philadelphia. It was a discouraged group of athletes that returned to New York for the final home stand of the season.

There would soon be equally bad news from the turnstiles. When the Giants started west, many New Yorkers still believed, against considerable evidence, that "...the nine would make a good fight for the championship."[25] No one was so foolish as to think that now, and fan interest decline sharply. Attendance at the Polo Grounds began to fall off, and there were few games in August and September that drew as many as 1,500 people. Moreover, the metropolitan newspapers started to skimp on their baseball coverage, and what there was emphasized the poor attendance and the sloppy play at the Polo Grounds.[26] Day was discovering that it was hard to love a loser.

Nonetheless, in spite of injuries, poor pitching, and general discouragement, the Giants played winning baseball toward the end of the season. But the boys could not get out of sixth place. They widened the gap over seventh place Detroit, but they failed to gain on Buffalo in fifth. When the season ended on September 30, with a victory over Detroit, the Giants were in sixth place with a record of 46 victories and 50 defeats. They were sixteen games behind first place Boston.[27]

It had been a disappointing season. In the spring, as the Giants defeated the Metropolitans and the fans listened to Day's propaganda, most people had assumed that the team was pretty good. The fans expected a contender, perhaps even a champion. They had neither. Now and then, when the Giants had a spurt, the fans were greatly encouraged, and renewed their hopes for a winner. Then, as the Giants fell back, the fans groaned and the press denounced the counterfeit heroes. Disillusionment is always difficult.

Although everyone had hoped for more, sixth place was about where the team belonged. The Giants were very spotty. The club had a few outstanding players — Buck Ewing, Roger Connor, John Ward, and Smiling Mickey Welch — but the rest were merely adequate. Some, like Clapp, Troy, Caskin, Humphries, and Pearce, were not even that good. Moreover, the Giants' pitching was thin. Ward had a sore arm, and only Mickey Welch was left as a major league pitcher. Just as serious was the team's fielding, which was genuinely bad. The Giants made far too many errors, and they lost the bulk of their games in the field.

These weaknesses showed up in the Giants' record. Although the team played nearly .500 baseball, it did so only by beating Philadelphia in twelve out of fourteen games. Against the rest of the league, the Giants did not do so well. The Giants were also particularly bad on the road, a weakness common to poor teams. Their two long western swings produced seven victories and twenty-one defeats, and the only reason the Giants did even that well is that several games were rained out. The home park, and Philadelphia, kept the Giants in the league.

In spite of his problems, John B. Day did have reasons for hope. He had the nucleus of a good team, and some of his best players were just entering their prime. Buck Ewing had his best year in 1883. He hit .303 and led the league in home runs with ten.[28] John Ward was slowly making the transition from pitching to the infield, which he would do brilliantly. Smiling Mickey Welch was also getting steadily better. His 27 victories were the most since his rookie year, and his record was a considerable improvement over the 14 and 16 mark of the previous season.[29] Finally, Roger Connor demonstrated again that he was an established major league star. He hit a robust .357, by far the leading average on the team.[30] For Connor, as well as for Ewing and Welch, 1883 had been his best year in baseball, and no one doubted that they would all be even better the following season. Thus, all Day had to do was prune the bums, hire a better manager, and wait until 1884, when his team would paralyze the league and astound humanity by driving for the pennant.

Beyond this, the Giants had been a distinct psychological success. Baseball was popular in New York; it had been ever since the amateur days before the war. As early as 1858 thousands of people had traveled miles to the Fashion Race Course in deepest Queens and paid fifty cents to see a championship series between New York and Brooklyn.[31] Since Hulbert had kicked the Mutuals out of the National League in 1876 for refusing to complete the schedule, there had been no major league baseball in the big city. New York fans had felt the loss; they wanted to see Cap Anson and King Kelly, and they wanted a local team to root for. The Giants satisfied both demands and became quite popular. The better players were local heroes, and their pictures hung in the gaudier saloons. The new celebrities took to hanging out in Nick Engel's Home Plate Saloon, where they drank, swapped stories, and talked baseball with the fans. Almost overnight the Giants became an accepted and important part of the local scene.

No one attained celebrity status faster than John Montgomery Ward. An adept and hustling ball player, he quickly became an immense favorite with the kranks and press:

> (Ward) is, at present, the finest general player in the country. His base-playing is fine, fielding perfect, batting good, and there is not a better base-runner in the country.[32]

The approval of his playing was quickly reinforced by Ward's suave and elegant manner. He began to go to the theatre. He entered Columbia law school. He made his personal friends among the stock-brokers, lawyers, and businessmen of New York. He was part of the process by which the Giants became fashionable.

The popularity of the players was tempered, of course, by the uncomfortable fact that they were losing ball games. However, all of the recriminations, excuses and analyses of defeat could have been avoided if Day had not made a couple of crucial mistakes before the season had even begun. Day wanted an experienced major league manager for his new team, so he shunted the manager of his independent Metropolitans, "Truthful James" Mutrie, off to his club in the American Association. Mutrie had been an infielder and manager for amateur and minor league teams in New England before coming to New York in 1878. He canvassed many of the wealthy men in town, trying to sell them on the idea of putting a team in the National League to replace the departed Mutuals. He promised them fame, fun, and profits. The New York moguls, however, had seen plenty of country boys come to the big city, hawking this and promoting that, and they were unconvinced by Mutrie's vision of baseball as a business. But Mutrie persisted, and eventually he persuaded John B. Day to back the independent Metropolitans. They played exhibition games with National League teams, as well as with such squads as the Hop Bitters Nine, whose main function was to promote a peculiarly revolting patent medicine. By 1881, Mutrie's troops were the best independent team in the country, and they were also making money. In 1883 the Metropolitans went into the American Association as a sort of junior edition of the Giants. Mutrie remained as the Metropolitan manager.

By 1883 Mutrie had come a long way in the world. He was no longer a hayseed immigrant to the big city. By luck and pluck, through energy and talent, he had become something of a public figure in New York. He was a large, handsome man, with a stylish handlebar mustache. He affected the executive dress of the times, top hat and a cut-a-way coat, and he never changed into a baseball uniform. Before the game he would stride up and down in front of the stands, roaring: "Who are the People? We are the People!" The slogan became the Giants' trademark.[33]

Mutrie was not just a clever promoter; he also knew a great deal about baseball. He had managed winning teams in New England, and he was to do even better in the American Association. He brought his collection of cast-offs and pick-ups home in fourth place with a record of 54 and 52. He had only one real major league player, Tim Keefe, who had been with Troy and had also been shunted off to the Metropolitans by Day. Keefe had a very good year, winning 41 games while losing 27, and he led the league in earned run average. Without Keefe the Metropolitans would have been nowhere, so Mutrie used him practically every day. If only the Giants had kept Keefe and Mutrie, they would have challenged for the lead. "If only...," "would..."—nothing is so soothing to the baseball fan as the conditional subjunctive, with its implied promises of a golden future ... next season.

CHAPTER THREE
THE BUILDING YEARS

I

The city which welcomed the Giants and the Brooklyn Bridge was undergoing stupendous change, as great and as rapid as any in the Gilded Age. The shift from a rather aristocratic Anglo-Dutch commercial town to a monstrous, sprawling, industrial multinational depot for a tsunami of immigrants had been underway for a generation by the eighties. Set aside for a moment the moral implications of all this; the merely physical overwhelmed the observer. The dirt, the noise, the traffic, the constant crowds of people, the endless process of tearing down and building up simply assaulted the viewer. These alone were enough to convince anyone that the future would be altogether different from the past. There was a new world coming and coming fast.

Everyone could see this, of course, but few were prepared for the implications, municipal, cultural, or psychological of such massive change. In New York, it appeared that as soon as anyone, anyone at all, was pleased with the way things were, then everything changed until even the memory of stability had fled and adjustment alone was permanent. Many observers thought that change was unrelenting, menacing, even, in their bleaker moments, apocalyptic. If the world itself was not ending, then the old and better ways certainly were.

This view was not altogether divorced from reality. Mark Twain did not describe the nineteenth century as "raging, tearing, booming" for nothing, and modern social historians have confirmed this description. And yet, appearances both confirmed and obscured reality. While much was different from what had been, other things seemed curiously stable. Had Fernando Wood been reincarnated to run for mayor in 1912, he would easily have recognized New York as a changed city, but he would also have found that his political instincts and methods still worked. A backward glance brings an appraisal close to Tennyson's final view of Ulysses:

Norfolk and Hester streets: 1898. The lower east side, packed with Italian and Jewish immigrants. Many began to climb to prosperity by operating a push-cart (collection of The New York Historical Society).

> Tho' much is taken, much abides, and tho'
> We are not now that strength which in the old days
> Moved earth and heaven: That which we are we are.[1]

One of the things which had not changed much, and which perhaps abideth always, was urban violence. There had, certainly, been some retreat from the massive riots of the previous generation, when general municipal order had been threatened. In July, 1857, the Dead Rabbit riot had lasted several days and defied official efforts to put it down. It involved politics; the Dead Rabbits were affiliated with Tammany Hall while their opponents, the Bowery B'hoys, had Know-Nothing connections. It involved turf; the Dead Rabbits were from Five Points and the Bowery B'hoys were from the Seventh Ward. It involved the police, hated by all and now caught in the Tammany split over the power and ambitions of Mayor Fernando Wood. It involved gang loyalty, and heat, and poverty, and booze.[2] But even this major disturbance was dwarfed by the Draft Riots in July, 1863, which added race to the previous problems and lasted five days, cost 105 lives, and had to be put down by the army.[3]

If the scale of urban disorder had waned since the War, the amount had not. The Dead Rabbits and the Bowery B'hoys had vanished, but the Fourth Street Tunnel Gang had succeeded them.[4] Commanded by Richard Croker, later Tammany Sachem, the Tunnel Gang played an important role in the elections that solidified Tweed's rule in the city. They voted early and voted often, and kept the opposition away from the polls.[5] Though the Tunnel Gang was tough enough, the lower east side after the War was dominated by a brutal Irish gang, the Whyos. They were not alone; the Five Pointers, the Gophers, the Eastmans and the Gas House Gang competed with them for turf and pelf, but the Whyos were reputed to be the worst. It was said they would enroll no member who had not murdered his man. They hung out in a Bowery dive called the Morgue, whose proprietor said his liquor worked equally well as embalming fluid. The Whyos were relatively indifferent to politics and concentrated their efforts on murder, prostitution, saloons, extortion and the usual forms of robbery, mugging and mayhem.[6]

New York also excelled in those branches of crime that did not involve massive and habitual violence. The city was home to Ann Trow Lohman, who, under the *nom de commerce* of Madame Restell, was the foremost abortionist in the Republic. Madame Restell practiced a profession not only contrary to the penal code but also to the moral law as most New Yorkers then understood it. Yet her services were so essential and effective that, though often denounced, she never lacked for clients. The authorities might disapprove, but they did not interfere, and Madame advertised her services openly in the newspapers as a "female physician." Eventually she became extraordinarily rich, and, in the mid fifties, built a five-story mansion at 657 Fifth Avenue on the corner of 52nd Street. Her closest neighbor was St. Patrick's Cathedral, for the rest of the town was still over ten city blocks south. Safely ensconced in her new mansion, one of the finest homes in the city, she flaunted her presence by taking daily carriage rides up the Avenue, accompanied by liveried footmen. When the northward expansion of the city caught up to her, by 1870, the value of her residence increased stupendously, but her social acceptability did not. Nonetheless, she continued in business until 1878, when she was arrested by Anthony Comstock, the permanent secretary for the New York Society for Suppression of Vice. This was the end, for Madame Restell committed suicide rather than face the relentless Comstock. But her profession survived her, though her successors lacked her flair and notoriety.

Equally celebrated, though in another line of work, was Frederika "Marm" Mandelbaum, New York's (and the nation's) foremost fence. A large, matronly woman (hence her nickname) she was admired and trusted by everyone for both her judgment and character. She lived at 79 Clinton Street at the corner of Rivington, in the very heart of the Lower East Side. Marm ran a haberdashery as a front, but the real business consisted of processing and disposing of about 10 million dollars (200 million or more in constant dollars) worth of stolen goods. She lived above the business in absolute luxury and enter-

Fifth Avenue: 1883–1884. How the wealthy lived. Looking north toward Central Park from 51st Street, one sees the mansion of William K. Vanderbilt, St. Thomas Episcopal Church and the Fifth Avenue Presbyterian Church. In the distance is the Metropolitan Museum. The line of mansions on Fifth Avenue began with Madam Restell in the 1850s, and lasted until the 1920s (collection of The New York Historical Society).

tained lavishly, including at her table both crooks and cops, to say nothing of the Tammany politicians from the Tenderloin wards. Every now and then she was molested in her work but was ably defended by equally famous and adept attorneys Big Bill Howe and Little Abe Hummell. She was reputed to retain them for a yearly fee of $5,000, a sum in excess of what any ball player earned in the early eighties. Finally, in 1884, a reform movement prosecuted her in a serious manner. She fled to Canada with those assets she had not transferred to a daughter. The fencing business, of course, continued at a brisk pace, though not nearly so honestly or efficiently. This caused great regret to crook, cop and politician alike. They claimed that it increased crime and reduced the trust necessary for commercial transaction.

The efforts of the police to control urban crime and violence were sporadic, generally ineffective, and substantially diluted by graft. The police were an integral part of Tammany Hall, and their primary duties had little to do with the actual solution of crimes. The fundamental police function was to work with the ward boss, seeing that voters voted right and that those who received municipal largesse, such as saloon licenses, supported Tammany. Beyond that, the police kept general order, making sure that the "criminal classes," that is, the poor, did not riot and preyed mostly on each other. Periodically, of course, business as usual was not enough, as public outcry against vice and crime forced action. The police response was simple and direct. Some salient brothels, saloons and fences were temporarily closed, and all known criminals were arrested and/or clubbed into submission. In this respect, the police took their cue from Inspector Alexander S. Williams, whose famous obiter dictum maintained that "There is more law in the end of a policeman's nightstick than in a decision of the Supreme Court.[7]

This realistic sentiment came from the heart. Williams was a large man who excelled at mayhem. He had begun his police career on August 3, 1866 and had risen to captain in 1871. His initial success in police work came from clubbing senseless a dozen thugs, and he continued to favor that technique. Police work, of course, consisted of more than battering toughs and hoodlums, and Inspector Williams also employed graft and protection racketeering while captain of the 29th precinct in the New York Tenderloin district. Contemporaries viewed his clubbing of miscreants with indulgence, even approval, but drew the line at graft. Charges of graft were preferred against him nearly twenty times, but he always escaped. The Lexow Committee investigation in 1894 into police corruption singled Williams out for both brutality and dishonesty. The Committee wondered how Inspector Williams, on a small police salary, could afford a seaside estate in Cos Cob Connecticut, as well as thousands of dollars in bank accounts. His reply that astute speculation in real estate in Japan had enriched him was not entirely convincing, but he again escaped prosecution.[8] When he retired from the force in 1895 to go into insurance and become a millionaire, his departure was genuinely regretted. "Clubber" Williams had run a tight precinct, given protection for graft received, and his native preference for battery and mayhem over the criminal justice system had inspired respect from gangsters and made the streets safer. It was not for nothing that James McCabe's guide book to New York, published in 1872, frequently emphasized both the vice and the dangers of the big city.[9]

Today the Clubber Williams style would be called police brutality and would be vigorously condemned with paroxysms of moral outrage by both press and courts alike. Certainly, Williams' policing fell far short of the civil liberties guaranteed by the Constitution and Bill of Rights, as well as possessing an incurable bias against the poor, the ignorant and the helpless. Still, unhappy experience with an expensive and ineffective criminal justice system, a rising crime rate and a distinct career criminal class has caused many to reconsider wholesale condemnation of the Clubber Williams technique. Savagely discriminatory, it was also cheap, non-bureaucratic, instantly effective, a marked improvement over the massive riots of the previous generation, and was possessed of a firm moral certainty as to who the bad guys were. The Clubber could hardly have survived repeated public exposure of his massive graft if he had not had strong public and political support for his style of copping.

New York politics seemed also to belong to those things which abide. Bosses might come and bosses might go, some into retirement (or Congress, which was the same thing), some to the Bench, and some to jail. But machine politics remained. And there were always reformers to oppose the machine. Their names might change, but their ideals, aims and methods did not. It had been this way when Tiemann ran against Wood in 1856, and it would be the same when the century turned. Tammany was the climate, reformers merely the weather.

When seen from this perspective, a view based on social and institutional structures rather than the frantic succession of elections, urban politics appears as a system, and a stable and effective one at that. A modern scholar has succinctly described it. In general,

> ...local political leaders championed their constituents' cultural values and sought to preserve them through policies concerning education, leisure, liquor, and social behavior.
>
> Throughout the century, the most pervasive economic (and social) role of government was the promotion of development by distributing riches and privileges to individuals and small groups.[10]

This distribution of benefits, the common coin of urban government, ranged from railroad concessions to Commodore Vanderbilt, to saloon licenses to the less favored but still propertied, to jobs sweeping the streets for newly arrived immigrants. Those in power asserted that this system was essential for government itself in a variegated and heterogeneous land. Urbanization meant an accommodation of "interests," from merely surviving to big money and big business. Scuttles of coal, help with the rent or a job from the ward boss were "interests" every bit as much as contracts for street railways. Building the physical fabric of the city was also certainly an "interest," and a more important one than abstract theories of "good government," whatever that

Essex Market Police Court: 1892. Behind the court building rises the wall of the Ludlow Street Jail, where Boss Tweed was incarcerated. The Police courts were where most immigrants came to settle their disputes (collection of The New York Historical Society).

might be. The bosses and politicians of the city were usually too preoccupied or inarticulate to put such sentiments into the proper baroque Victorian English, but they practiced them and the voters understood.[11]

It was certainly that way in New York. Machine politics survived the spectacular rise and fall and rise of Fernando Wood, and the even more stupendous episode of the "Tweed Ring."[12] There were reformers and proponents of "good government" who supposed that the fall of the "Ring" meant the end of the urban machine, but they were as wrong as it was possible to be. The shattered ranks of Tammany Hall were knit together by the hard and autocratic Honest John Kelly, who restored discipline, replaced the fallen or demoralized ward leaders, and began to win elections. The good government men found they had to try again, and they did, in the election of 1886. The Giants might have been a sad disappointment that year, but the mayoral election, as they used to say, was a whiz-bang. Theodore Roosevelt, recently returned from the west, ran for the Republicans. The call for reform was so strong among the Democrats that Tammany Hall acquiesced in Abram Hewitt as its candidate.[13] Labor and assorted liberals and socialists ran Henry George.[14] After a furious campaign, in which Tammany went all out for Hewitt as the least of the evils, the Democrats won. Hewitt got ninety thousand votes, while Henry George, who came in second, had sixty eight thousand.[15] Even in reform the machine had won. The New York election provided anterior confirmation of Italian political wisdom. "Se vogliamo che tutto rimanga come e, bisogna che tutto cambi."[16]

By the eighties New York politics had fallen firmly into the pattern of machine against the patrician reformers. Thus elections were more than a clash of parties or factions; they were also a clash of social attitudes and ideals. The machine politicians relied on distributive government with jobs for constituents and favors dispensed, wards organized down to the tenement, and due regard paid to the moral and social sensibilities of the voters. The ward heelers attended all marriages, funerals, christenings, graduations and fires, and were assiduously attentive to the clergy. In an age before "safety nets" and "social contracts" and welfare, the ward politicians were the primary social service agency in urban America. They gave every appearance of being the only Americans interested in the welfare of the new immigrants, and, in a general way, they were.

In return, the machine politician exacted only votes, and a general social tolerance for vice and graft, both "honest" and the usual variety. On top of that, the machine threw in, virtually for nothing, public order maintained by casual police brutality and rudimentary public education. Not a bad deal, all things considered, maintained the machine politicians, and, in the Gilded Age, most urban voters agreed with them.[17]

Reformers, however, did not agree with them. During the Gilded Age, when socialists and labor politicians were *rarae aves* and political curiosities, the politically significant reformers were genteel, elite patrician liberals. They alone posed a serious challenge to the machine, not because they could compete in organization or campaign promises, but because they held the moral high ground. At a time when most Americans thought urban government was very bad indeed, patrician reformers stood for good government, honest, cheap and efficient. This was an appealing platform, sufficiently seductive to win newspaper support, the business interests and political independents. The Victorian patrician reformer saw politics as

> ...a series of little morality plays, (and) he instinctively stepped forward to play the role of Virtue. He possessed a wonderful confidence in his own power to distinguish between right and wrong. As a member of the "better classes," he boasted a courageous independence and integrity of purpose that ordinary men lacked.... As guardian of the right, he proposed to broadcast his influence for decency throughout society. No economic, political, or social evil would escape his attention.[18]

Good government, however, proved easier to demand than to define. Did good government mean inexpensive government, along with its corollary, low taxes? The trouble with this view was the major social services were inadequately provided, or left undone altogether. Police, fire protection, streets, drainage, rapid transportation and communication all depended on heavy municipal outlays. Nonetheless, cheap government was tried. Brooklyn, during the regime of Martin Kalbfleisch, 1868–1871, was governed with real economy and an appalling mess in municipal services. The police were corrupt, and the streets were open sewers. A Brooklyn paper described them:

> In the gutters at various points is a slimy mass, made up of water from the houses familiarly known as "slops," a dirty, greasy, noisome fluid thickened with the dust of the pavement, garbage, and the refuse of the table, fragments of rotting meat clinging to old bones, fish heads and fins....[19]

Well, what about efficiency? Surely, that would work. Again, Brooklyn provided instruction in reality. A new municipal charter that went into effect in 1882 gave great appointive and administrative power to the mayor, and the mayor who won the 1881 campaign was the reformer Seth Low. A Columbia graduate and scion of an old and wealthy commercial family, Seth Low garnered the support of the Republicans, the Citizens Committee, and the city reformers. With the Democratic machine of Boss Hugh McLaughlin on the defensive, the result of pervasive graft and misgovernment, the forces of reform won the most important election in post-war Brooklyn. It was, said Brooklyn minister Wayland Hoyt, "...a new day in municipal affairs, and ... a flaring beacon beckoning to right politics the land over."[20]

Low was certainly an excellent mayor. For four years he struggled with the problems of governing a major Gilded Age city. He did not steal, and he kept his subordinates from doing so. He appointed men regardless of party, monitored continuously the work of the government, and strove for the moral and physical betterment of Brooklyn. He integrated the city's public schools and provided free text books for the students. He had storm sewers built in the "flooded district" and improved and extended the streets. He reorganized the tax system and collected arrears. He improved the police department and made liquor licenses much harder to get. He undertook a city fire inspection and bought a fireboat. He cleaned the streets, drained sewage ponds, and began systematic vaccinations for children. Of course, none of this was free. Expenditures went up and taxes did also.

In 1883, when Low ran for a second term, there was a referendum on the reform administration. It was an exciting campaign, as McLaughlin's machine, now in fighting trim, made a contest of it. The machine, while admittedly corrupt, was not without weapons. There were many disappointed potential officeholders who were "aching to serve the people." Germans and Irish had been offended by the attack on saloons. Reform cost money, and taxes remained high and were actually collected. So, while Seth Low won, his majority was cut from over four thousand to 1,843. Efficiency and reform, while it might produce "good government," was, compared to the machine, cold, impersonal, and unlovable.[21]

That lack of loveliness symbolized the basic problem that patrician reformers faced. Certainly, they offered some of the elements of better government. Efficiency and honesty are qualities not always to be despised. But the psychological disabilities of the patrician reformers were overwhelming. For the reformers were engaged in a moral, not a political, crusade, the objects of which were the great mass of urban immigrants. The reformers found newer Americans to be morally deficient. E. L. Godkin, editor of the Nation, caught the right note: "We must openly acknowledge that a very large proportion of our voters are ignorant and grossly corrupt persons, to whom the rule of a Boss is entirely acceptable."[22] Boss rule was the result of the fact that "...the vicious and ignorant are united solidly, while the intelligent and virtuous are split up into many sects and parties."[23] But things went deeper than that. Propensities to "bossism" were only the political facet of a general moral depravity among the urban masses that made the city a "moral blight and a social menace."[24]

Needless to say, the immigrants did not concur completely in the patrician liberal analysis of urban problems. The newer Americans did not regard themselves as children of a lesser god. They acknowledged their poverty and worked hard to correct it. They cherished their religion and supported it lavishly. They saw they must organize to prosper, even to survive. Mutual aid societies of all sorts flourished mightily, as did ethnic newspapers, journals and theater. A few were drawn to labor unions. But for all there was the urban political machine, which provided a few with jobs, a few more with help in dire times, but mostly treated the immigrant as a person of dignity, worthy of respect. Patrician reformers, smugly conscious of their unattainable social superiority, could never grant that simple respect. The more honest among them, such as Seth Low and E. L. Godkin, never even tried. They simply looked down from a great height on their dirty and rowdy charges and tried their best to lead them to the Puritan joys of Protestant respectability.

So lines were drawn, definitively so in the eighties. The patrician reformers were campaigning against the city itself, that great new social fact of Victorian America. In that respect, at least, their intuition was right. Politics may have reflected continuity, but the city was the quintessence of change. Those who talked (complained usually) about the huge size of massive change were right. The irony of it all was that those who defended the city, the machine politicians, had no ideas on how better to run it and never thought of what it might become, while those who attached the very idea of city, the patrician reformers, speculated continuously on how to improve both city government and the lives of urban inhabitants.

And so we are brought back to the metaphor used earlier to describe city politics; Tammany was the climate while reform was merely the weather. This comparison of the greater with the lesser does not refer primarily to structure, to political institutions, though Tammany certainly had a permanent

The Battery: 1883. The old fort of Castle Garden is in the center foreground. From 1855 to 1890 it was the place where immigrants, including Irving Berlin, landed in New York (collection of The New York Historical Society).

system of clubs and ward heelers, while the reformers had to start nearly from scratch at each election. But the two systems essentially mirrored each other. The Tammany forces were more coherent and better organized and better led, but they were not a different type of political structure from the various reform clubs and papers. And the patrician reformers, though sloppy when it came to details, were as persistent and durable as Tammany. No Tammany politician had as extended a political career as Seth Low. Nor does the above-mentioned metaphor deal with ideas. The reformers had as clear a view of how the city should be governed as Tammany; indeed, the reformers presented an urban vision that was more coherent, more thoughtful and more serious than anything Tammany could muster. Again, we return to Seth Low. Ultimately, the reasons why Tammany was the basic force in city politics came down to the immigrants, to their number and to their ethnic and religious and linguistic diversity, and to the endless stream of their coming. The patrician reformers, with their idea on honesty, economy and efficiency, were interested in administering the city. Tammany, with its continuing network of clubs and ward bosses, was interested in people. The reformers claimed, correctly as the first 15 years of the new century demonstrated, that good government would help everyone. But it was too remote. The immigrant needed personal assistance, needed it now and needed it bad, and, while Tammany was woefully inadequate and promised far far more than it could deliver, still, the machine tried and sympathized.

Change in the city came from more than mere growth. Technology in the eighties was already becoming a primary factor in shaping the social future. In 1882 Thomas Edison threw a switch in the offices of J. P. Morgan which turned on the power for the Edison Illuminating Company, the first electric utility. You didn't have to be a genius to figure out the importance of that event; plenty of people besides J. P. Morgan thought electricity had a future. The same year an invention then seven years old went into mass production. With lawsuits out of the way, Western Electric received a contract to make telephones for the Bell Company. The impact of that invention on the city was clearly going to be something else again, as Perlmutter used to say. That new world was coming from more than one direction at once.

Small things changed as well as big. If urban violence abideth always, styles in mass entertainment changed quickly. This was certainly true for the eighties of the last century. The first vaudeville tour was organized in 1886 by B. F. Keith and Edward F. Albee, the Keith-Albee Circuit. Its success meant the beginning of the end for old-timey minstrel shows, which seemed increasingly quaint and out-of-fashion. Buffalo Bill Cody opened his Wild West show in Omaha in 1883, bringing a substantially sanitized version of the west to urban America. The Giants were simply part of the new style in urban entertainment.

And all the while the city grew. While the vaudevillians were shufflin' off to Buffalo the population of Manhattan grew by about 600,000 people, from 1.9 million in 1880 to about 2.5 million in 1890. While retired cowboys rescued wagon trains in the Wild West show, the city pushed north. The rich migrated to Fifth Avenue. Developers were building flats all the way to Harlem, previously a separate village. The Giants were part of this northward movement. The Polo Grounds were at 110th Street. Fashion and good sense demanded such a location. It was important to be up-to-date in New York City.

II

"Wait till next year!" is the mournful cry of baseball fans everywhere when their team finishes deep in the second division. That thought occurred to Day also as he contemplated the changes he must make to win. John B. Day was eager to do all that money and baseball judgment required. He wanted a pennant as badly as the kranks; indeed, he was himself a krank of exceptional enthusiasm and devotion.

Like many an owner since, Day began by unloading his manager, John Clapp. He was not alone. Left-handed catcher Jack Humphries went to Washington in the American Association. Day also decided to part with Tip O'Neill, whose efforts as a pitcher in the National League had not been spectacular. The St. Louis Browns of the American Association grabbed O'Neill and turned him into a feared hitter, one of the leading stars of that powerful club. Day had thought that O'Neill was too weak to compete in the National League. It was one of his worst mistakes.[25]

There were also additions to the Giants. James L. Price was hired as the new manager. He was not a player, so his duties on the field were to be handled by the captain. That position was also changed. Buck Ewing was removed and John Ward took his place. Beyond this, the Giants brought three new players into the league. Edward Begley was hired as a pitcher, taking O'Neill's job of giving Welch and Ward a rest now and then. Day also added two infielders, Danny Richardson and Alexander McKinnon, hoping that they would help strengthen the team where it had been weakest.

These changes in the team were matched by changes in the National League itself. There were no new clubs, a rarity in the days when franchises failed regularly. But the rules were altered. The main changes concerned pitching. One was a mere adjustment, but the other was a revolution. The number of balls for a base on balls was reduced from seven to six, giving marginal assistance to the hitter. The main help went to the pitcher. He was now allowed to throw overhand. This meant that pitchers could throw harder, with a more puzzling delivery, and could get more variety on their curves.[26] There was another aspect to the rule change, one that was not immediately apparent. The new overhand motion put a considerably greater strain on the pitcher's arm, and he could no longer pitch every day or so. Gradually, over the course of a decade, clubs came to have pitching staffs, not just a couple of men who alternated day in and day out. For the Giants, however, that was in the future. In 1884, the pitchers would be Welch and others.

The revamped Giants opened their second season with another extravaganza at the Polo Grounds. A large crowd, about 10,000 people, began to arrive as early as one o'clock, three hours before the game. By game time, people were standing six deep along the foul lines. When the home-town troops appeared, they were greeted with thunderous applause. On Opening Day, the true krank is always certain that this is the year.

The Giants began the season against the powerful Chicago White Stockings, always one of the best teams in the National League. But Anson's boys played badly that afternoon. King Kelly made two errors, Larry Corcoran gave up six walks and sixteen hits, and the Giants pounded Chicago, 15 to 3. By the ninth inning the kranks, savoring the victory, began to get out of hand. Those in the stands started throwing cushions on the people standing around the base lines. The standees heaved them back. The game had to be halted, and Ward came in from center field to quiet the crowd and clear the field.[27] As the jubilant fans poured out of the Polo Grounds to home and saloon, few doubted that they had seen a great team win.

The fans were not totally wrong in their convictions. The Giants were better than they had been last year and proceeded to prove it by winning their first twelve games. For a fortnight the Giants were the best team in baseball. They were hitting well and were getting excellent pitching, but the biggest improvement was certainly the fielding. In 1883 the Giants had been making six to eight errors a game, and now they cut it back to one or two. It was a different club from the one that limped home in sixth place last year. The kranks were delighted.[28]

Hopes ran higher than reality, a frequent event in baseball. The Giants were certainly better, but the team still had serious weaknesses. Pitching was the salient difficulty. Smiling Mickey Welch had an excellent year; he won 39 games and had an earned run average of 2.50, but he could not pitch every day and the Giants had no one to support him. Ward had come to the end of his pitching career. He won only three games, all during the team's opening spurt. Begley repeated the experience of Tip O'Neill. He was wild and erratic, and he collapsed completely in the last half of the season, winning his last game on July 15. Throughout August and September the Giants were desperate for pitching. Even Buck Ewing pitched a game, and lost it. Mike Dorgan was brought in from the outfield and put in the box. He was not as bad as one might have expected, winning eight and losing six, but no one mistook Dorgan for Welch. Providence might win the pennant with one pitcher, Old Hoss Radbourne, but the Giants needed a deeper staff.[29]

Catching was also a problem. Ewing could not catch every day, so the Giants tried a succession of substitutes, all poor. Finally, in desperation, the Giants brought Humphries back. His batting average was a modest .094, but he was the best the team could find. Beyond all this, Buck Ewing had a bad year. His hands hurt him much of the season, and his batting average fell off to .277. Buck also hit three home runs.

In spite of the disappointment freely voiced by krank and sportswriter, the Giants had had a pretty good season. They were no longer one of the weaker teams in the League. The boys won 62 games and lost 50, playing exactly .500 baseball after their opening twelve game winning streak. The Giants spent most of the season in third place, and they finished it tied for fourth with Chicago.[30] Providence won the pennant, its second and the last that club would ever win. The Rhode Island team was carried to the top by Old Hoss Radbourne, who won a staggering total of 60 games while losing only 12 and posting a 1.38 earned run average.[31] It was the most stupendous season a major league pitcher would ever have, and the more balanced effort of the other teams could not prevail against it.

Although the Giants had had a successful year on the field and at the gate, the season ended on a sad and pathetic note. The manager, James L. Price, was caught embezzling club funds. Indeed, he was caught twice. His early season graft was forgiven, amidst many promises to reform. But Price did not reform, at least not for long. On the last road trip, which began on September 17, he was caught again, and Ward, the team captain, took over direction of the team and the finances for the western trip that closed the season. Price was fired in Detroit, and he remained there to avoid prosecution.[32]

In the theater, which also reflected closely American mores and aspirations during the Gilded Age, such conduct was common. W. C. Fields, reminiscing about his days in vaudeville on the road, commented that it was expected the manager would steal the funds and leave the actors broke and stranded somewhere in the sticks.[33] Apparently Day did not expect this, nor did anyone else. In baseball, embezzlement was considered a serious offense. The reason seems simple. Baseball did not have higher ethical standards than did theatrical road troupes. But it did have more money invested.

III

When the 1885 season began, both the Giants and the National League had a new look. The Cleveland club had folded, stunned by the loss of several of its best players to the outlaw Union Association. Anxious to replace Cleveland with a strong western club, the National League took in St. Louis from the collapsing Union Association. Only a year earlier, the president of the National League, A. G. Mills, had vowed to ban Henry V. Lucas, the St. Louis owner and founder of the Union Association, from Organized Baseball forever. But the National League magnates saw things differently from Mills, and now they welcomed Lucas and his team into the fold. Furious at this retreat from principle, Mills resigned in a huff, and was replaced by his weak and incompetent secretary, Nick Young. For the National League owners, of course, it was no longer a question of Lucas' enticing players to break their contracts, or running a competing league, or disrupting the established fabric of major league baseball. It was now a matter of business, and the magnates majestically ignored their former condemnation of Lucas as a thief and a cad.[34]

In the midst of the maneuvering over the collapse of the Union Association, the Giants were busy acquiring new players and strengthening the team. The most controversial deal was with the Metropolitans. The Metropolitans had won the American Association pennant, but they had lost money. This puzzled and irritated Day, who thought the fans ought to support a winner. If New York would not support American Association baseball, Day wanted to get his best men over to the Giants, who were making money. The problem was the ten-day rule. If Day released players from the Metropolitans, he had to wait ten days before signing them on as Giants. In the interim, of course, some other club could offer them a contract, and Day would have to pay heavily to keep men he already had. However, his craft was equal to the situation. He sent manager James Mutrie, infielder Tom "Dude" Esterbrook, and pitcher Tim Keefe on an ocean voyage to Bermuda, ostensibly as a reward for winning the pennant. While on the high seas, Mutrie released Esterbrook and Keefe, and ten days later all three signed Giants contracts at a nice raise. The American Association was outraged at this slippery deal. It crippled their championship team, demonstrated the dangers of multiple ownership, and proved to everyone that the National League was the superior circuit. It also exposed the Association's weakness in the biggest and most important baseball market in the nation. But what could be done? Short of denouncing the National Agreement, nothing. There were threats of this, which would have meant a bidding war for players, but the American Association was too weak financially to consider it seriously. Day, meanwhile, stuck to his deal, maintaining its legality and blandly wondering what all the fuss was about. The Giants already had enough clout in National League councils to gain support, and Mutrie, Keefe, and Esterbrook stayed with their new club.[35]

There were other new Giants as well. James O'Rourke came from Buffalo, where he had hit .347 the previous season. "Orator Jim" had always been one of the game's best players. He was a man of leadership and education, being both lawyer and a civil engineer. He had managed Buffalo for four years, but the Bisons, who were losing money steadily, were forced to send him to New York. O'Rourke added the outfield strength that allowed Mutrie to move Ward to shortstop. The Giants also obtained veteran Joe Gerhardt from Louisville in the American Association. "Move-up Joe" took over at second base.[36] Finally, the club sought to solve its catching problems by buying Tom Deasley from the St. Louis Browns. Deasley, a good journeyman catcher, had tried to evade the reserve rule, which bound a player to sign again with the club that owned him or not play at all. Deasley had had a specific statement written into his contract releasing him at the end of the season. The American Association nullified this early attempt to evade reservation, but Chris von der Ahe, the Brown's president, wanting to get rid of a dissatisfied player, traded Deasley to the Giants.[37]

These substantial personnel changes had enormously strengthened the Giants, who were now, for the first time, a really good team. Not surprisingly, they got off to an excellent start. They defeated Boston on opening day, 2 to 1, as Smiling Mickey Welch pitched a no-hitter.[38] The Giants were in first place at the end of May, and they were only a game behind Chicago at the end of June. By July it had become a two-team race, with the White Stockings usually in the lead.[39] Both teams played superb baseball, winning about three-fourths of their games. Periodically, the Giants made a run at the lead. Over the July 4th holidays the Giants polished the White Stockings off, winning three of the four games. When they left Chicago the Giants were only a half game out of first place.[40] With the fantastic pitching of Welch and Keefe and the team's big hitters, it seemed only a question of time until the Giants swept past Chicago. But the White Stocking refused to crack. Although the Giants kept on winning — they were 38 and 13 on July 12th and 47 and 15 two weeks later — Chicago stayed a game ahead.

The New York kranks were wildly excited. They had never seen anything like it. Could the Giants actually win? James Mutrie commented that:

> Every mail brings me letters asking information about my club and its prospects. Total strangers accost me in the street and ask the same question and I am waylaid in hotels and buttonholed for an hour at a time by enthusiasts on the National Game. The interest is not confined to the sporting fraternity. Staid businessmen and persons who would not touch any other sport seem to be deeply interested in the struggle.[41]

The fans did more than accost Mutrie. They came to the Polo Ground in record numbers, crowding the stands even for games with the tail-enders. On July 19 there were about 4,000 kranks to see the Giants defeat last place St. Louis, 3 to 2, with a run in the ninth inning. Two days later the Giants did it again. Three thousand people watched the "gilt-edged nine" score two runs in the ninth and defeat St. Louis, 3 to 2. Among the delighted spectators were two stars of the hit musical play, "The Black Hussar," Digby Bell and DeWolf Hopper.[42] Both were rabid kranks and personal friends of John Montgomery Ward, who was now an established member of New York society.

The growing connection between the Giants and the New York stage was reinforced during the remainder of the summer. On July 22, the entire company of "The Black Hussar" attended the game as guests of the management.[43] When the Chicago White Stockings came into the Polo Grounds on August 1, both teams went to a special night at the theater. It had become an appropriate way for the Giants to honor their guests and adversaries. The New York club was equally popular with the brokers on the Stock Exchange. As early as 1884 large delegations had started coming regularly to the games, which began at four o'clock, after the Exchange had closed. By 1885 some of the brokers closed up early and went to the game.[44] The Giants were not only popular, they now had become fashionable.

The kranks' excitement reached a peak with a crucial home game against Chicago on August 1, 1885. It was the biggest contest on the Polo Grounds since Grant had graced the opener. The elevated lines put on extra trains, and every hack in Manhattan headed north toward Harlem. There were 13,427 paid admissions, and thousands simply climbed the fence. The crowd was ten deep around the entire playing field. When the Giants appeared their fans gave them a mighty cheer and urged them on to victory. Smiling Mickey Welch did not pitch his best game, but he hung on to win, 7 to 6. After the game ended the crowd milled around the Giants' dressing room, cheering their favorites for half an hour before heading home. It was a happy group of kranks. Buck Ewing's mascot had bet his whole wad and won $4.50; other New Yorkers had done even better.[45]

As the boys continued to win, the New York management became much more sanguine about the pennant:

> Do I think the New-Yorks will win the championship, answered Manager Mutrie yesterday in response to a question put to him by a *Times* reporter.

> That is a hard question to decide. Chances are a little against us, but I have every confidence in my players. They are the pluckiest set of men in the country. If the race comes to a very close thing near the finish, the odds ought to be in favor of my players. They never lose heart like the Chicago men. One thing, however, is certain: the New-Yorks will make a strong fight for the championship and they will leave nothing undone to accomplish their object.[46]

By the end of August, Truthful James was even more optimistic. He oozed confidence and commented that, "...if [his] boys continued to play as at present, the pennant was theirs to a certainty."[47]

The players were equally outspoken, though their comments ran more to laments than boasts. The Giants may have had pluck, but Chicago apparently had the other Horatian Alger requirement, luck. Jim O'Rourke said disgustedly that Chicago was "...the luckiest club in existence," and John Ward had the same opinion. After two late season losses to the White Stockings, Ward said wearily, "It is impossible to beat fate. We lost both games by hard luck."[48] It was a sad anticipation of a future player who said that he would rather be lucky than good.

The season reached its climax with a four game series in Chicago during the week of September 27. It was the next-to-last week of the season, and the Giants rolled into Chicago riding a seven game winning streak. They were only two games out of first place. If the Giants won three out of four they would tie Chicago; if they won them all they would have a two game lead and the pennant. The whole season came down to four games in Chicago.

Everyone in the Giants' camp was optimistic. Their team had been beating Chicago all along, and no one saw any reason why it could not be done again. James Mutrie was emphatic. How many games would the Giants win in Chicago? Well,

> three, perhaps four. I shouldn't be a bit surprised if we won all four. To use a sporting expression, the Chicagos are quitters, or, in other words, they are afraid to meet my men.[49]

That was the prevailing opinion in New York.

The decisive series began on September 29. Eight thousand fans jammed into the Chicago park, including some two hundred who had taken a special train from New York. Those who couldn't afford such a trip gathered around newspaper bulletin boards or in saloons where the score was posted by inning. New York was the local betting favorite, 4 to 3. Confidence ran almost as high as hopes. But for the New York fans the bad news came early. In the opening game the White Stockings scored four runs in the first inning, and Smiling Mickey Welch went down to defeat, 7 to 4. There was worse news the next day. The White Stockings won again, 2 to 1. That was the pennant, and everyone knew it. There were only six games left to play, and the Giants were four behind Chicago. Only a few people appeared at newspaper bulletin boards in Park Row to watch for the score of the third game, which Chicago won, 8 to 3, and there was nobody at all to cheer when the Giants won the series finale, 12 to 8.[50] It was all over, and the Giants had come in second.

There was immense jubilation in Chicago at the dramatic end to the pennant race. The White Stockings' fans had won their bets, and the boys had beaten back the upstart Giants. Local pride at this example of baseball superiority was even expressed in poetry. The Song of Hiawatha was pressed into service to celebrate the great Chicago triumph:

> From the East came the Manhattans,
> From the land of the Knickerbokah,
> Came with mighty talk from Mutrie,
> This Iago, the great boaster,
> Saying: "We will teach these gophers,
> Feeble gophers of the prairie,
> How to wield the heavy willow,
> Teach them what the game of ball is —

In the end, of course, it was the proud New Yorkers who learned what the game of ball was. The White Stockings

> Slaughtered there the proud Manhattans.
> Slaughtered them as they were running,
> Took their scalps and all their wampum.[51]

A second poetic effort had fewer literary pretensions, but it did express the Chicago view of things, as well as the peculiar American practice of turning every occasion to commercial profit. Hartley's Photographers took the opportunity to celebrate both the White Stockings' victory and their own pictures:

> The hearts of our boys are buoyant as cork
> They have grandly and signally beaten New York...
> While Chicago's brave boys shall keep the ball buzzin'
> Hartley's Cabinets remain two Dollars a Dozen.[52]

Naturally, there was great debate in New York as to why this disaster had happened. A *New York Times* writer apparently thought the Giants should have won them all. The Giants "...have lost games with comparatively insignificant nines...." And why had that happened? The *Times* critic was both forthright and evasive. "Exceedingly bad judgement in a certain quarter..." was his verdict.[53] The *Tribune* had a different view. While agreeing that something was wrong, the *Tribune* correspondent thought "...that there ought to be better teamwork and the players should show more vim...." He varied this theme with the coda to the effect that "...the New-York men have lost several games through overconfidence."[54] James Mutrie, once so hopeful, fell back on the player's lament. The White Stockings, he said, were "...rattling good ball players, but they are lucky, wonderfully lucky, and luck goes a long way in a ball game."[55]

None of these excuses was fully satisfactory, because nothing was wrong with the Giants. They had won 85 games and lost only 27, which was .759 baseball and the best record the team would ever make.[56] Mickey Welch had had the best year of his career, winning 44 games while losing only 11. Between July 18 and September 4 he won seventeen games in a row. Tim Keefe did not do badly either. He started slowly but finished the season with a record of 32 victories and only 13 defeats. Roger Connor led the league with a .371 average. Both Ewing and O'Rourke hit over .300. Beyond that, the team had generated enormous fan interest, drawn huge crowds, become fashionable, and made a pot of money for John B. Day. It was hard to complain after all that.

IV

The Giants, said James Mutrie, "...will win the League trophy of 1886 to a dead certainty."[57] Most New York fans agreed. After all, Chicago could not keep winning as they had; luck, just confounded incredible luck, had kept them going this long. The same fans, however, saw nothing incredible or lucky about the Giants continuing to win three games out of four. Thus, by simple baseball logic, next year's pennant was theirs.

The Giants faced a changed league in their renewed quest for the pennant. Buffalo and Providence, both victims of red ink, surrendered their franchises and were replaced by Washington and Kansas City.[58] The best Buffalo players were bought by Detroit. Known as the "Big four," the Buffalo infield of Dan Brouthers, Hardy Richardson, Jack Rowe, and James "Deacon" White was the best in baseball. Detroit had finished in sixth place in 1885. Thus reinforced, Detroit was clearly going to do much better this time around.

The Giants, however, stood pat. Both Day and Mutrie thought that the team did not really need to be strengthened. So the Giants opened the 1886 season with the same lineup as the year before, and, again, the boys won, defeating Boston, 5 to 4, with a run in the bottom of the eleventh inning. Just before darkness fell Ward singled, went to third on Gerhardt's double, and scored on Jim O'Rourke's fly ball. The twelve thousand or so fans gave a mighty roar of approval and trooped home in the spring dusk convinced that this really was the year.[59]

For the first couple of weeks it seemed to be. The boys played well and were in front when they started on their first western trip on May 10. Then the team began to slide. The Giants lost four straight games to Detroit and Chicago and fell out of first place, never to regain it. Injuries certainly hurt the team. Both Ewing and Deasley were out and O'Rourke was drafted to catch. Mutrie, as usual, attributed the Giants' failures to bad luck. But the sportswriters saw it differently. The team, they said, was demoralized.[60]

The Giants had too many good players, however, to collapse completely. By the end of May they were lodged firmly in third place behind Chicago and Detroit. The fans were still hopeful. On Memorial Day, about eight thousand kranks watched the Giants defeat Detroit in the morning game, and nearly three times as many appeared in the afternoon. The official count was 20,632 but this did not include the thousands who came in when the fence broke. The crowd was so large that reserve police had to be called in, and mounted troopers pushed the standees back so the players would have room for the game. It was the biggest crowd in the club's history, and it saw the Giants lose 5 to 1.[61]

Third place was the best the Giants could do. They stayed there for the rest of the year, gradually falling further and further behind the leaders. The team played in streaks, unable to find the winning formula of a year ago. The Giants finished the season with a disappointing record of 75 victories and 44 defeats, twelve and one-half games behind Chicago.[62]

It had been a difficult and confusing season for both fans and management. The Giants should have done better than they did: "That the nine as a team is phenomenally strong nobody can deny. That the players as individuals have no superiors is a fact that even the enemies of the Giants do not deny."[63] Newspaper rhetoric was supported by statistics. Tim Keefe had a fine year, winning 42 games and losing only 20. Roger Connor hit a robust .355. Jim O'Rourke and Buck Ewing raised their batting averages somewhat to .309 in both cases. John Ward raised his batting average 47 points to .273. With these key players having a good year, the team ought to be winning, not falling off 130 points in its won-loss percentage.

When asked why such a superior team was not winning the pennant, Mutrie had two stock answers. He might repeat his standard proverb that baseball was an "onsartain game." Or he talked about bad luck. No one wanted to hear that. The kranks wanted to know: "What was the matter with the Giants?" Some said one thing and some another, but two opinions seemed to be especially popular. Many thought that the players had the "big head," a common affliction of professional athletes. Others had a more sinister explanation. Internal dissension was ruining the team. No names were mentioned and the story was steadily denied, but the rumors continued anyway.

The search for explanation for poor performance, which has continued as an integral and essential part of the game, had a querulousness in 1886 that reflected both the newness of the game to New York and the inexperience of the kranks in the realm of krankdom. As a modern commentator has remarked, baseball is a game for adults because it is about losing, not about winning. This is not only existentially true, it is built into the nature of the game. Unbeaten seasons, an annual event in football and an occasional one in basketball, are impossible in major league baseball. Even the best teams lose about 40 percent of their games, while the average lose even more. Moreover, the game itself is a panorama of falling short of perfection. One never knows which small failing, the inability to advance the runner, missing on the first pitch to a hot hitter, juggling a two-out ground ball, will cost the game. There are, of course, dozens of these in every game; indeed, modest but meaningful imperfections are the very structure of play. And one of them will bring defeat, while the rare brilliant plays and perfect pitches seldom suffice as the margin of victory. Baseball, like life, is too hard for perfection, too hard to be about winning.

The kranks, who had been rooting for only four years, could hardly be expected to know that. They were still rampant front-runners, they still expected perfection, and they still thought that it was possible in baseball to win constantly. Experience had not confirmed in the new Giants' kranks what it would for the fans of the Cubs or the Red Sox: that losing must be expected and anticipated, and that there is no rational or athletic explanation for it. That is just baseball. Mutrie's remarks that baseball was an "onsartain" game were closer to the mark than the more specific and analytical efforts of the experts, which included, of course, all the sports writers and most of the kranks. But only experience would confirm the essential inexplicability of baseball, of why players perform well one day and poorly the next, of why the average player has a career year, of why the game is about the ways and styles of losing. But that was all to come. In the meantime, amidst lamentation and complaint, kranks searched for reasons within a mystery.

The criticisms and rumors, regardless of their accuracy, reflected the basic situation. The gilt-edged nine was not doing as well as the kranks, or the players themselves, thought they should. New players might help. Toward the end of the season, Mutrie signed a half dozen men from the Eastern League for delivery next year. One of these, Silent Mike Tiernan, an outfielder from Trenton, turned out to be a superb player. The others did not make it. Finally, the Giants bought an established star for the 1887 season. They got George Gore from the champion Chicago White Stockings. Albert Spalding was selling off his team, by far the best in the short history of major league baseball. King Kelly went to Boston, Pittsburgh got Dalrymple, McCormick, and Billy Sunday, and the Giants grabbed Gore.[64]

The changes in the New York team were minor compared to the new rules. Convinced that pitching dominated the game unfairly, the magnates altered things in favor of the hitter. Five balls were now required for a walk, instead of the seven needed the previous year. Even more dramatic, the hitter was now given four strikes instead of three. This incredible change was followed by another, scoring walks as base hits. Under the new rules there were bound to be plenty of walks, so everyone should have a nice high average. And they did. John Ward raised his average to .374 and Tip O'Neill of the Browns led the majors with an average of .492, a fat one hundred fifty points above his previous best. There was also a pitching change, and it was to be permanent. The old rule, dating from Cartwright regulations of 1845, of allowing the hitter to call for a high or low pitch was abolished. Now the hurler could throw the ball where he wanted, or, at least, he could try to. Only this, among all the rule changes benefitted the pitchers. The rest were to aid the beleaguered batter.[65]

As the Giants opened the 1887 season against Philadelphia in the rain at the Polo Grounds, the kranks and press alike were in a critical mood. They hoped for the pennant, they even demanded it, but they no longer really expected it. For some inexplicable reason, a simple thing like winning the pennant seemed to be beyond the team's capacity. The Giants began well enough, however. It was not a brilliant game, but Tim Keefe beat the Phillies, 4 to 3.[66] But the opening win was deceptive. The Giants never hit a winning stride, and, at times, their play was truly wretched. On May 10 the Giants lost to the lowly Washington Senators, 8 to 3.

> The New York team ... didn't play any ball to speak of.... There was ... as usual, no team play. By the most devoted admirers of the club, it could not be said that the New-Yorks played even a fairly decent game.... Ewing managed to catch the ball that some one tossed to him once, and held it, and the crowd cheered him vociferously.[67]

If that was the treatment meted out to the popular Ewing, the rest of the squad must have put in a long afternoon. The catcher on that nearly forgotten Washington team was a former boot shop hand at the Green and Twitchell factory in East Brookfield, Massachusetts. After playing with semi-pro teams around Boston, he caught on with Meridan and came up to the majors in 1886. His name was Connie Mack. The papers did not mention it. His decades of national celebrity were still in the future.

As the Giants continued to lose, the criticism became worse. One commentator announced that it

> ...cannot be denied that there has been too much lukewarmness in the management and too much indifference and laziness among the players. The New-York players have been flattered and petted until the high salaried and fortunate individuals have begun to imagine that they owned all Manhattan Island. Conceit and big head are unwholesome but nonetheless common vices of the successful baseball player of today.[68]

Complaint about players' salaries is not a new phenomenon.

Indolence, inflated salaries and the "big head" were not seen as the only causes of the Giants' misfortunes. The team had good players, but they were badly managed. The culprit was the captain, John Montgomery Ward. He was a favorite in New York theatre society, but he was not as well liked on the team. Some players resented his popularity, others his authority, others his aristocratic demeanor. He was supposed to be domineering and "overflowing with bigotry," whatever that might mean. A new captain was needed. Ward must go.

As the team continued to flounder, the Giants' management caught up with public opinion and began to consider replacing Ward. On July 12 the decision was announced. The team had lost seven of its last eight games and had fallen to fourth place, with a record of 33 victories and 29 defeats. The Giants were playing their poorest baseball since 1883. Ward could hardly survive that, and he did not. When asked about the rumors of Ward's removal as captain, Day commented:

> Yes, it's true. A change must be made at once. Ward is not popular with the players. Why, three of the men will not even speak to him. Ewing will probably be made captain tomorrow.[69]

Ward promptly denied the charges of player hostility. He wrote a letter to Day and sent it to the papers.

> The reports in the morning papers referring to my retirement from the Captaincy of the New-York team do an injustice not only to me but to the other members of the nine. I am represented by some as having resigned and by others as having been relieved of the position because of the hostility of several of the other players. The facts are these: I tendered my resignation some time ago at a time when the club was winning. I chose that time because I did not wish it said that I had deserted in a time of ill success. Yesterday, I again spoke to Mr. Day about the matter and insisted that I be relieved. I did not give as my reasons that I was on unfriendly terms with other members of the nine.... The statement that there are three men in the team who do not speak to me is entirely false. Indeed, I did not know I had an enemy in the team, and certainly there is not one who could not command my friendly services at any time.[70]

Perhaps, perhaps not, but hardly anyone believed it. The Giants were too good a team to be playing as badly as they had been, and there had been rumors about Ward's managerial problems all season. Beyond that, there was a general feeling that the team was not hustling, and most people thought Ward's failings as a captain caused this.

Although Ward had lost his job of captain, he remained a popular and exciting player. The day the news was released, Ward received tremendous applause whenever he came to bat or made a play in the field. The elegant shortstop rose to the occasion. He got a base hit, stole a base, scored three runs, and did not make an error.[71] And the Giants finally won a game, as Tim Keefe beat Pittsburgh, 7 to 3. The crowd loved it. Giants fans hoped that the worst was behind them, and the team would start to win as it had in 1885. But Ewing's stint as captain, though it was popular with the players, did not produce winning baseball. The team did climb into third place briefly toward the end of August, but by September 11 they were back to fourth to stay.

The most humiliating blow came in the last series of the season. Philadelphia came into the Polo Grounds and won three straight games to hammer the demoralized Giants firmly into fourth place. It was disgraceful. The wretched Phillies, whom the Giants had taunted by nailing brooms over the clubhouse door, symbolic of their intention to sweep the Phils out of the park, finished the season in second place. And to make it worse, the Phillies were a lousy team. They were brilliantly managed by Harry Wright, the last man from the fabled Cincinnati Red Stockings still active in baseball. And one Philadelphia player did achieve a sort of eminence. He was Sid Farrar, a journeyman first baseman but an exceptional father. His daughter was the diva Geraldine Farrar.

The Giants' fourth place finish, with a record of 68 victories and 55 defeats, had been cruelly disappointing.[72] It was also puzzling, for the Giants were not a poor team. One of the players, John Ward, had had a superb year, in spite of the uproar about his managerial abilities. He appeared in every game, was the team's leading hitter, led the National League in stolen bases with 111, and was generally considered the best shortstop in the league. He also had a flair for the spectacular. One June 6, against Philadelphia, Ward singled in the ninth inning, stole second base, stole third, and then stole home with the tying run. He capped the season off by marrying the actress Helen Dauvray, who had her own company, a large house on Fifth Avenue, and an impressive portfolio of stocks.[73]

The other players had not done so well, however. The team lacked a dependable second baseman and third baseman. Gerhardt and Esterbrook were released because they could not hit; O'Rourke and Ewing, who tried to take their places, could hit but could not field. Beyond that, Ewing was needed to catch, and Orator Jim was the Giants' best outfielder. Mutrie, Ward, and Ewing tried every combination they could think of, but the only thing that worked was Ward's moving Danny Richardson from the outfield to second base.

The most serious problem was pitching. Smiling Mickey Welch won 23 games and lost 15, a good record certainly, but not what it had been. Moreover, Welch could no longer pitch every other day; this was his eighth major league season and he was beginning to feel the wear and tear. He appeared in only 40 games in 1887, compared to 59 the year before. Tim Keefe took up some of the slack, winning 35 games and losing 19, but overhand pitching was ending the days of the two-man rotation and the Giants looked desperately for other pitchers. They had very poor luck. William George won 3 games, lost 9, and had some very rocky performances. On Memorial Day he walked 16 and scattered 26 hits in losing to Chicago, 12 to 11. Even when he won, George was far from impressive. On May 20 he beat Pittsburgh but hit three men and threw five wild pitches in the process. A late season reinforcement, Ledell Titcomb, won four games and lost three, which was not too bad.[74] Even with the addition of Titcomb, however, it was clear that the Giants needed additional pitching.

When the season ended finally, press comment was curiously restrained. The reporters had stopped calling the boys bums; they had been doing that all year long with no discernible effect. Now, they turned on the owner. John B. Day had given the city poor baseball and made a fortune from it. It was outrageous.

> The New-York Club, as it has been conducted during the past few years, does not deserve the liberal patronage bestowed upon it by the lovers of baseball in this city. It has been run in a loose, shiftless manner, which has disgusted every lover of the game in this neighborhood. The stock-holders have been fortunate, but if some change is not made before next season's campaign begins, the public will probably refuse to be further gulled and will stay away from the grounds.[75]

The reporter was not confident of constructive changes, however. He added that the New York club "…seldom tries to strengthen its nine…" until there were no good players left. The conclusion was plain. The Giants were going nowhere. What was the matter with the Giants? Well, there was no team spirit, no hustle, no will to win, player dissension, bad management on the field and worse off it; everything you could think of was the matter with the Giants, that's what.

Chapter Four
"WE ARE THE PEOPLE"

I

As the new baseball season approached, gamblers, sportswriters and kranks tried to predict the winner. Some favored the world champion Detroits and others the Boston Red Stockings, who were strengthened by the addition of Chicago's best pitcher, John Clarkson.[1] Very few were so rash as to pick the Giants, assumed by now to be a team with marvelous talent that could not win ball games.

For the guidance of the superstitious, which included virtually everyone in baseball, there were some Delphic omens. Rumors abounded that the Giants would lose the Polo Grounds, a victim of the northward expansion of New York City up the length of Manhattan Island.[2] The city was going to cut a street through the stadium. John B. Day eschewed the usual sunny forecasts and instead issued low commercial complaints. He objected to the National League schedule. The Giants had to open on the road. More, the home opener was against the Philadelphias, a team that did not draw well in New York. Still more, the big Independence Day games were to be played in Detroit, which had notoriously bad attendance. Worst of all, the Memorial Day games, though scheduled for New York, were against the drab Pittsburghs.

The most significant omens came from the team itself. John Ward and Tim Keefe were holdouts. Having had excellent seasons the year before, they now wanted $5,000 for their work, a right fair salary in the dear, dead days before taxes and before inflation. Neither got it. Ward, now a married man, had powerful reasons for wanting to get out of the house and go to work, so he cracked first. He signed on Opening Day, April 20, for $4,000.[3] Keefe held out a bit longer. He did not sign until April 27, also for a reported $4,000, and he did not pitch until May 1, missing the first two weeks of the season. To kranks mulling over the Giants' chances in the new season, the holdout of two such stars was a particularly disquieting fact.[4]

This year, however, the elaborate sifting of such straws and hints, normally an absorbing occupation for the baseball *cognoscenti*, was interrupted by an Act of God. New York was struck by the worst winter storm since Verrazano's voyage. The blizzard of '88 began early Monday morning, March 12. It started with a cold rain, which turned to sleet and snow as the temperature dropped and the wind rose. It snowed hard all Monday and on into Tuesday morning. When the snow finally ended there were two feet on the ground and the drifts were ten feet high. New York was paralyzed. As the snow had gotten deeper, discouraged horse car drivers had unhitched their nags and ridden them back to the barns, leaving cars stranded all about the city. The elevated trains were hours late and most just stopped running. Deliveries were halted, creating an immediate shortage of bread, milk, coal and newspapers.

In spite of the blizzard and gale winds, thousands of people tried to get to work. The few elevateds that ran were jammed with miserable and dedicated commuters. Most had to walk, however, which was no easy task in blizzard conditions. A few even crossed from Staten Island to Manhattan on a large ice floe that had jammed in the Narrows. These heroic efforts were generally in vain. The city simply shut down, and there was no work to be done when the men reached their offices.[5]

It took about a week to dig out from the blizzard, and the storm was the major topic of conversation for most of the month. But baseball was not completely forgotten; nothing so important can ever be absolutely abandoned. Day and Mutrie were busily strengthening the team. They added Ned "Cannonball" Crane to the pitching staff. The New England "phenom" was reported to have the fastest pitch in baseball. Two outfielders, Elmer Foster and Michael J. Slattery, were brought up from the minors. Mutrie also signed a third baseman, Elmer Cleveland, who had played in the old Union Association.

The rules were also changed, another step in an endless search for the perfect balance between pitching and hitting. This time the strikes were cut back from four to three, as they had always been before and always would be since. Indeed, three strikes has become a tradition so firm as to seem etched in stone, and not even club owners or Congressmen have suggested its change.[6]

The new players and the inevitable optimism that suffuses the beginning of a baseball season did not quite conceal a certain querulous spirit among kranks and sportswriters. The season would be played to mixed reviews. Gone was the exuberant joy of 1885, when the Giants had nearly won the pennant and the players had been unsullied heroes. Everyone had been more innocent then. Now they were disillusioned. They had seen good teams lose and had listened to years of lame excuses about bad luck. They wanted a winner.

> New-York wants the League pennant, and wants no more nonsense. It has had a sufficiency of the latter during the last four or five years. The players are well paid for their work.... President Day and Manager Mutrie owe it to the public, which has been so generous in the support of the nine, to see to it that those men do their duty.[7]

John Clarkson: 1888. Typical of the formal baseball poses of the time. Clarkson and Kelly turned Boston into a good team and their departure from Chicago opened the door for the Giants.

The season began well, however. The Giants won the opener, as they had every season before. This time Washington was the victim, as Ledell Titcomb pitched a three-hitter and won, 6 to 0.[8] All in all, it was a solid, satisfying victory. This happy beginning could not be sustained, however, and other, grimmer prophecies seemed borne out when the Giants opened at home. There was all of the usual ceremony. The stands were covered with flags and bunting, the Seventh Regiment Band played, and about ten thousand people overflowed the grandstand on to the field. But the crowd reserved its loudest cheers for John Ward, who was given a huge ovation when he appeared on the field. The message was unmistakable. Nothing short of the Pennant was going to justify the Giants' management. And the Giants lost. Philadelphia won the game, 5 to 3, defeating Smiling Mickey Welch. Moreover, the Giants played wretched baseball. They made eleven errors, three by Ward himself.[9] As Day, Mutrie, and Ewing headed home in the chilly spring twilight, they knew it might be a long season.

The reviews in the papers the next day were not encouraging. The fans, said the *New York Daily Tribune*, went home mad, certainly an understatement. As for the New York players,

> ...nine school boys might have done worse work than the Giants yesterday, but if they had they would have been so ashamed of themselves that they would not have dared to go home for their dinners.[10]

The day was not a total loss, however. On the evening of the game, the two teams were invited to Niblo's Theater to watch the play "Upside Down." Theater attendance had become a standard feature of big games at the Polo Grounds.

The most extraordinary result of the growing connection between baseball and the theater in New York came later in the season. It involved the Giants and the White Stockings, but only as spectators. The players were guests at Wallack's Theater for a special baseball night. On that occasion, DeWolf Hopper recited "Casey at the Bat" for the first time. He was already a music hall personality of some fame and he was to climb to even higher stardom in the operettas of Gilbert and Sullivan, but the baseball poem became his trademark. Hither and yon, early and late, DeWolf Hopper must have recited "Casey" a hundred-thousand times. As a long-run bill it rivaled even Joseph Jefferson in *Rip van Winkle*, and Bob Keeshan as Captain Kangaroo. It became one of the most celebrated acts ever seen in American theater.[11] The poem, and Hopper's innumerable renditions of it, were part of the process by which baseball became the national game that A. G. Mills claimed it to be at the Delmonico's banquet.

Although the Giants redeemed themselves somewhat in the following week by winning three games from Philadelphia and splitting a four-game series with Boston, the team was not playing championship baseball. The Giants started their first western trip firmly mired in third place with a disappointing record of seven victories and four defeats.[12] On the western swing the Giants slipped even farther behind. The boys returned to the Polo Grounds in fourth place, six games behind the White Stockings.[13]

The New York Giants: 1888. A formal portrait of the championship team in standard Victorian display.

Defeats on the field were reflected in criticism from the press box. Sportswriters' theories on the Giants' malaise ran from modest sympathy (the team had suffered injuries) to forthright condemnation (incompetence and bungling). But injuries and illness had been used too often to explain why the Giants were not winning. Something more fundamental must be wrong. It might be dissipation. There had been hints of that, twice, during this very season. Management denied them, of course. But Truthful James Mutrie did not seem very anxious to get to the bottom of the rumors. No, instead, Mutrie dismissed the tales of booze as unworthy of notice and fell back on his excuses about bad luck.[14]

Some critics were even harsher. The Giants were doing everything wrong. Ewing was playing an inept third base when he ought to be catching, which he did well. Connor was not hitting and Ward was suffering from a severe case of self-adulation. The rookies looked lousy. Ned "Cannonball" Crane

> ...was said to be the speediest pitcher in the country and was credited with such control of the ball that he could curve the sphere around the corner of a house and land it in a tin cup....

As it turned out, he could not do it. He was fast, all right, but he was wild. The two new outfielders were also disappointing:

> Foster has ... probably fewer base hits than any other regular player on the nine. He says that he has never batted so poorly before. But then he has never played in such fast company before. Slattery ought to be a second Tiernan in time, but that time is not yet.[15]

All of these problems, so frustrating, so undeserved by the faithful fan, had kept the Giants out of first place, where the Laws of Nature and Nature's God clearly intended them to be.

These speculations, though partly right, were not the whole story. The Giants simply had not yet jelled. Slattery, Foster, Cleveland, Crane, and Titcomb were all young, and no one knew if they were major league players. Nor were the regulars set in their positions. Ewing was playing mostly at third base and he even took a turn at shortstop. O'Rourke caught and played the outfield, where Mutrie was also using Gore, Tiernan, Slattery and Foster in every possible combination to find the right balance between hitting and fielding. Third base was a particularly troublesome spot, as Ewing could not field and Cleveland could neither field nor hit. Basically, Mutrie was having considerable difficulty in finding the best eight men to go with Welch and Keefe, the team's most dependable pitchers. In the meantime, of course, the Giants lost ball games.

Slowly, much too slowly for the kranks and sportswriters, Mutrie and Ewing fit the team together. Once the team came home, on May 26, it began to play better baseball. The lineup became more stable, with Cleveland getting a thorough trial at third base and Tiernan becoming a mainstay in the outfield. Ewing went back to catching. By June 3 the Giants had moved into third place, two and one half games behind Chicago. Buck Ewing was so encouraged that he announced that "...we are going right to the top now."[16]

Such optimism was a bit premature. By June 12 the Giants had again slipped to fourth place. The press once again began its litany of bad management and lazy play. The Giants, wrote one reporter, did not care whether they won or not. Sensitive to public opinion, Mutrie made a new effort to strengthen the team and win the press over. On June 16, he concluded a trade with Pittsburgh. Elmer Cleveland was traded for Arthur Whitney, a veteran infielder who could play third base and solve the Giants' most persistent problem.[17]

Whitney's arrival at the Polo Grounds was one of the reasons for the Giants midsummer success, but the pitching of Tim Keefe was more important. Sir Timothy suddenly stopped losing ball games. He beat the Phillies, 7 to 6, on June 23. It was not a great game; Keefe was hit hard in the last two innings, but he won and kept on winning. It was the beginning of a nineteen-game winning streak and the start of the Giants' rise to the top.[18] The winning ways had begun at home, but they continued on the road. The Giants began their second big western trip with an Independence Day double-header victory over Detroit, and they moved into third place, four and one half games behind Chicago. The real crunch, of course, came when the Giants played the White Stockings. On July 14, the New Yorkers lost the first game in a three game series. But Mutrie pitched Keefe in two consecutive games and the Giants won them both. When the team returned home on July 22, they were only two and one half games behind Chicago.[19]

Dispassionate observers attributed the Giants' victories to exceptional pitching and a newly stabilized lineup. The boys themselves, however, had a different explanation. They had finally acquired some good luck. It came in the form of a new and potent mascot, a freckle-faced street urchin from Chicago named Fred Boldt. When the team came to Chicago, Fred attached himself to the boys. After the Giants lost the first game, they chased Fred away, but Keefe's two victories changed their minds. They slipped Fred on the train to Pittsburgh, where the Giants kept on winning. Fred had to ride the rails to get to Philadelphia, but he finally arrived and the Giants won again. During the remainder of the road trip, the Giants lost only when Fred was absent. That was enough for Ewing, and he and some of the boys chipped in and fixed Fred up. They had him bathed, got his hair cut, and bought him some clothes. Ward, who lacked the common touch, was one of those who did not contribute, but most of the boys felt that with Fred Boldt on the scene, the Giants could not lose.[20]

When the Giants returned to New York they came home to a large number of delighted kranks and enthusiastic reporters. There were no more stories about mismanagement or players who did not hustle. Instead, the sportswriters wrote about the Pennant, and several papers carried a cartoon showing Mutrie for Governor, Ewing for Mayor, and Orator Jim O'Rourke for District Attorney. The kranks swarmed to the Polo Grounds to see the new heroes, so recently and dramatically transformed from bums and slackers. "You will have to go early if you want a good seat at the Polo Grounds about these times," said a stockbroker at the Exchange.[21] And it was true. Seven thousand kranks appeared on a Monday afternoon to see Tim Keefe (and Fred Boldt) defeat Boston, 2 to 0.[22] Those who could not get to the game jammed saloons that chalked the score inning by inning on a blackboard, a service sustained by small boys who commuted between park and bar. Others hung around the newspaper bulletin boards in Park Row, where the scores were posted on all the major games of the day. It was reminiscent of 1885, but this time the news was good. It was the Giants who were winning. After six straight victories over Boston and Philadelphia, the Giants were tied for first place with Detroit.[23] On July 31, the Giants won and Detroit lost, and the New York club was alone in first place at last.[24]

Once in first place the Giants began to win at an even more furious pace. On July 31 they began a ten-game winning streak that carried the team far ahead of its rivals. When they finally lost a game, on August 11, the Giants were six and one half games in front of Chicago. The last game in the winning streak was also Tim Keefe's nineteenth consecutive victory.[25]

While the season still had two months to run, the Giants' August spurt really decided the championship. Throughout the rest of August and September, the Giants were never fewer than six games in the lead. On October 4th, Cannonball Crane defeated the White Stockings, 1 to 0, allowing only one hit. It was the best game he had ever pitched. New York scored the only run of the game in the fifth inning when Arthur Whitney came home on a wild pitch.[26] The Giants had won the pennant at last.

There were celebrations, of course, but the joy in New York was somewhat restrained. Anticipation had absorbed much of the fans' emotion; after all, the Giants had led the league by a comfortable margin for two months. No one was surprised when victory finally came. But the occasion did require some formal acknowledgment. A delegation of Giants fans petitioned Mayor Abram Hewitt for permission to fly the National League pennant from the flagstaff on City Hall, but the mayor, who had a strong sense of Victorian proprieties and was a reformer to boot, refused outright. The benefit organized for the Giants' players by DeWolf Hopper and Digby Bell was much more successful. Held at the Star Theater, it featured champagne, entertainment, and the formal presentation of the pennant by Congressman Amos Cummings. It also brought in about three thousand dollars to be divided among the players.[27]

The Giants' victory also inspired both fans and sportswriters to search for appropriate explanations for the joyous event. This was, after all, essentially the same team that had limped home a weak fourth in 1887. The most common explanation was that the Giants were the greatest players in America. There was a modicum of truth to that; there always is when a team wins the pennant. Buck Ewing had done well, batting .306, and Roger Connor had hit 14 home runs. But the man who had had the best year was Tim Keefe. He had won 33 games, 19 of them in a row, and had only lost 11. He led the league in shutouts with eight, in strikeouts with 333, and in earned run average with 1.74.[28] His nineteen-game winning streak had provided the momentum for the Giants' midsummer drive from fourth place to the pennant. Keefe had pitched the Giants to victory.

There was another reason for the Giants' success, however. It was the decline of the Chicago White Stockings. During the early eighties Albert Spalding and Cap Anson had corralled a fair number of the best players in the Republic. The White Stockings had won in 1880, '81, '82, '85, and '86, and were unquestionably the best team in baseball. Then, after the 1886 season, Spalding began to break the team up. Some, like outfielders George Gore, Abner Dalrymple and Billy Sunday, were slightly over the hill but still had several good years left. But King Kelly was in his prime in 1886 when Spalding sold him to Boston, and John Clarkson, Chicago's best pitcher, also sold to Boston for $10,000, had many superb years left. Spalding and Anson could not find adequate replacements for these stars. Most of the new men, with the notable exception of outfielder Hugh Duffy, were just not as good as their predecessors.

It was not entirely clear why Spalding sold off his best players and crippled his team. Perhaps he was relieved to part with genial Kelly, whose *joie de*

The Chicago White Stockings: 1888. An informal portrait of the Chicago nine, which was past its prime as a team when this picture was taken. Not all of the roster was present, though several admirers were.

vivre contrasted so sharply with Spalding's rural, Protestant puritanism. Certainly Spalding was growing away from baseball. Once a player, then a club owner, Spalding, by the late eighties, was rapidly becoming a merchant-manufacturer of sporting goods. His shops could be found in major cities, and he had already formed his sporting goods trust with Wright and Ditson and with Reach. He now thought of himself as an entrepreneur, and winning baseball was less important than profitable baseball.[29]

The result was a shift in power in the National League. As Spalding scattered his stars, the Giants became the best team in the league. Composed primarily of veteran players, possessing both pitching and hitting, the Giants were the team to beat after 1886. In 1887 the boys were too preoccupied with internal disputes to play their best ball. But in 1888, with Chicago clearly declining, the Giants swept to another pennant.

Winning the pennant was not the end of the season, however. Even then there was a world series. Arrangements were then made between club owners, who decided on the format that would bring them the greatest profit. Negotiations between John B. Day and Chris von der Ahe, the owner of the American Association champion St. Louis Browns, produced easy agreement. There would be a ten game series, with the first team to win six being the champions. The first six games were scheduled for the east, four in New York and the others in Brooklyn and Philadelphia, while the last four would be played in St. Louis.

For Chis von der Ahe, the World Series of 1888 was another triumph in a baseball career composed almost exclusively of profits and glory. He was the major power in the American Association and the owner of its only good team. The Browns were phenomenally successful, winning the American Association flag four years in a row, 1885, '86, '87, and '88, and nearly winning it again in 1889. Moreover, they played Sunday baseball, had twenty-five cent admission, and sold beer and whiskey on the grounds. In some ways, the Browns were an adjunct to von der Ahe's saloon and grocery, a scheme to stimulate business in both stores. But by 1888 baseball for von der Ahe had gone well beyond being only a shill for business. He loved the fame, the glory, the recognition, and the admiration that came from success in sports. He was a cheerful, generous and expansive man anyhow, and the public gaze stimulated these good qualities marvelously. For the New York series, his first appearance in the leading city of the land, Vondy went all out. He asked A. H. Spink, the sports editor of the St. Louis Globe-Democrat to make the arrangements. These included a special train, complete with Pullmans, dining cars, lounges stocked with food and drink, and bunting proclaiming the Browns as the greatest team in the world. The whole thing cost him nearly $20,000, a big sum in those days. But von der Ahe paid happily. Nothing was too good for him and his boys.[30]

The fifth of these Paleozoic and rather haphazard world series began on October 16 at the Polo Grounds. Keefe was in the box for the Giants and Silver King pitched for the Browns. Both men were in good form, as the phrase then went. Each gave up only three hits. But Keefe was luckier. The Giants scored the winning run in the third inning without benefit of a hit. Mike Tiernan walked, stole second, and scored when the Browns' catcher threw the ball into center field. Keefe made the one-run lead stand up and the Giants won the opening game, 2 to 1.[31]

The outcome did not surprise the Giants' fans, nor did it particularly elate them. They were certain that the National League was the stronger circuit, a view fostered by the League leadership which treated the American Association with ill-concealed contempt. For the complacent Giants' fans, therefore, the series did not become real until the Brownies won the second game. Elton Chamberlain defeated Smiling Mickey Welch, 3 to 0. The Giants got only five hits. Vondy and the Browns' fans were delighted. Their secret doubts about beating the Giants were now gone. The players were toasted again and again in the bar of the Grand Central Hotel, and there were loud predictions, fortified with champagne, that the Browns were going to win it all.[32]

The happy champagne toasts on the evening of October 17 were to be the high point of the series for the St. Louis Browns. The Giants won the next four games to head west with a commanding five to one advantage. In the third game, Keefe was again the winner. The Giants won, 4 to 2, scoring twice in the first inning and again in the fourth and seventh, while Keefe held St. Louis to single runs in the eighth and ninth innings. This victory was followed by another the next day, as Cannonball Crane defeated the Browns, 6 to 3. The Giants made it three in a row as Keefe won again, 6 to 4. In the sixth game, played in Philadelphia, the Browns scored four runs off Mickey Welch in the first three innings, but the Giants came back to win easily with three runs in the seventh inning and five more in the eighth. The final score was 12 to 5.[33]

Although St. Louis kranks reassured themselves that their boys would play better ball at home, these were hollow hypes. The Brownies did win the first game in St. Louis, 7 to 5. But that was their last gasp. New York pitched Tim Keefe the next day and won easily, 11 to 3.[34] The Giants were the World Champions.

II

The 1889 season began in confusion for the Giants. Two players, Cannonball Crane and John Ward, had been part of the Spalding around-the-world tour, which did not end until April 13, barely two weeks before the new season began.[35] They were back far too late to do much training with the team. Even more distressing was the loss of a playing field. The old Polo Grounds at 5th Avenue and 110th Street was cut in two by a proposed new street. There had been hints that this might happen for over a year, but John B. Day, a Tammany politician, had tried to stop it. He had asked for an injunction preventing the Commissioner of Public Works from cutting the new street, or in any way interfering with the baseball park. Day was dismayed to find that there were limits even to the clout of a Tammany brave. On July 14, 1888, Judge Ingraham of the Supreme Court denied the injunction, and ordered the Commissioner of Public Works to put 111th Street through whenever it might be convenient.[36] Day was able to make it inconvenient for the rest of the 1888 season, but that was as far as he could go. His hopes of tying the matter up in court for another year failed. On February 8, 1889, Inspector McGuiness of the Bureau of Encumbrances spent most of the day supervising a gang of workmen who were ripping down the fence around the park in preparation for cutting the street through. In an effort to save his field, Day offered ten thousand dollars to city charities, but the adjacent property owners, the city aldermen, and the law were all against him.[37] After a month of effort he gave it up. The old Polo Grounds were gone.

When the 1889 season began, then, John B. Day had a championship team and no good place to show it off. His choices lay between Oakland Park in Jersey City and the old Metropolitan's stadium in St. George, Staten Island. Both were inconvenient and distant from public transportation. No matter how good the Giants were, Day was going to lose a fortune if they had to play in either spot all season.

There was also considerable doubt about how good the Giants were going to be. Ward and Keefe were again holdouts. Money was part of it, although Ward and Keefe were among the highest paid players in baseball. Moreover, both had outside business interests. Ward was a lawyer, and Keefe had real estate investments and ran a sporting goods store at 157 Broadway. He furnished the Giants with their uniforms. For Ward, especially, the estrangement ran much deeper than money. Ward was president of the Brotherhood of Professional Base Ball Players, and he took an anti-management view of the business side of baseball. Furthermore, Ward had been feuding with the New York management for years. He had not forgiven his removal as captain in 1887 nor Day's opposition to his participation in the Spalding tour. After the 1888 season Ward had stated publicly that he did not wish to play any longer with New York. Day was quite aware of all this, and he tried to sell his star shortstop before the season began. He set the price at $12,000, saying that anyone, even the powerful Boston Red Stockings, could have Ward. Both Boston and Washington made a major effort to sign Ward, with Washington agreeing to make Ward manager. At the last minute, however, Ward became coy. He retracted his refusal to play another year in New York and stated that he would retire and practice law if traded. No team was willing to take that chance. So Ward and Day reopened negotiations, and, on opening day, Ward signed. Two weeks later, on May 9, Keefe came to terms.[38]

Thus, when the new season opened, the Giants were not ready, either emotionally or professionally. The first game was on April 24, and it was played at Oakland Park in Jersey City. Three thousand forty-two fans jammed into the small, rickety structure to watch the Giants meet the Boston Red Stockings. New York lost. Boston took an early 8 to 1 lead and hung on to win, 8 to 7, the Giants' first opening day defeat.[39]

Nothing about that day was satisfactory. The boys had lost, the New York kranks were unable to see their heroes, and the club was losing money. One more game in Oakland Park was all the disgruntled Day could stand. He promptly moved the team to St. George on Staten Island. But the St. George park was no better than Jersey City. It, too, was small and inconvenient. It was also low, right off the water. This was fine in good weather. The fans sat in the grandstand and looked out over the playing field to the ships in New York harbor. It made a nice backdrop for baseball. But there was not much good weather during the spring of 1889. It rained almost constantly and the field was frequently flooded. So poor was the drainage that the club had planks placed over the swamp in the outfield, and the fielders slipped and skidded over them in their efforts to catch the balls that came their way.[40]

For the Giants the rain was an inconvenience, but in other parts of the

Republic it brought incredible tragedy. On May 31 an earthen dam on the south fork of the Conemaugh River broke after an exceptionally heavy storm. A tidal wave swept down the narrow Conemaugh valley to Johnstown, burying the town under thirty feet of water and muck. So powerful was the flood that it literally scoured the Conemaugh valley down to the bed-rock, carrying houses, factories, trains, trees, dirt and debris to deposit it on top of what little was left of Johnstown. About 2500 people perished in the flood, including many whose bodies were buried so deep that they were never found. The property damage ran into the tens of millions, including most of the homes in the valley and its two largest industries, the Cambria Iron Works and the Johnson Company, which made switches, curves, and frogs for street railroads. The desolation was complete. Many were dead, and those who had survived were without food, home, clothes, or jobs.

The catastrophe was so stupendous that it caught the attention of the entire nation. Relief trains started for Johnstown on the day of the flood, and they came in droves from much of the nation. Over three million dollars in cash was collected, some of it from Europe, along with dozens of train loads of food, blankets, clothes, tools and medicines. The Pennsylvania Railroad donated thousands of man-hours of labor and tons of equipment to the process of repair and cleanup. Clara Barton, an exceptionally efficient and unpleasant woman, came in person to lead the Red Cross effort. The relief program was absolutely massive.

Equally impressive was the reporting of the disaster. Reporters, photographers, even artists headed for Johnstown as soon as they heard about the flood. When they saw the destruction they realized that this was the biggest story of their lives. They set out to do it justice. Fact, rumor and fabrication poured from Johnstown in an endless stream of purple prose, and worse. Horror struggled with bathos in the Johnstown dispatches. "The phrase 'no pen can describe...' kept cropping up again and again, but the pens kept right on describing."[41] They described the flood in newspapers, books, novels and poems. In the end the torrent of words and pictures conquered the torrent of water and debris. The Johnstown flood left the realm of horror and entered that of folklore. Its epitaph became one of the three genuine American proverbs: "Don't spit on the floor. Remember the Johnstown flood."[42] By 1900 that simple slogan was emblazoned in every saloon in America.

For the dedicated Giants fan the flood was only a transient diversion from an exceptionally unsatisfactory season. The problem of a decent park remained unsolved. St. George was virtually under water by the middle of May and the Giants tried to regain possession of the Polo Grounds. Day instigated a petition from the inhabitants of the neighborhood to the effect that low toughs were hanging around the deserted park to the evident disturbance of the public repose. This ploy failed. Next, Day put pressure on the Board of Aldermen, who voted not to grade the new street in 1889. That helped, but it did not give the Giants permission to play on the Polo Grounds, and without that permission Day was stymied. Finally, he gave up trying to pull strings and began to look for another location. After a couple of weeks he found one, at 155th Street in the lee of Coogan's Bluff overlooking the Harlem River. The contracts were signed on June 22, and teams of workmen started at once to get the place ready for the Giants' return on July 8. Day was delighted, and so were the players and fans.[43]

Problems with the park, while extremely vexing and costly, were only part of the trouble. The other part was the team. It was playing badly and losing games. Pitching was the main problem, as it usually is. Keefe signed late, on May 9, and only pitched four games before June. Ledell Titcomb was released on May 16, a victim of terminal ineffectiveness. This threw the burden on Welch and Crane, and they needed help. Buck Ewing pitched a couple of games, and Gil Hatfield, a reserve infielder, pitched six. They were not as bad as everyone had feared; between them they broke even, but it was not the same as seeing Tim Keefe in the box. Thus the Giants staggered badly in the early going. Most of June was spent in fourth place, even though Keefe was back. Not until the last week in June did the boys begin to look like the National League champions. They won eight of their last eleven games on the road to come home in solid possession of third place.[44]

Although the team was struggling, newspaper comment tended to be exceptionally kind. Instead of the normal denunciation, the sportswriters leaned in the opposite direction. They made excuses for the fallen idols:

> As soon as the Giants' pitchers Welch, Keefe, and Crane recover from their troubles, the New-York team will make a much better record than it has been doing of late.... The champions are doing better team work than they ever did before....[45]

This contribution was followed by another layer of soft soap:

> Should the Giants even get within hailing distance of the Boston men, that aesthetic team will shake with terror and like cowards slink out of sight. The Giants have more pluck ... in their little fingers than the Boston players have in their whole bodies.[46]

The testing time for this extravagant praise would come when the Giants returned to New York and played at the new Polo Grounds. For weeks the players, kranks, and management had been saying that the Giants would win if they could only get out of that wretched Staten Island mud puddle. Now they were. On July 8 the Giants returned from their western swing to a brand new park.

The first game was against Pittsburgh. The kranks came out in record numbers. Over ten thousand jammed into the park and several thousand were turned away. DeWolf Hopper was there, as was a contingent from the Stock

The Polo Grounds, New York, 1902. Coogan's Bluff and the "el" train are visible behind the field. Northeastern Manhattan was only partially developed as late as the turn of the century, and the Giants played "out of town" (collection of the New York Historical Society).

Exchange who presented Buck Ewing with a watch. Many of the kranks who could not get into the park climbed to the top of Coogan's Bluff and watched from there, a site that promptly acquired the name of dead-head hill. This mass of close-packed humanity roasting in the summer sun wanted a New York victory. They got it. The boys beat Pittsburgh, 7 to 5, with Cannonball Crane getting the victory in spite of hitting several Pittsburgh batters.[47]

The new park seemed to be just what the Giants needed, for they won nine of their next eleven games to move into second place, just a game behind the slumping Red Stockings. The fans expected to see New York in first place shortly. Excitement and confidence reached the point where New York sportswriters were assuring the kranks (and themselves) that Boston could not win:

> Moral courage and confidence, so conspicuous in the New-York team, is sadly lacking in the Boston nine. Some of the players of visiting teams have told the writer that half of the Boston players firmly believe that their team cannot win the championship.[48]

It was a little early for such boasting. With the Giants only a game behind the leaders it was New York, not Boston, that stumbled. The Giants fell four and one half games behind the Red Stockings by the end of July. Mutrie moved quickly to strengthen his team. He acquired Hank O'Day, a veteran pitcher from the Washington club.[49]

On August 4 the Giants started on a long western trip, and a sizable crowd of kranks gathered at Grand Central Station to see the boys off. And the Giants did well, winning eight of the twelve games in the west. The road trip ended with a three-game series in Boston. Again, a crowd came to the station to see the boys off. The mood was solemn. This was a crucial series. Boston had a one and one half game lead, and the Giants would have to win all three games to go into first place. The Giants fell far short of that. The first game ended in a tie, but Boston won the next two. New York had fallen three and one half games behind the Red Stockings.[50]

It was a chastened group of athletes who returned to the Polo Grounds, but they were not so discouraged that they stopped winning. Indeed, they played better baseball than Boston. Slowly, the Giants gained on the leaders. By September 4, New York was only a game out of first place. When the Giants finished their home season with two victories over Chicago on September 14, they were only half a game back.[51]

The crowds at the Polo Grounds reflected the excitement of the closest pennant race in National League history. Eight thousand fans turned out on a dreary autumn afternoon to watch the Giants close out their last home stand against the White Stockings. Ten thousand had watched the Giants win a Labor Day double-header from Pittsburgh, and a three game series with Boston drew over thirty-one thousand kranks. Day, of course, was delighted. So were the property owners around the Polo Grounds. Baseball had driven their property values up. It had done the same thing for the elevated line. All those baseball passengers had provided a large and unexpected profit.[52]

When the Giants left for their final western trip on September 15, the kranks were pessimistic. They feared a slump on the road. The next day, however, the Giants defeated the Washington Senators and moved into first place as Boston lost. It was not a safe or commanding lead, only half a game, and, while the Giants kept winning, so did Boston. The Giants won twelve games in a row. Boston won thirteen. By September 26, with less than ten days to go, the two teams were tied for first place. It was an anxious time for Giants' fans, as they watched the bulletin boards in saloons and the newspaper office.[53]

Then the Giants stumbled. On October 1 they lost to Pittsburgh and fell a game behind Boston. But it was only temporary. The next day Cannonball Crane defeated Pittsburgh, 6 to 3, while the Red Stockings lost to Cleveland. It was the most crucial defeat of the year for Boston. Not only did they fall out of the lead, but King Kelly showed up for the game drunk. He sat on the Cleveland bench and made obscene comments on the game. As the Red Stockings fell behind, Kelly shouted. "You never win when I don't play! Kelly is King! I am a King!" In the sixth inning he tried to assault the umpire when a close call went against the Red Stockings, and the police grabbed him and threw him out of the park. When he tried to get back in the kranks jeered him, telling the King to buy a ticket or walk it off. It was a sad afternoon.[54]

When the lead changed hands on October 2 there were only three games left. Both teams won the first two. It all came down to the last day of the season. Boston was only two percentage points behind New York. Both teams pitched their best, Keefe for the Giants and Clarkson for the Red Stockings. Again, crowds gathered on Park Row to watch the bulletin boards, and the faithful were rewarded with good news. Boston lost to Pittsburgh, and the Giants defeated Cleveland, 5 to 3. The Giants were still the champions. The kranks celebrated by singing their new ditty:

> There are no flies on us
> For we are the People!
> There are no flies on us
> There may be one or two
> On Kelly and his crew
> But there are no flies on us![55]

Popular enthusiasm ran high as it had in 1888, and several hundred people came to the Erie terminal in Jersey City to welcome the Giants home. Nearly all of the players were there, the only significant exception being John Montgomery Ward who was planning for the new league to be run by the players. The kranks called for speeches, and James Mutrie made one. This last trip, he said,

> has been one of the most remarkable ever made by a ball nine. We played ball that surpassed anything that I ever witnessed.... That last game in Cleveland was the greatest ever played. The spirit of our boys manifested itself there. They went to do or die.... On that occasion I really felt proud of the boys.... This contest has been a grand one and the Bostons deserve credit for the close race they gave us. The Bostons are good players but we are the people.[56]

As in 1888 there was a world series arranged with the champions of the American Association. For the first time since 1884, this was not the St. Louis Browns. The Brooklyn Bridegrooms, so named because several of their players had recently been married, beat the Brownies out by two games in the last week of the season. The fact that Brooklyn would be the opponent added interest to the series, but the National League fans still felt that their entry was clearly the better team. That smugness received a severe jolt when the Giants lost the first game of the series, 12 to 10. Keefe was in "poor form," and the Bridegrooms hit him hard and often. Even so, the Giants were ahead until the last inning, when Brooklyn scored four runs and won the game.[57]

Expectations in Brooklyn rose magnificently after that victory, and more than sixteen thousand kranks crammed into Washington Park or sat on the fence to see the Briderooms do it again. But this time the Giants won. Mutrie pitched Cannonball Crane on the theory that blinding speed was needed to win. Crane did very well indeed, giving up only two hits as the Giants won easily 6 to 2. The series was even at a game apiece.⁵⁸

This renewed the Giants' confidence, and Buck Ewing boasted before the third game that he would bet one hundred dollars to a toothpick that the Giants would win again. Buck was fortunate there were no takers, because the Giants lost, 8 to 7. Disregarding his own theories about fastball pitchers, Mutrie started Welch. Smiling Mickey was hit hard. This loss was followed by another. Mutrie went back to his theories about speed and called on Crane, but this time the Cannonball did not have it. Brooklyn won, 10 to 7, and went ahead in the series, three games to one.⁵⁹ The series had become much less the sure thing it had so recently seemed.

In an effort to bounce back Mutrie bypassed his aces, Keefe and Welch, and again pitched Crane. This time he won, 11 to 3. Encouraged by Crane's performance, Mutrie started another reserve pitcher, Hank O'Day. He pitched a superb game, and the Giants won in the tenth inning, 2 to 1, as Ward drove Slattery in with the winning run. Confident now that he had found the winning touch, Mutrie sent Crane back for a fourth game. The Cannonball was only modestly effective, but the Giants scored eight runs in the second inning and won easily, 11 to 7. Sensing that the Bridegrooms were on the skids, Mutrie sent Cannonball Crane back to the box for his fifth start. The Giants scored ten runs in the first three innings to help him out, and Crane coasted to a 16 to 7 victory. One more win would do it, and Mutrie pitched Hank O'Day. O'Day had been an important part of the New York pennant drive, winning nine games and losing only one while with the Giants. He had also been exceptionally effective in the series. O'Day had never pitched better baseball in his life, and Mutrie was confident he could win. And he did. Brooklyn got two runs in the first inning, but O'Day shut them out for the rest of the game. Meanwhile, the Giants pecked away, getting single runs in the first inning, and again in the sixth and seventh, to win the game and the series. For the second year in a row the Giants were World Champions.⁶⁰

The Giants and their kranks celebrated victory in the usual way. The players met the day after the series ended and split up their share of the proceeds. It came to $380.13 a man. There was also the benefit. It was organized by DeWolf Hopper and Nick Engel, proprietor of the Home Plate Saloon, a favorite hangout of the boys. The benefit was a huge success. Everyone applauded the Giants enthusiastically and assured the players that they were the toast of the town. Over the stage hung a huge banner with the Giants' slogan printed on it. "We are the People."⁶¹ But the benefit was one of the last times that proud boast would be heard. No sooner had the world series ended than the revolt of the Brotherhood of Professional Base Ball Players broke over the major leagues. The focus of the struggle would be New York, and the leading victim would be John B. Day and his Giants.

CHAPTER FIVE

THE BROTHERHOOD WAR

The reserve lists for the 1890 season were published on October 20, 1889, while the world series was still in progress. The New York list included all of the regulars and most of the reserves, fourteen men in all. Along with the published lists came a letter to each man reserved.

> You will please take notice that the New-York Ball Club hereby exercises its option for your services ... and does hereby now employ you under the provisions of said contract and retain your services for the season of 1890....[1]

The boys had received such messages before, of course, and they had always come in to negotiate. But not now. This time, under the leadership of John Montgomery Ward, the vast majority of players had resolved to found their own league as a final remedy against practices they felt to be mean and needless abuses.

I

The Brotherhood of Professional Base Ball Players had been in existence for several years by the fall of 1889. It had been founded on October 22, 1885 in New York, and was, from the first, dominated by the New York players. Ward became president and Tim Keefe was the secretary. The original members included Joe Gerhardt, Buck Ewing, Roger Connor, Danny Richardson, Smiling Mickey Welch, Mike Dorgan, and Orator Jim O'Rourke. The principles and objectives of the new organization were set down in a few sentences. The Brotherhood wished

> To protect and benefit ourselves collectively and individually. To promote a high standard of professional conduct. To foster and encourage the interests of the game of baseball.[2]

The immediate cause of the formation of the Brotherhood was the National League limitation rule, which stated that no player could be paid over $2,000 a season. Adopted on October 16, 1885, the limitation rule was designed to help the weaker clubs, which could not afford the salaries paid in New York, Chicago, or Boston, and to increase profits everywhere by halting what the magnates saw as an ominous trend of continually rising salaries.[3]

In spite of players' fears, the limitation rule was a dead letter from the day of its adoption. The owners cheated. While assuring each other that they were following the rule, they paid their better players substantially more than the limitation allowed. On the Giants alone, O'Rourke made $4500 in 1885, while Ewing made $3100, Ward and Keefe $3000 each, and Roger Connor $2200.[4] Considering the team's artistic and financial success, it was impossible to imagine these salaries falling to comply with the new limitation rule. And they did not. They rose. By 1889 Ewing and Kelly were making $5000, and a score of men made $3500, while the average salary in the National League was over $2000.[5]

Beyond that, the magnates were never able to persuade the fans that salaries ought to be so tightly limited. The owners did their best, subjecting the public to a river of propaganda. As he did with temperance, Spalding led the way. He maintained that the "...rivalry for the possession of the best players each season has been from the very outset an obstacle to the equitable arrangement of the salary question...." Salaries, said the magnates, have come to be based on all the player could squeeze from any club that would hire him. This, Spalding thought, was manifestly unreasonable. "Reasonable" salaries should be based on a player's value to the club, an

> ...equitable estimate of a ball player's worth on the basis of the relation it bears to that of any other occupation he might be competent to engage in.... Here is a ball player, who, as a street car driver or conductor, a brakeman, a porter, or an assistant at some ordinary trade in which, at his work as a common day laborer he can only command ten dollars a week for his services, and to earn that has to work laboriously from ten to fifteen hours each day; and yet this self-same individual is taught by unscrupulous or short-sighted rival clubs to believe that he is treated harshly if he is not readily given $2000 as a salary for six months work as a ball player, in which his work is comparatively a pleasant recreation, requiring but two or three hours of easy work each day.

Indignation was followed by homily.

> Experienced players ought by this time to have practically realized the fact that it is far more to their advantage in every way for them to accept a moderate salary from a sound organization, which has an established reputation for fair dealing with its employees than to sign for a salary double in amount offered by a less reputable club.[6]

There was a world of hypocrisy, self-serving, and class bias contained in that view, and the kranks knew it. Why should not players be judged on their skill in the field, their value to the team? There were many players worth more than the $2000 salary limit, and the kranks thought they ought to be paid what they were worth. There was, of course, great disagreement as to just what that figure might be, but the magnates were never able to justify their arbitrary limit.[7]

It was not until 1887, when the Brotherhood had over ninety members, that it made much of a stir in baseball. It petitioned the National League for official recognition at the winter meeting to the intense displeasure of league president Nick Young, who at first refused to deal with what he called "a secret organization." But Albert Spalding, who had been a player, understood the lack of wisdom in that attitude. He talked to Young about it, reminding him that Ward had attended a rules committee meeting the previous year as a Brotherhood delegate. After listening to Spalding, the league president so far reversed himself as to invite Ward and his players' committee to attend the National League meeting and discuss things.[8]

The conversations that November were restrained and decorous. The Brotherhood wanted the reserve rule specifically included in the contract, and it wished the annual salary written in as well. This meant the abolition of the limitation rule, for many players were paid over $2000 a season. Ward argued that it was a dead letter anyway, and a needless irritant to the players. Further, the Brotherhood requested that no one be reserved at a lower salary then previously paid.

The magnates bargained a bit, but they made substantial concessions to the players' point of view. The owners agreed to change the contract to read:

> 18. It is further understood and agreed that the said party of the first part (the club) shall have the right to reserve the said party of the second part (the player) for the season next ensuing....
>
> That the party of the second part shall not be reserved at a salary less than that mentioned in the 20th paragraph herein except by the consent of the party of the second part.[9]

On the limitation rule the magnates hedged a bit. They agreed to put the true salary figure in the contract but only if the American Association concurred. In return for this agreement, the Brotherhood accepted the reserve clause and a scale of fines for dissipation.[10]

These agreements, however, were built upon a foundation of sand, in spite of the fact that the changes suggested by the Brotherhood strengthened baseball's traditional system of doing business. It was the fact that the players had proposed them that irritated the owners. So, bit by bit, they reneged on their deal. Before the 1888 season started, the owners informed the Brotherhood that the American Association was unwilling to abandon the limitation rule, so the National League could not do it either. Then, after the season ended, the magnates announced that some players would indeed be reserved at a lower salary than they had previously earned.[11] In the course of a single season the magnates had broken their entire bargain.

For the players, the retreat from agreement and amity was slower and more cautious. There was no revolt in 1888. The players were not ready for one, either psychologically or organizationally. But the broken agreements did serve to focus the players' attention on the reserve clause, which had been resented for several years. As early as 1884, Ward had attacked reservation. In a letter to the *New York Clipper*, Ward had called the reserve rule a usurpation of players' rights. He advised players that they could break it if they wished. It had no moral or legal weight.[12]

The short and comparatively mild statement was followed by one much more harsh. In a letter published on July 17, 1887 in the *New York Times*, Ward set forth some basic complaints about the reserve clause. The first was the sale of players' contracts. This issue had become critical when Spalding had sold King Kelly to Boston in the spring of 1887. The price for Kelly's contract was $10,000, a truly stupendous sum. How did Spalding get that much for the King? It was from the reserve clause. Boston had purchased the rights to Kelly's services forever.

> It is not the ordinary assignment of a legal contract claim for future service that makes the price, but the anticipated operation of the reserve rule. The rule, therefore, is being used not as a means of retaining the services of a player but for increasing his value for the purposes of sale. This is a clear perversion of the original intent of the rule.

The injustice was even clearer when one realized that King Kelly got no part of the purchase price. It all went to Spalding. Kelly did get a substantial salary boost; the publicity attending the sale made that inevitable, but a less renowned player might not get even that.

Moreover, the sales system took no account of the player's preferences: "no matter how many reasons for wishing to go elsewhere, he is forced to go to his purchaser or nowhere." And, as the league magnates knew, very few players had sufficient resources to go nowhere for any length of time.

This system, evil enough in itself, was recently twisted to include further abuses. When a club failed, as Kansas City and St. Louis did after the 1886 season, its players did not become free agents. Instead, "the avarice of the clubs was equal to the occasion, and the League itself, [whatever that might mean] reserved these men and peddled them out at so much per head." Of course, the man had to go where he was sent, and the club that bought him could offer any contract it wished. If no club wanted him he could not play in the major leagues. He was reserved out of a job.

Finally, clubs had begun an undesirable practice known as "loaning."

Under this system one club would loan a player to another, keeping the right to recall the player at a stated time. The reserve rule, and the threat of the blacklist, made it impossible for a player to refuse such an arrangement.

All of these practices — loaning, sales, reservation, blacklists — had reduced the player to the status of a serf. And these practices must be abolished. They were illegal and unjust. But the prevailing system of "baseball law"

> ...has become so rooted that heroic treatment may be necessary to remove it; but go it must, like every other, founded upon so great injustice and misuse of power. The only question is, Whence shall the remedy proceed? Shall it come from the clubs, or from the players, or from both?...[13]

In this salvo, which preceded the meeting with the owners by only a couple of months, Ward called for the reform of the reserve system, not its abolition. He admitted that reservation was needed to protect the value of baseball stock, as "...the defection of a few important players might render it worthless."[14] He had pursued that line in meeting with the magnates. But in 1888, under the impact of the magnates' duplicity, Ward and the Brotherhood began to take a harder line. By the end of the season they had decided that the personal liberty and individual rights of the players could be protected only by destroying the reserve rule. Ward was going to take it to court. He would ask for the right to sign with the club he chose and would ask the court to restrain the National League from preventing him from playing. Furthermore, all members of the Brotherhood would be asked to refuse to sign their new contracts until the test case was settled.[15]

But the test case was never made. Ward denied that one was even being prepared.[16] Instead, the players signed their contracts though Ward himself, for the second year in a row, was a holdout. Moreover, Ward went on the Spalding tour around the world, and Brotherhood affairs were left in limbo for the winter of 1888–1889. League affairs were not, however. Taking advantage of Ward's and Spalding's absence, the magnates in their meeting in November passed the Classification Plan. It was the invention of John T. Brush, owner of the Indianapolis club and arose from the demand of the weaker franchises for some league assistance. The plan, a change in section 29 of the league constitution, proposed that all players be grouped into five classes based on the player's ability, record, personal habits, and attitude. The classes were to be as follows:

A	$2500 salary	
B	$2200 salary	
C	$2000 salary	
D	$1750 salary	
E	$1500 salary[17]	

Approved overwhelmingly by the magnates, this plan included everything the players disliked about the current system. The Brush Classification Plan had the threat of blacklisting, reservation at lower salaries, the club's degrading interference with a man's personal life, and management evaluations made on the basis of such intangibles as attitude toward one's owner and the game.

When Ward heard about it he wanted to leave the tour at once, but Spalding persuaded him to continue. When he returned in April, 1889, however, Ward began a series of conferences with members of the Brotherhood to determine what ought to be done about this latest outrage. A strike was considered but voted down. The Brotherhood preferred further negotiation. In its meeting on May 19, 1889, it appointed a committee headed by Ward to discuss things with the magnates. The players wanted the new classification rule repealed, and an end to the sale of contracts, and immediate action on these complaints. After their last experience with the magnates, the players were hostile and suspicious:

> Salary limits and classification systems ... are schemes devised by mean managers who want to keep the men down to rock-bottom prices in order to enable them to pocket big dividends.[18]

On June 25 Ward and his committee met with Spalding and laid their demands before him. The Brotherhood wanted action right now. It was important, Ward said; the players were serious and would not be put off. For once, Spalding's instinct failed him. He was a naturally optimistic, cheerful, and expansive man, and those qualities overruled his judgment. Everything was going to be all right, he told himself. So he countered the players' demand by saying that the issues ought to be put off until the regular meeting of the National League, after the season. When Tim Keefe, the secretary of the Brotherhood, heard this, he said only, "The League will not classify as many as they think."[19]

After the meeting with Spalding, the Brotherhood turned rapidly to a new plan. Amid many comments to the effect that the players would do nothing, Ward and his lieutenants pushed secret efforts to form another league. They searched for backers who would supply the capital to start the new circuit. Their first success was in Cleveland, where street railway magnates Tom and Albert Johnson were quite interested in backing a new club in a new league. In his later years (1901–1909), Tom Johnson would be reform mayor of Cleveland and engage the Interests in spectacular and ferocious battles mostly devoid of results. But before he succumbed to the gospel of reform, Tom Johnson had been an important and significant figure in the traction (street cars) industry, where his efforts to improve the technology and to lower the costs actually brought people the benefits that his bawling for reform only promised. In 1876 young Tom Johnson had gone into business for himself, borrowing thirty thousand dollars from his former employer, Bidermann du

Pont. Johnson purchased the street railway system in Indianapolis. He turned that deteriorated road into an efficient and profitable business, and three years later he obtained a traction franchise in Cleveland, where the street railway business was dominated by Mark Hanna. The twenty-five-year-old tycoon had a tough time with Uncle Mark, who controlled the city council and used his political pull to oppose Johnson's applications for city franchises. By 1882, however, Johnson had won out and was established, with his brother Albert, as a successful and enterprising Cleveland traction magnate.

The reasons for Tom Johnson's rather startling success seem to have been twofold. The first involved technology. Johnson was an inventor as well as an executive. As early as 1876 he had invented a new and improved fare box. It held the coins in a glass case, in full view of everyone, thus reducing the opportunities for conductors to pilfer and passengers to ride free. By the middle eighties Johnson had come up with an improved design for curves, frogs, and switches, all to be made out of a particularly hard and durable steel. Thus, his roads had better equipment that lasted longer and needed less maintenance than his rivals'. Beyond that, Johnson was a "street railroad man," not a politician or a lawyer who had happened to invest in traction companies. He knew his business better than his competitors, and he worked harder at it than they did. He pioneered the free transfer system and the single fare, and he pushed his rates as low as possible so as to attract as many riders as he could. In a long struggle, therefore, Tom Johnson would prevail.

By 1889, Tom, Albert, and their brother Will Johnson had gone well beyond their Cleveland base. They held franchises in St. Louis and Brooklyn, and Tom had gone into the business of manufacturing traction equipment. In partnership with Arthur Moxham, he had established a steel plant in Johnstown, Pa., to manufacture the curves, frogs, and switches he had previously invented. Just before the plant went into full production it was devastated by the Johnstown Flood. But Johnson, a man of buoyant and optimistic temperament, rebuilt and made money both from the factory and a land development connected with it.[20]

Like the Johnson steel enterprise, interest in baseball had grown out of street railways. Along with everyone else, the brothers had noticed the surge in baseball attendance during the eighties. Most of those people went to the game by street car. Having a ball park on one's line meant a major boost in the endless struggles among the various traction interests. For the Johnsons, this fact had been illustrated in four major league towns—Cleveland, Indianapolis, St. Louis, and Brooklyn. Thus when Ned Hanlon approached Albert Johnson with a proposal that he back a club in the new league, the traction magnate was interested. He envisioned huge profits. Tom advised caution, but Albert was entranced. He liked baseball and enjoyed hanging around with the players, and he thought the reserve clause was both illegal and immoral. So in he went.

The South Ferry Elevated "Y": 1894. The end of the elevated line in lower Manhattan. Behind the "el" is the Coney Island Ferry and the Victorian splendor of the Barge Office, which was briefly, around the turn of the century, the predecessor to Ellis Island. The "el" was New York's first attempt to solve the twin problems of urban traffic and the need for speed of transportation within the city (collection of The New York Historical Society).

Once committed, Albert Johnson was heart and soul with the Brotherhood. He helped the players with the organizational details. He made trips to Boston, New York, and Philadelphia, sounding out eastern investors on the Players' League. He helped sign players for the new enterprise. So efficient and energetic was Albert Johnson that by the end of the 1889 season most of the preliminary organizational work was done, and the Players' League was close to being a reality.

It was still a secret, however. Ward did not merely want to compete with the National League; he wanted to put it out of business. Therefore, the less warning the league magnates had, the better. There were rumors, of course, but nothing definite was known until early September, when a reporter for *Sporting Life*, the major contemporary journal of organized sport, wormed the story out of a player. Within a fortnight, Will Johnson had confirmed it in an interview with *The Sporting News*.[21]

Faced with this news, most of the National League magnates remained publicly hopeful that the Brotherhood scheme would collapse. Nick Young, the league president, talked about business as usual. But no one expected leadership from Nick. Albert Spalding was the man who mattered. What would he do? Spalding made a few reassuring comments to calm the nervous and then wrote to Ward suggesting a meeting between the Brotherhood committee and the National League to resume discussions of the players' grievances. Ward's reply was ominous. It said that the

> ...grievance committee ... appointed last May ... had been unable to obtain a hearing from the League and having so reported on July 14 was discharged.[22]

There would be no discussions.

For the next month the attention of baseball men was divided between the game on the field and rumors of trouble. It was the most exciting pennant race the National League had ever seen, but the pennant race and the world series could not completely overshadow the Brotherhood. Although every game counted, Ward and his lieutenants continued to work on their plans for a new league. They particularly wanted John B. Day on their side. He was popular with the players and paid the highest salaries in the league. He had frequently expressed disapproval with salary limitations and the sale of contracts. Moreover, his defection to the Brotherhood would certainly bring the strong and profitable New York Giants into the Players' League *en masse*, which would insure the financial success of the new league and would probably ruin the old. Brotherhood representatives tried hard to persuade Day to join their side, and Ward gave Day advance warning about the New Players' League. But Day, though continuing to criticize his fellow magnates in the National League, declined to desert them. His loyalty to the National League almost certainly saved it from collapse and destruction.[23]

Day saved an institution that was doing almost nothing to save itself. By the end of the season the National League had done nothing more than release a statement claiming that Ward, Hanlon, Keefe, O'Rourke and the other Brotherhood leaders had fomented revolt only to save their jobs. They were getting older and would be in the minors in a couple of years. While there could be no more doubt that many players were planning to secede from Organized Baseball, the magnates felt, on the whole that it might be "...a good thing for the League to get rid of all the dead wood it has been carrying for so long — and there is considerable of it — and start with younger players and healthier salary lists...." Finally, the National League made a promise to the fans. The established clubs would continue in business. "Most assuredly, prices will be cut down until we play with open gates if necessary."[24]

Although there were numerous and accurate new leaks, the players' plans were made fully public only with the meeting of the Brotherhood in New York on November 4. The new Players' League was to be composed of eight clubs: New York, Brooklyn, Boston, Philadelphia, Chicago, Pittsburgh, Cleveland, and Buffalo. The players would sign a three year contract at their present salaries, after which they would become free agents. If they then decided to change clubs the consent of the league was needed. The players also received some protection they had not had in the National League. They could not be released before the end of the season, and the blacklist was abolished. Moreover, both the new league and the individual clubs made provision for some control by the players in management decisions. Each club was to have an eight man board of directors, four of whom were elected by the players while the other four represented capital. The league would be directed by a board of sixteen, two from each club, with one chosen by the players and the other by the financiers. The directors would choose the league president and would also serve as a supreme court on all matters referred to the league's attention.

The financial relationship between the players and their backers was extremely complicated and departed considerably from Ward's original proposals. Ward had envisioned a cooperative enterprise, with eight clubs pooling their revenues and the player-owners drawing their salaries from the common treasury as a form of profit sharing. No single individual or corporation would be responsible for the players' salaries, and the players themselves would no longer be employees but partners in the profits and risks. Cooperation had a brief vogue in the eighties as an alternative to unions, strikes, and increasing class consciousness of workers. Ward, who had some of the characteristics of an advanced thinker, was quite taken with it. He had always thought of baseball as a profession, not as a craft, as a career, not as a job, and he desperately wanted the Brotherhood to be something besides a labor union. A cooperative Players' League was the answer to his hopes and aspirations.[25]

Ward's opinions were not shared by the capitalists who were prepared to invest in the Players' League, and they demanded some changes. The pooling arrangement was abandoned at once, and each team became responsible for its own receipts, expenses, and profits. The home and visiting team shared equally in the gate receipts, but the home team kept the income from concessions. The income of the club was to be spent in accordance with a clear system of priorities. First came the ordinary expenses of playing the game — travel, rent for the park, paychecks for the employees. Then came the salaries of the players, which were to be met from the gate receipts only. Then, each club was to contribute $2,500 to the league. After that, any money would be split up, with the first $10,000 going to the stockholders, the next $10,000 going to the players, and the remainder divided half and half between all the league clubs and the players. Even this system was modified before the new season began. In December, 1889, the investors agreed to create a fund of $40,000 to provide working capital and to assume responsibility for payment of the player's salaries.[26]

Along with these plans for a new major league came the formal public announcement, inevitable in a scheme that would depend for its success on the favor of the fans. The Brotherhood manifesto was primarily a recitation of the inequities of the National League:

> There was a time when the League stood for integrity and fair dealing. To-day it stands for dollars and cents. Once it looked to the elevation of the game and an honest exhibition of the sport; to-day its eyes are upon the turnstile.... measures originally intended for the good of the game have been perverted into instruments for wrong.

These measures were, of course, the reserve rule and the sale of contracts. The players had tried to negotiate on these matters with the magnates, but the magnates had "broken faith" with the players. They had refused to consider the players' grievances as a serious matter, and the players had been forced to leave the National League and go it alone.[27]

This document, written by Ward, was a graceful and concise statement of the players' position, though it failed to mention that the corporate structure of the Players' League was a frank imitation of the National League. The cooperative organization that was to have distinguished the Players' League did not survive the initial meeting. In only two particulars did the new circuit differ from the old. These were abolition of the sale of contracts and the prohibition against releasing a player before the end of the season. The reserve rule was abolished only in name, not in fact. Each player was bound for three years in a single contract, and the average major league career lasted only five or six years. Thus, most players would become free agents only once, and even then their change of club would require the approval of the league.

Within a week of the Brotherhood meeting, the two major leagues held their annual conventions. The National League magnates, who were most seriously threatened by the Players' League, were close to panic and ready to do anything to save their ship. Instead of standing with the American Association in defense of their established position, they committed felonious assault upon the younger circuit. They persuaded two of the strongest franchises in the American Association to shift over to the National League. Brooklyn and Cincinnati suddenly applied for admission to the National League and were accepted immediately. These two profitable franchises replaced Indianapolis and Washington, both of which had been losing money steadily. This crippling of their circuit naturally infuriated the other American Association magnates. They promptly refused any cooperation with the National League in the war against the Brotherhood and talked ominously about future conversations with the Players' League.

Having strengthened themselves for the struggle, the National League magnates turned to deal with the Players' League. They appointed a War Committee, composed of Spalding, Day, and Col. John Rogers, of Philadelphia, to direct the campaign and plan strategy. They decided to lure their players back with high salaries, despite public denials that anything of the sort was contemplated. They made plans for lawsuits to force their players to stay in the National League, a tactic much favored by John B. Day. They abolished the classification system, which had been the proximate cause of the revolt. They offered three-year contracts to the defecting players, thus matching the Players' League contract. They agreed to pay a player's expenses home if he was released on the road. And, finally, they modified the sale of contracts, giving the player some voice in where he went. When the meeting ended, the National League magnates felt they were ready for war, and so they issued a press release denouncing Ward as a hypocrite and a fool, and promising a further and fuller statement in the near future.[28]

That further statement was published on November 21 by the War Committee. The manifesto, which was designed as a direct answer to Ward's statement for the Brotherhood, began by asserting that the National League had no apology to make for its methods or record. The National League "...stands today, as it has stood, sponsor for the honesty and integrity of Base Ball." The League had been founded in 1876 to rescue "...the game from its slough of corruption and disgrace...." The League, upon its organization, abolished pool-selling and open betting upon its grounds, prohibited Sunday games and prohibited the sale of liquors...." The manifesto further claimed that the players owed their professional dignity and "munificent" salaries to the National League, which had saved the National Game from

> ...destruction threatened by the dishonesty and dissipation of (the) players, and which, by stringent rules and ironclad contracts, it developed, elevated, and perpetuated into the most glorious and honorable sport on the green earth, will still, under its auspices, progress onward and upward, despite the efforts of certain overpaid players to gain control it for their own aggrandizement.[29]

The league *pronunciamento*, while florid and self-serving, did state the key issue: control of the game. Ought the players to do this, or should the business arrangement inaugurated by Hulbert in 1876 continue? The magnates, of course, believed the latter. They founded their case on two major assertions. The first was that they had saved baseball from certain ruin at the hand of the players, who were unreliable, dishonest, and given to booze. The players had controlled the game once, the magnates said, and they had nearly run it into the ground. Curbing the players' propensity to sin was essential if the game were to survive, and this is what the magnates had done. They had also made it profitable. They had put baseball on a "business-like" basis. They had paid the players' salaries, built the parks, assured the fans that the scheduled games would actually be played, and had enforced the rules. This was the magnates' second point, and they never tired of saying that they had rescued baseball from financial doom as well as moral iniquity.

The magnates' case reflected the views of their most substantial member, Albert G. Spalding. He had come into the game as a pitcher, the best in the seventies. It was Spalding's decision to sign with Hulbert and Chicago for the 1876 season that had led to the breakup of the National Association and the formation of the National League. In Chicago Spalding had pitched the White Stockings to the pennant in 1876, and soon thereafter moved from active playing into management. He succeeded Hulbert as owner and president of the Chicago club in 1882. Owning the club was only a small part of his business interests. On February 3, 1876, Albert and his brother, Walter, had opened a sporting goods store at 118 Randolph Street in Chicago. They stocked the usual run of fishing tackle and such, but Spalding's name over the door identified the shop with baseball. And it was baseball that turned A. G. Spalding and Bros. into a national business. In 1877 the firm took its first step. It received the right to publish the official National League Guide. Spalding, of course, used that little book to advertise his products as well as the National League.

The firm also quickly turned the corner from retail shop to manufacturing. In 1878 it received the contract to supply the National League with baseballs. In order to convince league officials to use his ball, Spalding offered to supply them free, and, in addition, pay the league a dollar a dozen. His friendship with Hulbert made acceptance of this offer inevitable. For Spalding, it was a bonanza. He now advertised his baseball as "official," and he began to sell it everywhere. He sold so many that his own plants could not manufacture enough, so, in 1880, he subcontracted with his major competitor, A. J. Reach and Co., to produce the Spalding baseball. By 1885 Reach's capacities were strained, so Spalding put up the capital to expand operations in return for half of Reach's stock. It was the first major corporate acquisition by the Spalding brothers.

The Spalding store carried more than baseballs, of course. It sold bats, gloves, catcher's masks, uniforms and shoes for the players, automatic turnstiles for the gate, ball and strike indicators for umpires, and grandstand cushions for the fans. By the middle eighties the firm was also a major retail outlet for guns, with a catalogue running over twenty pages. It ran a publishing house called the American Sports Publishing Company. In addition to the baseball guides, Spalding published a *Library of Athletic Sports* as well as *Journals* on summer sports, field sports, fishing and cycling, and he issued guides to new sports as they caught on (football, basketball, tennis, golf, etc.) In each book there were prominent advertisements for Spalding products.

Spalding added to his retail stores as well as to his publishing and manufacturing interests. In 1885 he opened a huge emporium in New York.

> Our patrons will no doubt be pleased to note that we have established in New York a store fully as large as our Chicago house.... We shall carry duplicate and complete lines of Base Ball and all Sporting Goods in either house.[30]

This was such a success that the firm added fourteen new stores in the next year. They stretched from coast to coast and gave Spalding and Bros. a dominant position in the retail business of sporting goods.

This retail dominance was soon extended to production. In 1892 Spalding effected a major reorganization of the firm's manufacturing and selling of sporting goods. A. G. Spalding and Bros. absorbed several smaller companies. These included Wright and Ditson, the manufacturer of tennis balls and equipment; the remainder of A. J. Reach; Peck and Snyder, a New York firm that manufactured skates; the St. Lawrence River Skiff, Canoe, and Steam Company; and George Barnard and Co., which made sporting clothes and uniforms. The whole thing was capitalized at four million dollars and incorporated under the laws of New Jersey, then notoriously lax in its disclosure requirements. The various components of the corporation continued to function separately, manufacturing and marketing their products, but it was all controlled by Spalding.

Even this large corporation was not the end of Spalding's industrial expansion. There was one sporting activity that the company did not control. It was bicycling, which was the leisure craze of the nineties. The firm did manufacture bicycles, of course; by 1894 advertisements for Spalding bicycles appeared regularly in the major newspapers. But Spalding wanted to control the entire industry, and, by 1898, after years of work and negotiation, he created a bicycle trust, the American Bicycle Company. Spalding was its president. It was the culmination of a quarter century of effort, planning, and executive skill. Albert G. Spalding had built a virtual monopoly of sporting goods in America.

The Spalding trust was a pioneer in American business, the first leisure conglomerate. One of his businesses published the rules and records of every organized sport in America. Others manufactured and sold every possible type of leisure equipment. Spalding's companies grew because leisure was becoming more common in America, at least for the bourgeoisie, largely because of industrialization and urbanization. Increasing numbers of people could afford a summer at the shore or in the country. Those who could escape the city in the summer did so, partly for status, partly as a respite from the crowded, ugly, dirty cities that characterized industrializing America. The increasingly affluent and leisured middle classes needed something to do during these vacations, since idleness was contrary to the mores of the Gilded Age. Sports helped fill that need, and Spalding was the first to understand the business possibilities inherent in that trend.

His grasp of the impact of leisure activities went well beyond merely creating a monopoly, which was the standard drive of American businessmen during the Gilded Age. He carried his insight into community planning and real estate deals. In 1891 he and a partner bought a ranch in New Mexico, where they planned to build a sports resort. Outside of Chicago he planned a model town, to be called Spalding. He laid out streets and lots, and included several baseball diamonds. Outdoor sports needed room, and Spalding made sure his suburban community would have that room. If his plan succeeded, it might be the beginning of a trend for new forms of suburban development. It might convince other municipalities to build bicycle paths around playgrounds. Spalding's companies could hardly fail to profit from that.[31]

But more than money was involved in all of this. Spalding was a believer in the virtues of sport and recreation. His model town plan had no jail. Wouldn't need one if the kids were exposed to healthy and ethical competition in baseball. Properly conducted, sports would build the moral fiber of America. Properly conducted. For Spalding, that meant in accordance with contemporary canons of business. The National League clearly and perfectly fit both of Spalding's cherished beliefs. The Players' League violated both. That meant it had to be a war to the end, and Albert G. Spalding's authority, both moral and financial, were great enough to commit the National League to that policy.

II

The trouble with total war, from the National League point of view, was that the Brotherhood was better prepared to fight. Ward and his lieutenants had been preparing for six months, and they had lined up solid support among both players and backers. Nor had they ignored the press, for the new league would depend for success in no small measure on the opinions and articles that appeared in the major metropolitan papers. Finally, as a lawyer, Ward was convinced that the reserve rule would never hold up in court; thus the National League would be forced into open competition for baseball talent with the well prepared Brotherhood.

Even before the formal organization of the Players' League was completed, the boys demonstrated their loyalty to the Brotherhood and their willingness to gamble on the uncertain prospects of the new circuit. On October 21, the day after the reserved players were notified that their clubs were renewing their contracts, few men had signed and even fewer said they were going to sign. In Chicago only Cap Anson agreed to a White Stocking contract, and a dismayed Spalding was "unprepared" to say which players he expected to get. In New York, no one signed. In Pittsburgh it was the same story, and Billy Sunday spoke for most of the boys when he told club president W.A. Nimick that he would play for Pittsburgh only if "the Brotherhood matter is settled satisfactorily." Generally speaking, it was the same for every National League club but Indianapolis.[32]

On November 2, two days before the Brotherhood meeting to establish the new Players' League, the National League magnates learned the extent of the damage. Brotherhood secretary Tim Keefe released tentative rosters of the Players' League teams. The eight clubs, in New York, Boston, Buffalo, Brooklyn, Pittsburgh, Chicago, Cleveland, and Philadelphia, were well stocked with players. Each had at least twelve established major leaguers under agreement to sign contracts for the 1890 season as soon as they were offered. The New York club contained the heart of the Giants' championship roster. Buck Ewing, captain of the new Players' League team, Orator James O'Rourke, Danny Richardson, Tim Keefe, Hank O'Day, Cannonball Crane, Roger Connor, Silent Mike Tiernan, Smiling Mickey Welch, and reserve catchers Brown and Murphy were all on the list, and John Ward was to manage the Players' League in Brooklyn. If Keefe's list held up and the boys stuck with the Brotherhood, the Giants were utterly wiped out. It was the same for nearly all of the National League teams. Cap Anson was the only star the Brotherhood did not seem to have under contract.[33]

As soon as the standard Brotherhood contract was approved, on November 7, the actual signings began. This was the moment of truth, when all of the brave rhetoric about player solidarity and mutual faith must be translated into solid commitment. And, for the National League, the bad news rolled in steadily. Charles Comiskey, captain of the St. Louis Browns, joined the Players' League as captain of that circuit's Chicago club. He was the most popular and celebrated player in the American Association, and he added materially to the attractiveness of the new Chicago team, offsetting somewhat Anson's decision to stick with the National League.[34] Comiskey was followed by many others. On November 12 the papers announced that Buck Ewing had signed with the Brotherhood. Ten days later the news came that King Kelly had signed with the Players' League club in Boston, and he had started on a trip across the country to persuade wavering players to sign with the new league.

Estimates as to the number of players signed by the Players' League varied as propaganda, rumors, wishful thinking, and outright lies appeared interchangeably in the press. On November 27, the *New York Times* reported that the Brotherhood had corralled 73 men. In the *New York Clipper* of December 7, Ward boasted of having 65 players. *The Sporting News* sent letters to 75 players, and reported that 71 said that they were with the Brotherhood. The *New York Press* in mid–December counted 90 men signed to Players' League contracts and proceed to demonstrate its superior accuracy by listing them, club by club.[35]

If the lists of Brotherhood players varied a bit in detail, the general tenor of the articles was correct. The Players' League would have most of the major league players for the 1890 season, a fact amply confirmed when the new season began. Of the 123 men on the April rosters of the Players' League, over 100 had had former major league experience, the overwhelming majority in the National League.[36]

But the Brotherhood did not get everybody. Some men said they would never leave the National League, a view voiced by Chicago players Cap Anson, infielder Tom Burns, and pitcher Wild Bill Hutchison, a graduate of Yale. Nothing short of the collapse of Organized Baseball would drive them into the Players' League. Others, like Smiling Mickey Welch and reserve catcher Pat Murphy of the Giants, thought the whole thing over and signed with the old club.

When Murphy signed with the Giants in January, 1890, he told reporters that loyalty to John B. Day was one of the reasons he could not go with the Brotherhood.[37] Other New York players had the same attitude. Mickey Welch was one, and Gill Hatfield, a utility infielder, was another. Hatfield's comment to the press summarized the feelings of most of the New York Giants. He had no complaint to make of John Day, who was the best friend the players had ever had. Hatfield was

> "...in the movement heart and soul, but we don't seem to be treating our old friend right. Why, when I meet Mr. Day, I can't look him in the face. I feel ashamed."[38]

The National League magnates did not rely merely on the loyalty of their players. There were too few Ansons for that. They also offered large salaries and multi-year contracts to induce players to sign with their old clubs. These tactics were not without success. Silent Mike Tiernan, the quietest Irishman in baseball, or perhaps the world, made no statement to the press when he signed a three-year contract with the Giants. Others who were enticed to remain in the National League had more to say, much of it less than candid. John Clarkson, Boston's great pitcher, stated that "I have not signed with or been approached by the Boston Club. I am with the players, a Brotherhood man, and have signed the agreement."[39] Be that as it may, Clarkson and his battery mate, Charles Ganzel, had signed with Boston in the National League within a week of that statement.[40]

There were other players who weighed the odds at the last minute and decided to remain with Organized Baseball. Pebbly Jack Glasscock, shortstop for Indianapolis, deserted the Brotherhood and signed with the National League. Beyond that, Pebbly Jack helped persuade teammates Jerry Denny and Henry Boyle to do the same thing. This drew an outraged response from the Brotherhood leaders. Buck Ewing snapped that "Glasscock is a traitor. We are not disappointed, though, for we expected him to desert us."[41] Tim Keefe and John Ward echoed the same harsh sentiments, adding that the trio had profited dishonorably from the troubles in baseball. But Denny had an answer for that:

> Baseball playing is my business, and I expect to make money out of it, and for that reason I don't want to jump into an airy project at the sacrifice of what I now have.[42]

Denny had the same opinion of the Players' League financial arrangements as Day or Spalding. He preferred to have his salary guaranteed, under the old system, warts and all, rather than take a chance on sharing in the

"Pebbly" Jack Glasscock: 1888. Glasscock came to the Giants in 1890 as part of the National League struggle to strengthen the Gotham nine against the Players' League competition.

profits. He was not alone in these misgivings, which the National League magnates stirred up as best they could. They persuaded a few men who had signed Brotherhood contracts to jump back to the National League. Their most notable success was Big Sam Thompson, a Hall of Fame outfielder for the Philadelphia Phillies. By Thanksgiving, the National League counter-offensive against the Brotherhood had begun to pay off. Twenty-three men had signed with their old clubs, and others had promised that they soon would. When the season began, the National League had sixty major league players on its teams.[43]

These sixty men were not evenly distributed among the eight teams, however. By far the most successful in persuading its reserved players to remain were the two teams that came over from the American Association in

November, 1889. Brooklyn, which had won the Association pennant in 1889, had clearly the strongest team in the National League. The Bridegrooms had kept nearly all of their former players and added only one man without previous major league experience, the future manager of the 1914 Miracle Braves, George Stallings. Cincinnati was almost as strong. Though the Queen City did not have a good team by 1889 standards, the Reds looked considerably better in 1890. They had only four rookies, and the rest were established, though not outstanding major league players. Some of the old National League clubs were also able to field respectable teams, though they had only fragments of their former teams. Boston kept four players, as did Cleveland and Chicago, while Pittsburgh had only two. Philadelphia retained its best player, Big Sam Thompson, and added a spectacular newcomer from the collapsed Kansas City franchise in the Americana Association, Hall of Fame outfielder Sliding Billy Hamilton. Boston still had John Clarkson, who had won 49 games in 1889, and was strengthened by the addition of several exceptional minor league players, including Hall of Fame pitcher, Kid Nichols. The Beaneaters also acquired a new and astute manager, Frank Selee. Indeed, to some observers, Boston looked strong enough to challenge the Brooklyn Bridegrooms for the pennant.[44]

No one made such predictions about the Giants, although they had more major league players (11) than any of the old National League clubs. The New Yorkers had been hurt more seriously by the Brotherhood than any other team. They had lost most of the stars from the 1889 champions, keeping only a fading Mickey Welch, reserve catcher Pat Murphy, and the regular right fielder, Silent Mike Tiernan. New York was, of course, the center of the Brotherhood movement, and its leaders, Ward, Keefe, and Ewing, had a great influence on their colleagues. Some of the Giants like Roger Connor and Gil Hatfield, were reluctant to go to the Players' League, but they went nonetheless. Day was fortunate to win back the three men he did.

The National League could not, of course, let the Giants collapse completely; it was too important and strategic a franchise for that. So, when the National League cut back to eight clubs, on March 22, 1890, lopping off Washington and Indianapolis, the Giants were given the pick of the Indianapolis players. Nine men were assigned to New York, including the two Brotherhood "deserters," Denny and Glasscock. The Giants also received two young players of great promise, pitcher Amos Rusie and outfielder Jesse Burkett, known as the crab because of his penchant for extended complaint. No one thought that the nine Indianapolis transfers would make up for the lost heroes, but they were considerably better than the motley collection of muffins that Mutrie had been able to collect on short notice. Day, however, did not have the money to pay for his nine new men, and the Indianapolis owner, John Bush, took a note for $25,000. It was a bad omen for the new season.[45]

There was more to the war between the Brotherhood and the National

League than competition for players. A second front opened immediately, a propaganda war for the loyalty and support of the kranks. Public opinion would be a decisive factor in the success or failure of the Players' League, everyone knew that, and both sides strove mightily to justify their own actions and paint their opponents as evil, grasping, dishonorable men. The Brotherhood leaders were ingrates, rebels against legitimate authority, conspirators, anarchists, and troublemakers, said the National League magnates, and they would lead baseball straight to ruin. Not so, said Ward and his friends. The National League owners were greedy men, who had oppressed the players, lied to them, and had no intention of redressing legitimate grievances. The players would be less than men if they stood for that sort of thing.

The initial salvos came in the form of the official pronunciamentos, one from the Brotherhood on November 21. Although these were primarily pietistic statements, the National League homily to the faithful drew a chorus of commentary from the Brotherhood people. "Well, now," said H. M. Love, president of the Players' League club in Philadelphia,

> ...that is a nice statement to issue. So we are conspirators and wreckers! Well, I am willing to let the public decide whether the backers of the New League are not as honorable gentlemen ... as those now composing the League.[46]

Fred Pfeffer, the Chicago second baseman and enthusiastic Brotherhood leader, had an equally snappy retort. "Well, I must say those self-glorified magnates throw bouquets at themselves in great style." He then added, "...that the players were justified ... is more than proven by the fact that the League has now eliminated from their contract the obnoxious classification rule, and has moderated the sales system."[47] The official response came from John Ward. He began with the assertion that

> If anything further were necessary to show the desperate state of mind into which the old League magnates have fallen, this last appeal to the public has furnished it. In its statements of fact it is the weakest, and in its misstatements the strongest yet issued. The League committee has taken pains to point out how much the players owe to the league, but omitted to mention how much they themselves owe to the players.

After blaming the whole mess on the National League, Ward promised that the players would do all in their power to preserve the purity of the game, "...to elevate it above a mere speculative enterprise, and to place it on the level which our national game should occupy."[48]

These official and semi-formal bulletins had only a limited effect, however. Many papers refused to waste space on the full text, and some forgot to mention them altogether. And, in any case, they appealed only to the already converted; those in the other pew dismissed them as pure drivel. It was the daily papers which really mattered; these and the three major sporting journals, *The Sporting News*, *New York Clipper*, and *Sporting Life*. It was here that the cast of public opinion would be set, and the participants in the struggle had relatively little control over it.

In this forum, curiously, the battle was essentially a tie. The National League magnates, with their entrenched position as established capitalists facing uppity and ungrateful workingmen, should have been given the benefit of the doubt everywhere. Considering the general climate of opinion on labor-management questions during the Gilded Age, Spalding, Day and his cohorts should have been able to assume the high ground of moral superiority. That did not happen.

The magnates did fairly well in the daily papers in the major league cities, though even here praise for the National League position was often tepid and far from unanimous. In New York, the influential W. I. Harris of *The Press* took an anti-Brotherhood position. He criticized the Brotherhood contract, saying that it did not guarantee the players' salaries and was not much different from the old National League pact. Harris freely predicted that the Players' League would have serious financial problems. He treated the Brotherhood leaders with more sarcasm than respect, and he did not believe that the players were oppressed slaves. But Harris was a realist. He was not one to praise the generosity or disinterestedness of the National League magnates. Like *The Press*, the *Sun* took a National League position, but other New York papers were more circumspect. The *Times* and the *Daily Tribune* rarely ventured an editorial comment and generally confined themselves to reporting what happened.[49]

The National League magnates fared somewhat better with the western papers. In Cleveland, where the Johnsons had run afoul of Uncle Mark Hanna, the *Leader* took an anti-Brotherhood position. In Cincinnati, the *Enquirer* stuck with the National League team. The Pittsburgh *Post* also remained a National League paper.[50]

This adverse reaction in the daily papers bothered John Ward quite a bit. He was a sensitive man, who believed firmly in what he was doing. He did not like to be called John "Much-Advertised" Ward, and he resented the implications that he was a shyster in it for personal gain and that the Players' League was a swindle. While on a swing through the mid-west, Ward complained that

> ...we are being unfairly treated in some quarters. We don't expect everyone to agree with us, and we do not object to fair criticism, but when a few subsidized ... correspondents start in to flood the country with misrepresentations concerning our plans and movement, it is time to hit back.[51]

Ward assured the Clipper that the Brotherhood was doing well, that the Players' League was legitimate, and that it would be run in a business-like manner by businessmen.

Ward could hardly have failed to be pleased by the stance of three major sporting journals. They tended to side with the players. Here, the magnates' past duplicity and arrogance caught up with them. The *Clipper* was the most discreet, giving extensive reportage of the events with a minimum of editorial comment. But the *Clipper* was not totally neutral. In a staid but sarcastic paragraph it denounced contract jumping:

> No one questions the integrity of the National League magnates, yet it hardly seems the proper thing for some of these gentlemen to stoop to means that in any way cast a reflection on their transactions. The fact that some of them have been guilty of encouraging their old players in dishonest dealings by inducing them to sign a second contract is not commendable.[52]

The Sporting News was far more vigorous. Always a critic of Spalding, it had mercilessly ridiculed the tour around the world, and it now took delight in reporting Spalding's outrage at the Brotherhood plans. Spalding was having "conniption fits" and was wild with indignation, the paper reported with glee. Well, he deserved every bit of it, said *The Sporting News*, taking a high moral line. He was a mean and niggardly man, who had "skinned" the Chicago kranks on the "cushion and score card racket." Everyone of honor and conscience could see that the players were in the right.[53]

Sporting Life also took the players' side, though not without saying that the Players' League would probably not prevail against the National League. But editor Francis Richter was a personal friend of John Ward, and he was dubious about the National League claims to purity, honor, and righteousness. This shocked the National League men, but it was not totally unexpected. Richter had never been an uncritical booster of the National League policy, and he had always been critical of the reserve rule. But his lack of support hurt the National League. *Sporting Life* was the nation's most influential baseball paper, and Richter was widely known as a man of honor and intelligence.[54]

Public opinion would be decisive if the war went on long enough, two or three seasons, perhaps. In the short run, however, something else might be more important. That something was the law, which, as Alexis de Tocqueville remarked, was the automatic American response to every major difference of opinion. The National League magnates were rather reluctant to use the courts; like Ward, they had doubts about the validity of the reserve rule. Still, by December the magnates did not see what else they could do. The Brotherhood had signed most of the best players, had crippled the best teams in the National League, and the Players' League seemed to have solid financial backing. If the National League owners were going to save the 1890 season, the law it had to be.

The first tentative step in this direction was made by Albert Spalding himself. In a moment of indignation he said that he would enjoin any of his players who refused to sign with the White Stockings for the 1890 season:

> When the men signed our contract last year it was under the agreement that we had the right to reserve them for this year. I have notified every one of the players that they must come to the front and sign for the next year. I'll fix them if they don't, for my attorney assures me not one of them will be able to play ball in Chicago when I serve the injunction, and you can bet your bottom dollar I will preserve my rights.[55]

But Spalding did not serve his injunction. Instead he dispatched Cap Anson to persuade the players to stay with the White Stockings. And he made no further references to the law.

John B. Day, however, had far greater faith in the courts than Spalding, and far greater need of them as well. In contrast to Anson, his team leader, Buck Ewing, had gone over to the enemy. Late in October, therefore, Day consulted the eminent New York law firm of Evarts, Choate, and Beaman. They were cautious, as is the lawyer's wont, but they did tell Day what he wanted to hear:

> It was, of course, perfectly legal for the players to have bound themselves to the club by a contract for the season of 1890 .... Now, if the contract had absolutely bound the players for the seasons of 1889 and 1890, this right of injunction would have been just as good in the second season as in the first.

Therefore, the players had to stay with the Giants for the 1890 season, and, Evarts, Choate, and Beaman concluded, "...in our opinion, the courts ... would enjoin them from playing during that season (1890) on any other club."[56] That opinion was so satisfactory to Mr. Day that he gave it to the papers, and waited confidently for the players to see the light and come in and sign.

The players however, reassured by Ward, did not come in and sign their contracts.[57] So, National League magnates made preparations for opening a third front in the baseball war. In their plenary session in New York on November 15, the league owners appointed a Law Committee, composed of Col. Rogers of the Phillies, Charles Byrne of the newly acquired Brooklyn Bridegrooms, and John B. Day. The committee was authorized "...to act and to formulate and carry out the best methods of enforcement of said contractual rights (reservation) of said clubs.[58]

The Law Committee did nothing for about a month, but by early December the magnates could wait no longer. On December 11 the Law Committee called on Evarts, Choate, and Beaman, whose earlier opinion had been so soothing. Mr. Beaman saw them, listened to an extended recitation of the magnates' case, repeated his previous views, and said that he would begin immediately to draw up papers for a test case, probably against Ward or Ewing.

This was no secret from the Brotherhood, of course. On December 17, the new Players' League established its own Law Committee, which included

John Ward. Ward's committee reported that Judge Henry Bacon of New York had been engaged as general counsel for the Players' League, and would defend any player sued by the National League. At the same meeting former Judge Henry Howland, who was Ward's personal attorney, delivered a strong statement against the legality of reservation. Thus armored with competent counsel and favorable opinions, both sides awaited the due process of law.[59]

No one had long to wait. On December 23 papers were served on John Ward. The Metropolitan Exhibition Company (the Giants) were asking for a preliminary injunction, forbidding Ward from playing anywhere but with the Giants until October 31, 1890. The case was scheduled for January 6, 1890, in the New York Supreme Court, before Judge Morgan J. O'Brien. When the case was called, the plaintiffs (Day and the Giants) asked for a three-day delay to allow their chief counsel, Joseph H. Choate, to be present. Neither Ward nor his attorney opposed the motion. In the corridors after the hearing reporters talked to the litigants. Both sides were confident of the outcome. They also wanted a speedy decision.[60]

There was some progress toward that speedy decision at the hearing on January 9. Mr. Beaman, speaking for the Giants, came straight to the point. The question involved was the construction of a contract and the application of the law, and that under the contract signed by Ward, his services could be retained during the coming season. Beaman went on to say that the baseball contract was much like a theatrical agreement between manager and actor, and the reserve clause was analogous to stock option on Wall Street. Moreover, Ward had a unique value to the Giants. He was the best shortstop in baseball and could not be replaced. His services, and those of the other stars, were essential to the club. The club lived off its attendance. That is where the money came from. Popular players like Ward brought people out to the games and were, therefore, the basic support of the whole fabric of Organized Baseball. Kranks would not pay to see muffins, as the phrase then went; they wanted to see the stars, like Ward. Without Ward, and the others, the Giants would be seriously weakened. Finally, Ward himself had given implied agreement to reservation in 1889, when he had drawn up a supplementary contract with the Metropolitan Exhibition Company. In this supplementary contract, the Giants agreed not to reserve Ward for 1890 at a salary of less than $3,000. This could only mean, Beaman argued, that Ward understood and accepted the fact of reservation.

Judge Howland began his reply by stating that the case dealt with more than John Ward and the Giants. It involved the National League, the Brotherhood, and the entire structure of baseball. To support this assertion Howland produced a bound volume of lengthy affidavits, signed by Ward and some of the other New York players. These documents gave a detailed history and analysis of the reserve clause, how it was established, how the National League had used it in previous years, and the abuses connected with it. Howland argued that these affidavits would illuminate the real meaning of reservation. Before he could begin reading them, however, Joseph Choate rose to object. He stated that these documents, which he now saw for the first time, amounted to a detailed history of baseball, and he needed some time to study them and make his reply. Howland said that the case should be heard now. It was vital for the defendant to have a quick decision. There was, Howland said,

> ...a struggle going on to secure players and there was a certain amount of intimidation being used that might seriously injure the defendant and the cause he represented.

Choate retorted that the intimidation was all on the other side; Ward and the Brotherhood were trying to break up the Giants.

Before the hearing deteriorated into a wrangle between the opposing attorneys, Judge O'Brien decided that Howland must let the Giants' lawyers see his file of affidavits, and that Choate and Beaman must file any reply they wished to make. The case would be resumed on January 16.[61]

When the hearing resumed after the week's delay, the courtroom was packed with baseball people. This was the crucial day, and everyone knew it. Howland had everyone's attention when he began his presentation. The case was

> ...based on a contract made April 23, 1889 for seven months' services, and which contained a clause known as the reserve clause. The entire case of the plaintiff rests on the construction to be placed on the word "reserve."

John Day and the National League claimed that "reserve" meant that the Giants had a binding option on Ward's services for 1890. To no one's surprise, Ward had a different view, and his lawyer presented it at length. Ward's statement affirmed that he had no obligation to the Giants under the reserve clause and that his departure would do no irreparable harm to the club.

Howland also submitted a long written brief. It made three basic points. The first was a request for an immediate decision in Ward's favor. A preliminary injunction, or even any serious delay in refusing one, would bring practical victory to the National League, whatever the final legal outcome might be. An injunction would cast a cloud over the legality of Players' League contracts, frighten investors away from the enterprise, and destroy the league. Howland also dealt with the meaning of reservation itself. The reserve rule, he argued, was a contract between clubs bound by the National Agreement. It meant that one club within Organized Baseball, that is, the National Agreement, could not sign a player reserved by another such club. Nothing more. A man could refuse to play, and the club could not compel him to do so. He could sign with a club not bound to respect reservation, one outside the National Agreement. Again, nothing could be done against him. Reservation, therefore, was a contract between clubs. Further, Howland claimed that the contract between Ward and the Giants lacked mutuality. It was completely one-sided, all in favor of the club. The standard player contract of the National League was

> ...grossly inequitable in terms, and therefore not enforceable in a court of equity. We have the peculiar spectacle of a contract which binds one party for life and the other party for ten days.

No contract like that was fair. It might be legal, but it was not fair and could not be enforced.

Finally, Howland made an extended oral argument. He treated the National League magnates roughly, deriding their claim that they were the guardians of the purity of the game. They were in it for the money, he said, and this suit for a preliminary injunction was designed only to destroy the Players' League and preserve the monopoly of Organized Baseball. He repeated the arguments in his brief and the affidavits, and again asked for a quick decision for Ward.

Joseph Choate then made the final arguments for the Giants. He denied that reservation was primarily an agreement between clubs. It was part of the contract between club and player. It did not merely mean that a man could not play with a National Agreement club that had not reserved him. It meant that he must play with the club that had reserved him and with no one else. Reserve, in short, meant just what it said. The meaning was plain and simple, just what everyone, Ward included, had always thought it meant. In 1890 Ward had to play for the Giants. It was a simple question of good faith. If this contract, so plain and obvious in its obligations, was overthrown, then ball players might as well have no contracts at all. This concluded the plaintiff's case and Judge O'Brien, after a full day in court, took the papers both sides had presented, and reserved his decision.[62]

Judge O'Brien delivered his decision on January 28, and it was a total disaster for the National League. He found for Ward. He would not issue a temporary injunction prohibiting Ward from playing anywhere but with the Giants. His Honor did find some merit in the National League case, but this just made the debacle complete. The judge agreed with Choate's contention that the meaning of reserve was clear and simple. It was just what plaintiff had said it was. Judge O'Brien, therefore, rejected Ward's contention that reservation was a contract between the clubs of the National Agreement and accepted the National League view that it was part of the contract between club and player. More, the judge denied Ward's argument that a temporary injunction was inappropriate in this case. A claim for personal services was exactly the kind of case for which a temporary injunction was the proper remedy. Still more, the judge agreed with plaintiff that the Giants would suffer seriously from Ward's defection. He compared the services Ward performed for the Giants to those of an actor or circus star.

In spite of this, the National League case suffered from two overriding defects. In the first place, the National League contract was vague and imprecise. It did not include the salary Ward was to receive. The judge was quite clear:

> Not only are there no terms and conditions fixed, but I do not think it is entirely clear that Ward agrees to do anything further than to accord the right to reserve him upon terms thereafter to be fixed.

Here the full irony of the case came home to the National League magnates. In 1887 Ward and the Brotherhood had insisted that the standard contract be made specific, including the salary terms. The magnates had agreed, and then went back on their word. Had they kept their promise to Ward, the contract would have passed muster on this point. The magnates were hoist on the petard of their own treachery.

There was a second problem with the standard baseball contract. It lacked fairness and mutuality. After reserving a player, the club need pay him no salary at all for the next year, having the right to release him before the season began. Moreover, and more seriously,

> ...we have the spectacle presented of a contract which binds one party for a series of years and the other party for ten days, and of the party which is itself bound for only ten days coming into a court of equity to enforce its claim against the party bound for years.

That could not be permitted. The injunction was denied, and the baseball contract was, in effect, declared null and void.[63]

The blow from this adverse decision was so serious that the National League met the next day to discuss it. Two full days of discussion failed to produce any new ideas on how to deal with the Players' League. The best the magnates could think of was more of the same. They would continue the attempt to persuade players to return, and John Day made a special trip to Cincinnati on February 17 to try and retrieve Buck Ewing. Day offered Buck $8,500 and a three-year contract. But the catcher turned it down, and Roger Connor and Danny Richardson also rejected Day's offers. Some of the magnates also continued to try the law. On February 6, Col. John Rogers of the Phillies filed bills in equity against three of his players who had signed with Philadelphia in the Players' League. This was Rogers' second go at the law; he had already filed against Bill Hallman, the Phillies second baseman. That case had not yet been heard, but the outcome of the Metropolitan Exhibition Company vs. Ward could hardly be encouraging for the National League.[64]

In spite of his defeat in the New York courts, John Day was also considering further suits. The failure to pry Ewing, Connor, and Richardson away from the Players' League made Day's situation truly desperate. He had only three men from his championship team, and the New York Players' League nine was clearly going to give him more competition than he could handle. There must be another effort in the courts. On February 27, therefore, he had papers served on Buck Ewing in a suit to enjoin him from playing anywhere but with the Giants. The case was to be tried in the United States Circuit Court in New York. Day had lost in the state court; the federal bench was his only hope.[65]

The case was heard before Judge Wallace of the United States Circuit Court in New York on March 14. Neither side presented anything new, either in brief or oral argument. The plaintiff repeated his interpretation of the reserve clause, a view that had already won support from Judge O'Brien in the New York State Supreme Court. Plaintiff again claimed irreparable damage in the loss of Ewing and argued that players had signed standard contracts before 1890 without being turned thereby into slaves. Mr. Choate closed for the plaintiff by asking for an injunction against Ewing, stating that without such an injunction it would be useless to continue the case.

The defense was equally repetitive, though with better reason, since its arguments had been so well received by Judge O'Brien. Again, the defense claimed that the contract lacked mutuality and fairness, and that it was fatally imprecise in its terms. The defense brief denied that the Giants would be badly damaged by the loss of Buck Ewing. Henry Bacon, Ewing's lawyer, also repeated Ward's interpretation of reservation. The reserve rule, Bacon claimed,

> ...meant simply an agreement on the part of one club to hold a player's services to the exclusion of the other clubs that entered into the national agreement. Mr. Day absurdly claims that the "reserve" clause gives him the right to Mr. Ewing's services against the world.

That line of reasoning had already been rejected by Judge O'Brien, and might well fail here also. Still, this was a new judge and a federal court. It would be better to include the entire defense argument, whether it seemed likely to succeed or not.[66]

The decision did not come until March 26, barely a month before the season was to begin. Again, it was a Brotherhood victory. Judge Wallace refused to enjoin Ewing, and for many of the same reasons that had appeared in the Ward case and in the dismissal in Philadelphia of the Phillies' suit against Hallman. Judge Wallace was not brief in his opinion, but he was decisive. He wrote that

> ...as the basis of an action for damages if the player fails to contract, or for an action to enforce specific performance, it (the reserve rule) is wholly nugatory. In a legal sense it is merely a contract to make a contract if the parties

> can agree. It follows that the act of the defendant in refusing to negotiate with the club for an engagement for the season of 1890, while a breach of contract, is not the breach of one which the plaintiff can enforce.

Therefore, the injunction was denied.[67]

There was a coda to this concerto for lawyers and baseball players. On March 3 the Giants asked Judge Lawrence of the New York State Supreme Court for a permanent injunction against Ward. The case was heard on March 24. The attorneys for the Giants made essentially the same points they had made before Judge O'Brien on January 16 and would make two days later in federal court against Ewing. When asked by the judge if there were any new facts that had not been presented to Judge O'Brien, Day's attorneys were obliged to admit there were none. Judge Lawrence then said that, were he to give an immediate decision, he would rule in favor of Ward. The Giants' attorneys asked him to reserve his decision until briefs could be filed, and the judge reluctantly agreed. John B. Day and his lawyers left the court in a low frame of mind. They admitted to reporters that they did not expect to win.[68]

Nor did they. On March 31 Judge Lawrence decided the case. His statement was brief, a single sentence. He clearly thought that the opinions of his colleague, Morgan O'Brien, and Judge Thayer of Philadelphia, were sound and inclusive. Therefore, Judge Lawrence denied the injunction. The decision came three days after Ewing's legal victory. It was the end of the National League's efforts to destroy the Players' League in the courts.[69]

When Ewing and Ward won their final legal victories, the baseball season was just three weeks away. The various teams had been south for spring training. Grounds keepers were getting the fields ready. Sportswriters were reporting the results of the spring games and speculating on how the teams and the players would do. Where would the Giants finish? Well up in the race? Few thought so. And the New Yorks in Players' League? Most freely predicted victory. It was time to put lawsuits and injunctions aside. Kranks had heard enough about player contracts, club and league management policies, and the diplomacy of baseball. Away with all that. Opening Day was three weeks off. But this season would be unlike any other in the short history of Organized Baseball. This season would be another front in the death struggle between the two leagues. This season would be as much a form of war as any day in court.

Play ball!

III

The 1890 season began on a dismal note. Only 4,644 kranks came to the Polo Grounds to see the Giants play Philadelphia. Their attitude was somber rather than festive. Uncertainty and apprehension were the dominant moods.

No one shouted the Giants' old slogan: "We are the people!" No one cheered the familiar heroes, so often victorious in the past. The parades and banners and civic dignitaries were missing this year. The ebullient and expansive James Mutrie seemed unusually subdued. Everyone just hoped for the best.

The New York faithful watched a virtually new team take the field on that cool April afternoon. Only Silent Mike Tiernan played from the champions of yesterday. The Giants started Amos Rusie, a young power pitcher just acquired from Indianapolis, and the unknown Dick Buckley caught in the place of the incomparable Buck Ewing. Instead of the massive Roger Connor there was a nobody named Crane; where the dashing Johnny Ward had once played, the kranks watched Pebbly Jack Glasscock. The new men aroused no enthusiasm that day. They lost a dull game to the despised Phillies, 4 to 0. The result was not unexpected. This new bunch were not the Giants.[70]

What excitement there was for baseball that day came from the crowd across the fence at Brotherhood Park. Over twelve thousand kranks came for the opening game in the Players' League schedule. They saw most of the familiar demigods and heroes, Ewing, Keefe, O'Rourke, and Connor, and they saw them lose 12 to 11. But the game was exciting and the mood festive. After all, these were the real Giants, who would soon round into form and win the championship.[71]

All of the dire predictions for the 1890 season were confirmed at once. The ersatz Giants were in last place after the season was only a week old, and they remained there for most of the first month. Toward the end of May the Giants began a spurt as the pitching suddenly and unexpectedly improved. Amos Rusie, who could throw as hard as anyone in baseball, began to look like the great pitcher he would soon become, while Smiling Mickey Welch showed flashes of his old form. The Giants won eight games in a row and climbed as high as third place for a couple of days. It was a brief, but heady, time.

The high point of the season came just before this short spurt. On May 12 the Giants played Boston at the Polo Grounds. Two of the best pitchers in the league, Amos Rusie and Kid Nichols, faced each other, and both were "in good form." Boston got just three hits off Rusie, while the Giants had only four. But one of those four was a home run in the thirteenth inning by Mike Tiernan, a stupendous drive over the center field fence that was the longest ball ever hit at the Polo Grounds. It won the game for the Giants, 1 to 0, and both kranks and sportswriters agreed that it was the best baseball game ever seen in New York.[72]

The glory of that game soon disappeared as reality reasserted itself. The Giants were a poor team, a patchwork of retreads, minor leaguers, and muffins, only slightly leavened by Smiling Mickey Welch, Silent Mike Tiernan and the Indianapolis stars, Amos Rusie, Jessie Burkett, and Pebbly Jack Glasscock. On Memorial Day the Giants lost a double-header to Cincinnati and started back down toward the bottom of the league. In two weeks they were in sixth place, and when the season finally ended they were still there. The team's record was 63 victories and 68 defeats, and the Giants finished 24 games behind pennant winning Brooklyn.[73] No one was happy with this, of course, but the general feeling was that Mutrie has done a good job with the material he had had.

The poor record on the field was more than matched by the poor showing at the box office. The attendance figures for New York were dreadful. Those reported, and they were certainly inflated, had the Giants drawing 60,667 kranks, an average of only 919 a game. This was eighty thousand fewer fans than the Players' League claimed to draw in New York. More to the point, it was 140,000 fewer fans than the 201,989 the Giants had drawn in 1889, when the average attendance had been 3,206 a game.[74] The difference between those figures speaks for itself.

Even during the height of the season the Giants played to an empty house. A series in July against the Chicago White Stockings, always a stellar attraction at the Polo Grounds, drew 1,727 kranks for the three games. On July 10, with Smiling Mickey Welch pitching against Pittsburgh, the attendance was 227, and that figure was probably inflated. The next day the Giants did better; 507 kranks, more or less, came to the Polo Grounds to see Amos Rusie pitch. League-leading Brooklyn drew 904 fans to an August game with the Giants. In only a dozen games all season did the Giants draw the 1,080 fans needed to meet expenses.[75]

John Day could not take this kind of loss forever, and by July he was virtually bankrupt. During July he called on his fellow magnates for help. Summoned to Brooklyn for a secret conference, several of the wealthier National League owners found that the Giants needed the huge sum of $80,000 to see the season through. Knowing that the National League could not survive without a club in New York, the assembled magnates reluctantly agreed to help. The Giants kept on playing, though their financial weakness could not be concealed from the press. Thereafter, the unfortunate New York owner was frequently referred to as John Busted Day.[76]

Day's plight was matched almost everywhere in baseball. As the 1890 season neared its end, the owners of the twenty-four major league clubs surveyed a terrain composed almost entirely of catastrophe. Peace and cooperation had become the overriding economic necessity. But for the National League the situation was even worse than profit and loss, or, rather, large losses and gargantuan losses. Between October 1 and 5, 1890, the Players' League bought the National League Cincinnati Reds from Aaron Stern for $48,000. Although Stern first denied the sale, and then said he had not thought that the Brotherhood men were serious in their offer, he ended by admitting that he had sold the club. It was only good business, he said, to cut his losses and get out while he could. Any other magnate so beleaguered would have done the same.[77]

The loss of the Cincinnati franchise put the National League at death's door, and the league owners met in immediate special session to discuss the catastrophe. Their meeting opened on October 8 in New York amid private predictions that the end was near and the National League was going under. The general gloom was lightened somewhat by two rays of real hope, however. Buck Ewing, the manager of the New York franchise in the Players' league, spent October 8 shuttling between John B. Day and E. B. Talcott, the managing partner of the New York Players' League club. Ewing was pushing the idea of consolidating the two clubs in the National League, and he found both Day and Talcott enthusiastic about the notion.[78]

On a more general level there were also signs of peace. Allan W. Thurman, owner of the Columbus club in the American Association, took the initiative in the search for peace. Thurman received assurances of good will from several Players' League magnates, who were in New York to keep an eye on the National League meeting, and he appeared at the National League meeting on October 8. He proposed that a joint committee from the National League and the American Association meet with the Players' League representatives to search for peace. There was some resistance to this idea, and the Pittsburgh and Cleveland owners uttered fighting words about no compromise with traitors, but no one paid any real attention to that nonsense. The situation was so serious that acceptance of Thurman's proposals was inevitable. The magnates appointed Spalding, Day, and C. H. Byrne of Brooklyn to meet with Thurman, von der Ahe and William Barnie of the American Association and Talcott, Wendell Goodwin of Brooklyn, and Al Johnson from the Players' League.[79]

The basic agenda for the conversations was set by Thurman, now styled by the press as the White-Winged Angel of Peace. At the National League meeting Thurman had presented a scheme for merging the three leagues into two through local consolidation of competing clubs. One league would have teams in New York, Brooklyn, Boston, Philadelphia, Pittsburgh, Chicago, Cleveland, and Cincinnati; the other, clubs in Boston, Philadelphia, Baltimore, Washington, Chicago, Columbus, St. Louis, and Louisville. Both leagues would be bound by the National Agreement and would play for the world championship after the end of the season. The White-Winged Angel was eloquent and persuasive, his plan made sense, and the economics of peace were compelling, so his proposals were accepted as the basis for discussions.[80]

The new peace committee met at once, beginning its discussions about 10:00 in the evening on October 9. Every delegate wanted peace, but the Players' League men were so desperate to cut their losses that they were prepared to agree to anything. Indeed, E. B. Talcott was already starting to sell the side out whether there was any general peace or not, as the Ewing shuttle diplomacy showed. Talcott had had enough of losing money in baseball. In addition to desertion in their ranks, the Players' League men faced the superior diplomatic talents of A. G. Spalding, who had had decades of experience in baseball negotiations. When Goodwin and Johnson incautiously revealed the true extent of their financial plight and desire for peace, Spalding, who already knew of Talcott's desertion, promptly stiffened his stance. He now interpreted consolidation to mean that Organized Baseball would absorb the Players' League. The Players' League magnates were not ready to go that far yet, at least publicly, so the meeting did not end in a general peace. The delegates did agree to a truce until October 28, during which time all player contracts were to be respected. The joint peace committee would reconvene again on October 22, when both the National and Players' Leagues would also be meeting. Finally, the joint committee said that consolidation terms would be set by the various clubs involved, an open invitation to the National League to continue subverting the weaker clubs in the enemy camp.[81]

Negotiations for consolidation between the two New York clubs now reached the agreement stage. With everyone in favor of peace and the joint committee encouraging local consolidation, the New York magnates were now confident that any deal they made would be accepted all around. On October 14 Talcott, a stock broker, went to see John Day, and the two then joined General E. A. McAlphin, T. B. Robinson, and Cornelius Van Cott, all stockholders in the New York Players' League club, in Postmaster Van Cott's office. They conferred for over an hour and emerged with a draft agreement. The two clubs were to be merged into one in the National League. The new club would be capitalized at a quarter of a million dollars, with the stock to be divided among the present owners of both franchises. The Players' League people would have the controlling interest. After their conference, both Day and Talcott expressed their satisfaction with the deal and said that they expected no further trouble from the players.[82]

This agreement signaled a death watch for the Players' League and the Brotherhood. Without a strong club in New York they could hardly expect a profitable season next year, making many of the other Players' League magnates desperately anxious to "get in out of the wet." Rumors circulated that in Pittsburgh and Brooklyn magnates were "getting together, and would soon consolidate clubs with the National League." Players were beginning to desert to their old clubs, the papers said, and the end was near. The stories were premature, but they were not pure fiction. The Players' League had begun to unravel. In city after city the rival magnates were beginning to reach an accommodation. After the New York agreement on October 14, it was just a question of time.

This was not immediately apparent to the leaders of the Brotherhood. Ward and his lieutenants wanted peace, but they still assumed that it would be a peace among equals. Ward offered a five-point program, including mutual respect of contracts, an end to competing playing dates in the same city, and a world series at the end of the season. At the Brotherhood conference, held in New York on October 20 and 21, the same attitudes prevailed. Still not realizing that it was all over Ward persuaded his troops to send their backers a resolution stating that the Brotherhood, in

> ...view of the many rumors current ... extend to you the assurance of their entire confidence in your ability to safely conduct the affairs of the Players' League.

This drew the desired response from the magnates. Your resolution they replied, "...now stimulates us to a still stronger effort for your interests in the future."[83]

Comforting communications failed to satisfy all the players, however. Many were suspicious, disgruntled, and nervous about the future, and they did not share Ward's belief that negotiations were going well. Many suspected that the magnates were in the process of selling them out, and these feelings surfaced at the afternoon session on October 21. The players demanded representatives on the joint peace committee, reminding their backers that they were stockholders also. After prolonged and serious debate, the players won their point, and John Ward, Ned Hanlon, and Arthur Irwin were added to the Players' League delegation. This was not done without misgivings on the part of several magnates, who declared that the older leagues would not continue the peace conferences under such conditions.[84]

These forebodings proved correct. When the joint peace committee reconvened on October 22 the National League delegates refused to continue discussions with any but the original Players' League delegation. In this they were supported by Thurman and his American Association colleagues. Al Johnson, the Cleveland owner, protested that the players were there as stockholders, not merely as players. But the White-Winged Angel and Spalding held firm. That made no difference, they said. The players were still players, no matter how much stock they owned. And, in any case, the original committee could not be changed. Johnson then complained that the older leagues had six representatives, while the Players' League had only three. Thurman and Spalding rejected this also. Each circuit had the same representation, Thurman held. It must be the original committee or nothing.

After nearly an hour of wrangling John M. Ward finally spoke. He admitted some merit to the Thurman/Spalding position but argued that the joint peace committee consisted of three separate delegations, which could be altered at will without changing the nature of the negotiations. And in this case, the addition of three players simply evened the sides, as the two older leagues were acting in unison. Ward added that joint representation was a fundamental principle of the Players' League and should be followed in this crucial meeting. He denied that the players would hinder or damage the negotiations, adding that they, not the magnates, had the greater proportional investment in the Players' League. Ward then accused the delegates from the older leagues of refusing to deal with the players because they were players. Two of the magnates, Spalding and Barnie, had been players themselves. Were they ashamed of that fact? Did they "...wish to go on record as saying that the occupation of a ball player bars him from business association with respectable men?"[85]

Ward's speech, like all of his public statements, was clear, pointed, and eloquent. But this time his eloquence and logic were wasted. He had missed the point. The magnates, like college professors, were impervious to shame. Moreover, the magnates were playing a game. The meeting was a charade, designed to conceal business rather than transact any. The real negotiations were going on club by club, with the demise of the Players' League and the Brotherhood the anticipated result. That process was already well under way.

Ward's speech changed no minds, of course. Spalding replied that it was all beside the point. The magnates had already agreed to settle things among themselves, "...on a purely business basis." Faced with this attitude, Al Johnson agreed that the committee could reconvene with its original membership, which would then decide on admission of the player delegates. When the vote was taken player representation was predictably defeated, six to three. This news was conveyed to the players, who replied that they could accept no negotiations in which they were not represented. This left the meeting deadlocked, and the formal peace sessions were over.[86]

The real peace negotiations continued, however. The Players' League was falling apart.[87] The first casualty had been New York, where Day, Talcott, and the others had been in substantial agreement since their meeting on October 14. During the first week in November, Talcott announced that the New York Players' League club had consolidated with the Giants. This was followed by similar news from Pittsburgh. On November 10 the Pittsburgh Players' League club merged with its National League counterpart. Thus, when the two circuits met on November 12, the National League in New York and the Players' League in Pittsburgh, the National League had already absorbed one quarter of its rival's clubs. New York and Pittsburgh promptly resigned from the Players' League. Moreover, National League magnates reported that the Chicago and Brooklyn clubs in the Players League were about to fold, the first by outright purchase and the second by consolidation. Finally, it was said, on good authority, that King Kelly was back in the fold. He was supposed to have signed with the Boston Red Stockings. Awash in good news, the National League magnates wore "smiles of satisfaction," and made plans for next season on the assumption that their rival was dead.[88]

It was a sound assumption, for the dominoes continued to fall. Chicago was next. Even while the Players' League was meeting, Spalding and John Addison, owner of the Players' League Chicago franchise, were negotiating a deal. The final settlement was held up until December 29, 1890; there was a serious wrangle over how much money was to go to Addison and how much to his players, whose salaries were in arrears. The final arrangement called for $18,000 to be prorated among the non-player stockholders, with about $47,000 to go to the players to pay their salaries, less ten percent, while the player stockholders were paid fifty cents on the dollar for their holdings. To close the deal, Talcott gave Addison $15,000 in stock in the consolidated New York Giants, while Spalding threw in season passes to the Chicago games.[89]

Brooklyn was the next of the Players' League franchises to fall. Wendell Goodwin, the major stockholder in the Brooklyn club, had long advocated consolidation. Like Talcott, he felt the wisest course was to give up the fight and join the National League. There had been sporadic conferences toward that goal since the end of the season. But negotiations had been difficult, and not until the beginning of January, 1891, was the deal completed. The two teams would be consolidated in the National League, where Brooklyn had just won the pennant. The National League owners, Charles Byrne, Joseph Doyle, and Ferdinand Abell, would have the majority position, while the Players' League people were allotted $40,000 of the stock of the club. The team would be managed by the arch-fiend himself, John Montgomery Ward.

But this deal, so long in negotiation, came apart almost at once. Some of the minority stockholders in the Players' League club, called "minnow magnates" by the press, were dissatisfied with the settlement. Led by Edward Linton, they claimed they were being sold down the river, as indeed they were. The minnow magnates went to court and got a temporary restraining order blocking the whole thing. In addition to this, Linton travelled to Boston on January 6 to talk with Charles A. Prince, owner of the Boston Players' League club. Linton joined Prince, Al Johnson of Cleveland, and the Wagner brothers in Philadelphia in promising not to settle the baseball war unless they were all satisfied with the terms. They implied that they were going to fight on, certainly with lawsuits, perhaps by joining the American Association, even continuing with a four team league if necessary.[90]

Linton's unexpected legal action, along with the increased solidarity and belligerence of the remaining Players' League magnates, both so disturbing to the hopes for peace, came on the eve of concurrent conferences of the three leagues, scheduled for January 12, 1891, in New York. But the appearances were more menacing than the reality. Linton's suit merely challenged the price being paid the minnow magnates for their stock; it did not challenge the consolidation itself. That was taken as settled. Brooklyn would play in the National League in 1891. To dispose of Linton, therefore, the Brooklyn magnates had only to buy him off, which they did on January 23.[91]

It was equally easy to deal with the problems in Philadelphia. The American Association expelled the Athletics, their Philadelphia club, for failing to meet their financial obligations, and the owners of the Players' League Philadelphia franchise, J. Earle and George Wagner, were slipped into their spot. The

Wagner brothers were given the Athletics name and players. It was another successful consolidation.[92]

The rest of the settlement, though not without some difficulties, also proceeded on the general assumption that the Players' League would disappear. Boston and Cleveland alone remained of the Players' League when the January meetings began. Their disposition depended on a major restructuring of the American Association, and that circuit's new president, Allan Thurman, bent his energies to that end. The Thurman plan required the three weakest Association clubs, Rochester, Toledo, and Syracuse, to resign from the league, making way for Association clubs in Chicago, Boston, and Philadelphia. This would strengthen the league and preserve the interests of Players' League magnate Charles Prince of Boston. Thurman's plan hit an immediate snag, however. Syracuse and Rochester seemed ready to die quietly, but Toledo did not. Toledo president V. S. Ketchem indignantly refused $7,000 for his franchise and obtained a court order forbidding the American Association from dropping his club. The Association thereupon commissioned Thurman, von der Ahe, and Barnie to "reason" with the defiant Ketchem. Their methods, their threats, their enticements were not disclosed, but after three days of "reasoning," the committee prevailed. The three clubs dropped out of the American Association for $24,000.

This was only half of the final battle, however. The American Association now had its house in order, but the National League did not. The Association insisted on a club in Boston, and Charles Prince insisted on a club in Boston as his price for peace. But the National League Boston magnates were totally opposed to an American Association club in their city. The Boston owners claimed that their territorial rights were sacrosanct and they refused to budge. It took Spalding several days to reason with the stubborn Boston owners, but in the end they gave way. The American Association could have a Boston club, but it must charge fifty cents at the gate, not the two bits customary for that league.

With Prince provided for, only Al Johnson remained out in the cold. There had been sporadic efforts by the National League to buy Johnson out, but these had not succeeded. In November, 1890, Johnson had turned down an offer to sell, and in January, 1891, the question came up again. Asked to name his figure for this Players' League interests, Johnson quoted $46,000. That was refused. After Boston and Philadelphia had been admitted to the American Association Johnson was given a counter offer of $29,000. He turned it down. After thinking it over, however, he changed his mind and accepted. But the National League committee, which was negotiating with Johnson, had also been thinking things over. Why pay Johnson anything? There was no longer any Players' League. What could Johnson do? So the National League reneged on its offer and refused to pay the $29,000. Outraged, Johnson went to court, and the case dragged on through the rest of the year. In the end

Johnson got something, the National League spent more on the case than it would have paid Johnson, and the lawyers, as usual, made more than anyone else.[93]

On January 16, 1891, the Players' League came to a final and formal end. The National League, with clubs in New York, Brooklyn, Boston, Philadelphia, Chicago, Cleveland, Cincinnati and Pittsburgh, signed a new National Agreement with the American Association, with clubs in Boston, St. Louis, Baltimore, Philadelphia, Columbus, Cincinnati, Washington, and Louisville. The baseball war was over. For the players there was a general amnesty. All of the Brotherhood leaders stayed in baseball, most returning to their old teams. Normalcy was what everyone wanted. John Ward caught the mood. At a wake for the Players' League held at Nick Engel's Home Plate Saloon, Ward proposed a toast: "Pass the wine around, the League is dead. Long Live the League."[94]

The collapse of the Players' League brought the end of the Brotherhood as well. None of its objectives had been realized, and the owners had refused to recognize its existence during the negotiations that dissolved its league. No one saw any further reason to belong, and the organization simply evaporated.

IV

As soon as it became clear that the Players' League was doomed, those interested in baseball began to look for reasons why. The most simplistic and self-serving answer came from the magnates' mouthpiece, Henry Chadwick. As editor of the Spalding Guides, he wrote that the lesson of the 1890 season was that there

> ...was but one course to pursue in the business of ... running ... professional clubs, and that was to manage the professional leagues and clubs on the basis of true business principles....[95]

The whole mess, Chadwick thought, the losses, the lawsuits, the bitterness, the loss of patronage, all of it

> ...arose from the selfish greed of a small minority of overpaid "star" players of the National League of 1889 who thought they saw an opening for their becoming wealthy club magnates in the place of being fancy salaried players, no matter what cost to the fraternity at large their efforts at self-aggrandizement were likely to lead to.[96]

This gratuitous sneering at the fallen enemy was not, of course, a serious attempt at explaining the rise and fall of the Players' League. In *The Sporting Life Guide*, John Ward attempted to evaluate as dispassionately as he could the causes of the Players' League collapse. Ward asserted that the Players' League had been

> ...founded on new principles, some of which, it is true, proved to be impracticable and had much to do with its failure; but in the main these principles were sound.

Moreover, the Players' League was

> ...a standing protest against the National League's harsh, selfish, and tyrannical rule. It represented the aspirations of the players for personal liberty and higher professional and social standing than was possible under the repressive League system.

But beautiful principles and noble aspirations were not proof against the world's problems, and Ward proceeded to name a few. The Players' League suffered from timid and inexperienced capitalists, who grabbed control of the league, mismanaged it badly, and then "...deliberately sold out the players and the Players' League."[97] Beyond the magnates' incompetence and treason, there were structural problems in the Players' League. The clubs were undercapitalized and did not have a contingency fund to cover unexpected expenses. By the middle of the season even the stronger franchises were running in the red. The financial pinch was aggravated by conflicting playing schedules with the National League, which cut patronage even further.

There were also problems in the game itself, Ward thought. The lively Players' League baseball, adopted to give Tim Keefe some business and to make the games more exciting, had damaged the balance between pitching and hitting. The changes made by the Players' League in the playing rules were, it turned out, ill advised. The double umpire system cost a lot of money, but it did not materially improve the quality of the officiating nor reduce the number of rhubarbs. Finally, the grounds were often poorly prepared and maintained, with a predictably adverse affect on the game. The players themselves, however, Ward absolved from the blame. They had been models of discipline and devotion, and had the magnates been worthy of them, the Players' League would not have failed.[98]

The secretary of the Players' League, Frank H. Brunell, also essayed a post-mortem, which appeared in the Reach *Guide*. Brunell agreed with Ward that the clubs had been undercapitalized; the capital fund should have been $50,000 instead of $20,000. Brunell also thought that the Players' League should have used only non-playing managers, despite the fact that Boston, Brooklyn, and New York, the three best teams in the league, were managed by active players. But, like Ward, Brunell thought the basic fault lay with the magnates. The New York and Brooklyn owners sold out to the National League for selfish reasons, and the Players' League negotiating committee was no match for the wily and experienced Albert Spalding.[99]

Correct and germane as these comments were, neither man, curiously enough, touched on a theme which was constantly played in the daily papers. Kranks were not interested in the sordid squabbles of the magnates, the sports reporters wrote. Nor did they care for the name calling, the double dealing, the lawsuits, and the financial problems of the great baseball war. The kranks were profoundly uninterested in the players' principles, and they were disgusted by the magnates' seamy treacheries. What the kranks wanted was baseball, preferably at the old stand with the old teams and the old players. When they did not get it, they blamed everybody and lost interest in the game. What was needed, the sportswriters felt, was to bury the magnates' quarrels in the back rooms and direct the kranks' attention again to the game.

Nor did the baseball men mention the split in the Brotherhood ranks which meant that the National League retained enough of its players to compete on the field. Having some of the best players was not enough; the Players' League, to succeed, must have them all. And it never got them. Labor solidarity, that chimera of the union organizer, was not achieved in baseball any more than it was in the textile mills or coal mines. The National League owners ultimately signed about a quarter of their players, more than the Brotherhood leaders thought they could. The National League, therefore, could make a plausible claim to presenting major league baseball. It was not as good as it had been in the past few seasons, but it was still recognizably of major league quality. And that, of course, was what Ward knew must not happen. Ward understood that success depended in large part on having most of the major league players; thus he and his supporters could argue convincingly that the National was no longer a major league. The only real major would be the Players' League, which had all of the best players, while the National would be presenting minor league at major league prices. This did not occur, and it was one of the salient reasons for the survival of the older circuit.

The overriding failure of the Players' League, however, was financial. Every other problem, administrative, political, professional, was insignificant when compared to the red ink. In boom times, when the financial outlook is optimistic, business losses, particularly in the first year of operation can be written off to experience and made up quickly by borrowing at favorable rates. But 1890 was not a solid boom year. The Players' League, born in times of high prosperity and great expectations, found itself in financial difficulty at precisely the time when the American economy began to turn down. The high point of economic activity after the depression of 1884–1886 was in July 1890.[100] The downturn came at a time when the economy should have been most buoyant; the third and fourth quarters of the year saw the sale of the harvest. Even worse, the slump in the real economy was accompanied by two sharp financial panics. Problems began in August. Tight money and a decline in the stock market touched off a wave of called loans. Interest rates on short-term loans shot up to 35 percent on August 20 and reached 186 percent the next day, a figure that borders on usury even by the slippery standards of modern loan companies. Intervention by the Secretary of the Treasury was needed to calm the panic.[101] Secretary Windom's action in offering to pay off some Treasury bonds and put some more money into circulation averted immediate disaster, though the New York Clearing House banks fell below their required reserves by August 30 and money remained tight for the better part of September.[102]

This brief unpleasantness was only the beginning. In November, when the fate of the Players' League was being sealed, the New York money market suffered a real panic. During the first week in November money became tighter, with interest rates advancing to about 25 percent for call loans. Things rapidly got a lot worse. Reserves sank sharply, and the New York Clearing House had to issue special loan certificates so that its member banks could pay off their obligations to each other without using cash, since all of that was pledged to depositors. The stock market slumped badly and banks began to close. The biggest failure was in London, where Baring Brothers and Company went under. Short-term money continued to become more expensive, again reaching the extravagant figure of 186 percent.[103] Under such conditions capitalists were no longer interested in investing in baseball, particularly with the massive financial problems the game was having. Many of those who had already invested in baseball became quite anxious "to get in out of the wet." And so they did.

The financial panic of 1890 sharply aggravated the fundamental economic miscalculation the Brotherhood leaders had made: they greatly exaggerated the basic profitability of baseball. Ward and his friends read newspaper stories about the huge profits in New York or Chicago, running close to $75,000 or even $100,000 a year. Occasionally, in New York, or Boston, or Chicago, or St. Louis, such profits were made. But they were not made there every year, and they were never made in Louisville, Providence, Detroit, Philadelphia, Indianapolis, Kansas City, Cleveland, etc. The Brotherhood leaders ignored the clear message of constantly shifting franchises. Clubs were always going broke, even winning clubs like Providence and Detroit. Most clubs never made much money, even in the best years, and some never made any. The constant financial losses were the basic reason for such things as large fines, road trip assessments, and the Brush Classification Rule. Under the best of circumstances baseball was marginally profitable, and it had only been even that since 1884. Baseball was a risky business, and for every Spalding there were fifty Lucases.

The Brotherhood people and their backers did not understand this. Some, like Al Johnson, thought of baseball as a street railway bonanza. Others, like E. B. Talcott, thought of baseball as an excellent financial investment. Few imagined that it might be a serious economic risk, which could only produce losses the first year when the cost of new parks was added to the normal running expenses. In 1890 there were no tax credits to offset real losses. The Players' League was founded on the incredible assumption that professional baseball was an eldorado. In fact, of course, it was just the opposite.

There is no substitute for victory, runs the military axiom, and there is no excuse for defeat. Yet the Players' League deserves better than the magnates' verdict of obloquy and oblivion. After having told themselves that the Brotherhood was a lot of damn nonsense and the Players' League had never had a chance because it was not conducted on "sound business principles," the magnates thought the best thing to do was just forget about it. But the Brotherhood was not just nonsense. It was founded to deal with serious grievances, the reality of which was demonstrated by the substantial support it received from the players. Nor was the Players' League inevitably doomed to failure. Most of its losses had come from capital investment in the parks, not in operating deficits. The established leagues had lost more money on running expenses than the Players' League had. Nor were the players inherently incapable of taking a hand in baseball management, as the magnates maintained. The magnates' opinion that the players were all roistering drunken louts reluctant to accept discipline or take responsibility was simply not true. Finally, the kranks were not as put off by the sight of players as stockholders as the National League owners pretended. Attendance at the Players' League games proved that.

In public, the National League owners had scoffed at the Players' League, saying that it was no real threat. In private, among themselves, they had a very different opinion. The Players' League might well succeed. The power of the magnates might be drastically reduced. They might go broke. In private, the National League magnates were thoroughly scared. But, although badly frightened and nearly ruined, the magnates survived. After their victory they recovered their former arrogance and looked forward to the new decade as an era of fun, profits, and total domination of the game. For the players, who had lost the war, the prospect was different. The veterans of the Players' League would soon view the '80s as the good old days, fondly remembered and gone forever.

> Backward, turn backward, O time in thy rush, make me a slave again, well-dressed and flush!
> Bondage come back from the echoless shore, And bring me my shackles I formerly wore.[104]

CHAPTER SIX

AN ATTEMPT TO RECOVER

I

The war with the Players' League was a watershed for Organized Baseball. It separated a period of growing prosperity from one of persistent poverty. It divided an era of sustained and successful improvement of the rules from a time of general professional conservatism. The Brotherhood struggle also changed the management structure of baseball, and abruptly halted the rise in players' salaries. Finally, it shifted the focus of power within baseball from the players to the owners, where it remained until 1975.

Sudden stabilization of the rules was the change most noticeable to the fans. Before 1890 there had been rule changes almost every year as the impresarios of baseball tried to achieve the appropriate balance between pitching and hitting. In the nineties, however, the pace of rule changes slowed abruptly. There was a major alteration in 1893, when the pitching distance was increased to sixty feet, six inches, and the pitcher was required to throw from the rubber. A second significant change was the introduction of the infield fly rule in 1895, the result of imaginative play by the Baltimore Orioles and indignant complaints from everyone else. The rest of the changes were largely technical, involving scoring or the clarification of rules already extant. Thus, by 1895, the game had solidified into recognizably modern form. Thereafter, changes would come in playing patterns and strategy, or in technology, rather than in radical alterations of the rules.

An unforeseen result of the solidification of the rules was the rapid growth in the number and importance of baseball statistics. Now that the performances of players could be compared over a number of years, sportswriters and fans collected masses of figures to prove who the best players were. By 1900 this tendency was well established. Fans became great collectors and quoters of statistics, and columns of exact figures became as important to the games as the ball and bat. By the turn of the century baseball had succumbed to the enticements of exact measurement, a development certainly compatible with the rest of American life.

Equally significant were the alterations in the management structure of baseball after 1890. For most of the eighties, when professional baseball had become firmly established as a commercial, artistic and psychological success, there had been two major leagues, the National League and the American Association. The League was stronger, having a solid majority of the better teams and players, but the Association survived and prospered, and on occasion (as in 1886) an Association team defeated the League winner in post-season championship play. But the two-league system, so beneficial to baseball and so satisfactory to the fans, survived the Brotherhood war by only a single year. Financial reverses had something to do with this, but the sustained hostility of National League owners to the American Association was an equally important factor. After the 1891 season the two major leagues were combined into a single twelve-club circuit, as the National League absorbed four Association franchises and bought the rest off. The kranks never liked this monopolistic arrangement. They missed the world series and they would not support teams mired deep in the second division. They criticized the twelve-club league relentlessly, and sportswriters echoed fan dissatisfaction.

The unhappiness of the kranks was reflected in the attendance. In 1891 almost every club in both leagues lost money, and in 1892 only Cleveland made a profit in the new twelve-club National League. Things were better for the next few years, particularly in 1893 when almost every club made money and the League paid off its debts. In 1897, however, the red ink rose again. In 1900 the situation had become so desperate that the magnates threw four clubs out of the league, primarily to cut expenses. During the nineties most owners, even those with winning teams, found baseball to be a parlous and profitless business.

In order to keep the losses as small as possible, the magnates did several things. One was to own more than one club. This drift toward syndicate control began in 1890, when the Giants bankrupted and several league owners invested in the ailing club. By 1900 this practice was the rule rather than the exception. Ferdinand Abel, the principal owner of the Brooklyn franchise, also held 40 percent of the Baltimore Orioles and was a minority stockholder in the Giants. The Robison brothers, Frank and Stanley, owned both St. Louis and Cleveland. Barney Dreyfuss owned both Pittsburgh and Louisville, and every club except Boston and Chicago had minority stockholders from among the other league owners. The object of all of this was simple: If a magnate diversified his holdings, owned stock in enough places, he was bound to make a profit somewhere.

An equally obvious money-saving move was to cut the players' salaries. This was not so easy to do in 1891. Magnates had offered long-term contracts to induce players to stay with the National League, and they had also given good contracts to secure the best men they could out of the rubble of the Players' League. In 1892, however, things were different. The number of players a club could have under contract was sliced to thirteen, and those players who were retained were forced to take a substantial, midseason salary cut. These reductions were deepened when the contracts for 1893 were sent out. Even the greatest players found that $2400 was the top salary offered, and many stars, like Ed Delahanty, a .400 hitter, were offered only $1800. It was take it or leave it. Most took it. What else could they do? The reserve clause, the owners' real and serious losses, the failure of the Brotherhood, their own inability to pursue any other trade, all combined to force the average salaries down below the 1885 level. And there they stayed until the formation of the American League in 1900 reintroduced competition for players.

The players not only lost money during the nineties, they also lost status and influence in the game. The old sense of community between owner and players, so obvious in New York, disappeared completely. Instead of being a junior colleague of the owner in their common enterprise, the player became merely an employee, regarded by the magnates as childish and potentially troublesome. Players no longer referred to an owner as "our good friend," which was Gil Hatfield's term for John B. Day. For their part, the magnates publicly stated that they were going to drive salaries so low that the franchises could not possibly lose money. Changes in attitude led to the creation of sharp social lines. Owners, even managers, no longer fraternized with their players. The easy camaraderie of Nick Engel's Home Plate Saloon, where Day and Mutrie drank with "the boys," was over. Buck Ewing, John Ward, Roger Connor, and Smiling Mickey Welch were heroes to Day, but their successors were only hired hands to the New York magnates of the nineties.

By the end of the 1891 season this change in attitudes was complete. Efforts by players and magnates to put things back the way they were had failed. The financial losses and emotional bitterness of the Brotherhood struggle were too great to be ignored or forgotten. Once the magnates had decided that the players were not heroes but wage earners, it was an easy matter to reduce them to that status. If the Brotherhood failure had demonstrated anything, it was that "baseball law," whether legal or not, was going to stand up. The reserve clause was used mercilessly to drive salaries down. Players were traded or sold with no apologies. Players were released at the end of the season to save the club a fortnight's salary. Fines were imposed for the slightest infraction, and poor Fred Pfeffer was exiled to Louisville, a baseball Siberia, for continuing insubordination. The Brush classification system was revived in reality, if not in name. Players who complained of the numerous instances of unfair treatment were told to look for another job and were reminded that there were many minor leaguers who would gladly take their place, at a lower salary.

There was some compensation outside the game for the players' deteriorated status within it. Players may no longer have been heroes to the club owners, but they still were to the kranks, especially the kids. Particularly in Baltimore, winning players became civic demi-gods. They were recognized everywhere. They were wined and dined and cheered and feted, and enjoyed such perquisites as having their pictures on baseball cards and opening their own saloon (John McGraw and Wilbert Robinson tried this and did fairly well with it). Most were not so favored by fortune or talent, but even the poorest players on the weaker teams had a small constituency of friends who looked up to them with admiration and envy.

These changes in the game were, for the most part, quite undesirable. The tendency toward interlocking ownership undermined public confidence in the honesty of the game, particularly when magnates shifted players from one of their clubs to another to assemble the best possible team in the town most likely to have good attendance. The kranks resented the replacement of open competition with syndicate management, and their interest in baseball declined. This increased the magnates' financial problems, which had given rise to interlocking ownership in the first place. The twelve-team league, with eight or nine uncompetitive teams each year, also intensified fiscal woes and increased the attractiveness of syndicate ownership. It was a vicious circle of magnate misgovernment and fan disinterest, and it was only broken by the successful establishment of the American League.

II

"United, Greater, Stronger Than Ever" read the banner over the Giants' clubhouse on opening day of 1891. Everyone connected with the club certainly hoped so, but there were plenty of doubts. No one was certain that the kranks had forgiven the catastrophe of 1890. The Giants' management, afraid that the kranks would not support the reunited team, arranged a magnificent display of opening day pageantry. The New York and Boston players met at Broadway and Wall Street and were driven uptown to the Polo Grounds in Tally-Ho coaches. Several amateur teams followed in carriages and on foot. The parading players were cheered the length of their journey to the Polo Grounds, which was handsomely decorated with flags and bunting. The Seventh Regiment band played as it had so many times before.

To Day and Mutrie's great relief, the Polo Grounds were packed with kranks. The official attendance was 17,835, the largest opening-day crowd in the club's history. Every grandstand seat was taken and the kranks stood around the outfield. The Giants responded badly to this massive show of support, however. They lost to the Red Stockings, 4 to 3, as Boston scored two runs in the ninth inning. It was an inauspicious beginning and a poor way to win back the fans.[1]

After the opening series with Boston the Giants went on the road. The boys played pretty good baseball, although the team was not without problems. Tim Keefe was out of shape. Buck Ewing had a sore arm and Orator Jim O'Rourke had to catch. He was too old to take much of that sort of punishment and had to take some time off to recuperate. Finally, Smiling Mickey Welch had a sore arm. In spite of it all, the Giants returned to the Polo Grounds on Memorial Day with a record of 14 victories and 15 defeats.[2]

Back in the Polo Grounds the Giants accelerated their winning pace. Starting with two Memorial Day victories over Cleveland, the Giants won 15 of their first 16 home games. On July 22 they were in second place, three games behind Anson's Colts, as the Chicago team was now called. When the Colts came to New York for a four-game series with the streaking Giants there was enormous interest in the games. The teams were now tied for first place. For a single weekend it was the old days; it was 1885 once again, when Keefe, Welch, and Ewing were young and no one had heard of the Brotherhood. Mutrie strode up and down the field, shouting his old cry: "Who are the People? We are the People!," and the kranks responded with roars of approval.

Caught up in the excitement, the Giants sustained the illusion. They did what they had never done before; they won four straight games from Chicago. Almost seven thousand fans saw Rusie pitch New York into first place in the opening game, as the Giants scored four runs in the ninth to win, 9 to 6. On June 13 Rusie pitched again, before 22,289 frenzied kranks, the largest crowd in the team's history. Again the Giants won, 8 to 7, as Connor, Tiernan, and O'Rourke, all heroes from the old days, each hit a home run. On Monday the Giants pitched their old stars, Keefe and Welch, and won again, shutting Anson's Colts out on two hits, 5 to 0. When the series ended the Giants were four games ahead of Chicago.[3]

That was the high point of the season for the Giants. Within a week they had slipped to a slim half-game lead over Chicago. But the boys did not collapse. They hung on to first place by a game or so for another month. They also won the big ones. In Chicago the Giants won two of the three games and clung to the lead a few days longer. Not until July 22 did the Giants drop out of first place for good, as Chicago took over.[4]

Thereafter the Giants' decline was gradual but steady. On August 10 they dropped to third place as Boston moved up. For a while the Giants remained within striking distance of the top; a single game out on August 12 and just two and one half games back on August 18. During the last six weeks of the season, however, the Giants slipped badly, and they finished the season in third place, 13 games behind pennant-winning Boston.[5]

The kranks and the reporters were profoundly irritated by this. All too often, the work of the Giants had not been "...what their friends would like it to be." This was particularly reprehensible since "The team is the strongest aggregation of players ever got together, and the players ought to be ashamed of themselves."[6] So should the management. Ewing was the particular target for this criticism. He was accused of not hustling and was warned that he was losing his friends in New York. Ewing's leadership was derided as so lax and uninspiring that the players all quit trying toward the end of the season. By the middle of September writers were openly stating that James Mutrie was the only Giant left who thought that the team had a chance to win the pennant.[7]

The major part of Ewing's problems with the kranks and the press stemmed from the fact that he spent most of the season on the bench. Buck insisted that his arm and shoulder really hurt, but few believed him. Finally, Buck endured an incredible cure, even for the crude therapy of the time. He went to a veterinarian, who gave Buck's arm the same torture inflicted on a horse with strained tendons.

He first put a plaster cast on Ewing's arm

> and then produced a hot iron which was placed on the plaster burning the flesh. Much pain and suffering was attached to it but Buck stood it heroically.... Ointment was then rubbed on the arm after which it was done up in heavy bandages. A mark will be left on his arm for life.[8]

Naturally, the treatment did not work. Buck might better have swallowed horse liniment, a favorite general purpose remedy of the time. But it did have a certain moral success. Gilded Age Americans were impressed with Buck's fortitude and they stopped accusing him of malingering.

The Giants' main problem, however, was age. Ewing's sore arm was a sign that he was past his prime. Both Roger Connor and Jim O'Rourke had also slowed down. George Gore could no longer play major league ball. And Welch and Keefe were about through. It was sad to see; they were exceptionally popular and had hundreds of personal friends in New York. Smiling Mickey had come with the franchise; there had never been a Giants team without him. Keefe, with his stylish pitching, impeccable appearance and elegant manners would be sadly missed. So would they all. The Giants were a young franchise, and this was the first time the fans had said goodbye to a host of veterans whom they had cheered to victory. The press tried to be hard and practical about it; if the veterans were too old then get new men. But the fans knew better.

> Remember...
> Buck Ewing, Rusie, Smiling Mickey Welch,
> Remember a left-handed catcher named Jack Humphries, who sometimes played the outfield, in '83?[9]

The departing heroes also included the manager, Truthful James Mutrie. John B. Day was loyal to his old friend, of course, but the new investors, Cornelius Van Cott, General E. A. McAlpin, and E. B. Talcott, were all cool to

Mutrie. At Day's insistence Mutrie stayed on as manager, but he was shorn of any real authority. Buck Ewing ran the team. By the end of the season Mutrie was all but forgotten, ignored by the fans and seldom mentioned by the press. When his formal dismissal finally came, it was only a confirmation of the way things long had been.

It was a sad and pathetic end to a successful managerial career. In his nine years as a major league manager Mutrie had won three pennants and two world series. Only once did he finish out of the first division and that was during the Brotherhood war. His winning percentage was .611, the second best in the history of the game. He had been the symbol of the Giants in their glory days with his top hat, his waxed moustache, and his constant cry: "We are the People!" And now he was gone. Truthful James Mutrie had become a victim of his own aphorism: "Baseball is an uncertain game".[10]

The whole sour season was summed up in a squalid incident at its close. It involved a close pennant race and the Giants' questionable participation in it. Toward the end of August King Kelly jumped from the collapsing Cincinnati franchise in the American Association to his old National League team, Boston. Kelly's presence made a difference and Boston began a sensational drive for the pennant. They won their last eighteen games in a row, including five from the Giants in the last week of the season. The Red Stockings passed Chicago and won the flag by three and one half games. The demoralized Giants had played listless and shabby ball in those games with Boston, and many of the best men did not play at all. After the season ended the angry Chicago President, James A. Hart, accused the Giants of throwing the games to Boston to prevent Chicago from winning the pennant. His statement was forthright and bitter:

> Were I under indictment for murder with the circumstantial evidence against me as strong as it appears to be against the New-York Club, I should expect to be hanged. From present information and from private advises from Boston, I cannot help but feel that there had been either downright dishonesty on the part of the New-York Club or gross incompetency on the part of those in control of the team.[11]

Hart wanted to know why the Giants had not played Rusie, Danny Richardson, Buck Ewing or Roger Connor, and why two of the games, originally scheduled for New York, had been played in Boston.

These were all good questions, so good that a special National League committee was formed to look into the possibility that the Giants had thrown the pennant to Boston. The Giants' management claimed that Buck Ewing had a sore arm and Danny Richardson and Roger Connor were out of condition and could not give their best. Amos Rusie was tired, and, in any case, he had already done a hard season's work before the Boston series. The two games had been transferred to Boston for reasons of money — to save on travel and play before larger crowds. What the New York management did not say was that the team had given up, that no matter who played, the team would have lost. No one likes to admit that. The Giants' explanations, though feeble, had some air of plausibility about them, and no one could prove that the team had thrown the games. The New York excuses were finally accepted. The pennant belonged to Boston.[12]

The bitterness in Hart's accusations reflected more than losing the pennant. There was the more serious frustration of losing money. After the catastrophic losses in 1890, the magnates had hoped to recoup 1891. They had not. The franchises were saddled with substantial debts from the rosters; Chicago, for example, had reserved twenty-three players before the 1891 season began.

Many men had signed multi-year contracts when they stayed with the National League. The results of this pressure were clear and inevitable. Only a couple of clubs made expenses. Chicago and Boston probably made some money. The Giants did not. Moreover, the losses in New York were felt around the league, as the poorer franchises counted on large gates at the Polo Grounds to pay for their road trips.

One obvious road to solvency was the reestablishment of peace between the National League and the American Association. The two circuits had spent the 1891 season in a cold war, resulting from the division of players after the collapse of the Players' League, but the pressures of financial reverses had forced both sides into a series of peace meetings. The two leagues were near agreement on August 25, when the news came that King Kelly had jumped from Cincinnati in the Association to Boston in the National League. The Association demanded him back, the League refused, and the talks collapsed.

But the logic of peace, backed up by another ruinous season, outweighed mere pique. In November 1891, when the National League held its annual meeting, there were Association owners on hand to talk peace. So successful were the conversations that a formal meeting was scheduled for December 15 to end the war. This time the magnates succeeded. The American Association, sinking in red ink, was dissolved, and four of its clubs were taken into an expanded, twelve-club National League. Baltimore, Washington, St. Louis, and Louisville retained their major league franchises, while the other four Association clubs were bought out for nearly $130,000. The National League assumed this debt, and announced a 10 percent levy on gate receipts to pay it off. To meet this assessment, the season was lengthened to 162 games and was split in two, with the champion of the first half meeting the champion of the second in a substitute world series.[13]

So major league baseball returned to the situation of the seventies, when the league had been new and most of the clubs were bankrupt. The National League once again held a monopoly of major league baseball. The magnates showed intense satisfaction at this development, so much in tune with business thought at the time. Now they could do what they wanted. They controlled the players, they were not in the least inhibited by the weak and pliant Nick Young, and they had their monopoly. The magnates looked forward to times of fun and profit.

III

The changes in the structure of the National League were almost matched by the alterations in the Giants. The new manager was Patrick Thomas Powers, who had seen service in the American Association and the Eastern League. Powers promised his owners that he could revamp the sagging Giants. He did his best, and the Giants began the 1892 season with several new players. He brought in some refugees from the defunct American Association, including catcher Jack Boyle, infielders Denny Lyons and Shorty Fuller, and a pitcher, Charles "Silver" King. Unlike the others, Silver King was a legitimate star. He was a bit over the hill now, but in 1887 and 1888 he had pitched the St. Louis Browns to the pennant, winning 45 games in 1888 and pitching against the Giants in the series. Even in his declining years, however, he was a welcome addition to a very thin pitching staff.[14]

To make room for the new men some of the veterans had to go. Roger Connor joined Tim Keefe in Philadelphia. Danny Richardson became the manager of the Washington team, a move ordered by the league to strengthen an obviously weak franchise. These changes meant that Powers had practically a new team. But did he have a good one? There was some apprehension among both kranks and press.

The expanded season began for the Giants on April 13 in Philadelphia. Amos Rusie pitched against Tim Keefe. Powers started a lineup that included his new acquisitions and some older Giants. The blend of the old and the new seemed to work well. The Giants won the game, 5 to 4, with an unearned run in the seventh inning. Only about 4,500 fans sat in a cold drizzle to watch New York win the rather routine game, a clear sign that the reorganized National League was already in financial trouble.[15]

Opening day at the Polo Grounds was equally uninspiring. The Giants began the home season on April 23 with two games against the wretched Washington Senators. The festivities were much less elaborate than previously. There were no parades or bands, and only about 9,000 kranks came to the Polo Grounds on a soggy day. The Giants split the two games.[16] It was a far cry from the gaudy and triumphant pageants staged in years past. Powers was not the showman Mutrie had been. These opening day victories were deceptive, and the Giants were soon losing more games than they won. By the first of May the team was mired in seventh place, and, when the first half of the split season ended on July 13, the Giants were tied with the St. Louis Browns for ninth place. They had the dismal record of 31 victories and 43 defeats.[17]

The second half of the season was somewhat better. Again, the Giants won the first game, 13 to 5 over Pittsburgh, but only 2,940 fans came to the Polo Grounds to watch it. This time the Giants won somewhat more often than they lost. By the middle of August the boys were in fourth place and had even, for one giddy day, climbed as high as second. This was the high point of the season for the Giants. The team could not keep up the pace. When the season ended, the Giants were in sixth place with a record of 40 victories and 37 defeats.[18] This was better than before, but it was clear to everybody that the Giants had a long way to go.

The kranks took continued defeat with great ill grace. They stayed away from the Polo Grounds in large numbers. Even the Memorial Day doubleheader drew only 8,500 spectators. Most of the home games were played before fewer than 2,500 persons, and by July the crowds were frequently less than half that size. By the end of the season, in spite of the improvement in the team, the crowds were smaller yet. On October 5, against Brooklyn, the Giants drew 616 fans; the next day they raised the total to 707.[19] It was like the Brotherhood year.

Equally important, the financial and theatrical fans who had done so much to make the Giants a part of New York fashion were rapidly falling away. DeWolf Hopper no longer went to every game. There were no brokers gathering in committee to present gold watches to favored players, nor were evenings at the theater an ordinary part of New York hospitality for visiting teams. The Giants were no longer "the people." They had become just another form of second-rate entertainment, fit only for the dedicated krank. A dismal lack of flair within management and persistent defeat on the field had dissipated the high gleam and polish of the former champions.

The press, of course, reflected this disillusionment. Criticism was immediate and constant, varying in tone from insult to indignation. Powers responded with a few mild excuses about bad weather and injuries, but he lacked Mutrie's taste for extended verbal complaint. Instead, stung by press criticism, he moved with exceptional vigor to acquire new players, a process which became the motif of the season. Powers began by releasing veterans. Smiling Mickey Welch was sent to Troy in the Eastern League. George Gore went to the Browns to finish out his last season. And Orator Jim O'Rourke was released, though not without incident. O'Rourke was hitting .304, but he was also in his twenty-first year of major league ball and he was slowing down considerably. On September 10, therefore, Powers released the Orator and assigned his contract for 1893 to Washington. O'Rourke was outraged. In a clubhouse scene he denounced Powers as a fool who was running the team into the ground. John Day, supporting his manager, suspended O'Rourke for insubordination and outrage to authority. After thinking it over, the Orator apologized to Powers and was reinstated. But he did not return to the lineup.

The press reported these events gravely and carefully. There was little feeling for the toll of time. One writer commented only that this meant "...the retirement ... of O'Rourke ... and, as sentiment does not win base ball games, the veteran with the exemplary habits must go."[20]

There was also a steady stream of new players. Most were marginal players who remained with the team a season or so and drifted off to the minors. Two of Powers' acquisitions, however, were men of exceptional ability. On the first of July he got Jack Doyle, who played with such ferocity that he gained the nickname "Dirty" Doyle. Powers put him into the lineup immediately, using him primarily as a catcher and an outfielder.[21]

Powers' other discovery was Wee Willie Keeler, one of the great players in the history of the game. Keeler was playing for Binghampton in the Eastern League when Powers purchased his contract. He was only twenty years old when Powers signed him, and he had been in professional baseball for less than a season. In Binghampton he had become an overnight sensation and was generally regarded as the best player in the league. When the Giants signed him the Binghampton manager said

> In Keeler, the New-Yorks have one of the very best all-around players in the profession. In all my experience on the diamond ... I have never seen a young man who impressed me so favorably.[22]

Physically, Keeler was a small man, about five feet, four inches tall, and he weighed less than 150 pounds. In an era of brutal, rowdy play, Wee Willie was a quiet, modest, self-effacing man. He never argued with umpires nor spiked an opponent deliberately. He rarely spoke to anyone on the field. When he hit, he choked up on the bat and tried to tap the ball just out of reach of the opposing fielders. He could bunt and steal bases, and he almost never struck out. The quiet man remained in the big leagues for nineteen years and compiled a lifetime batting average of .345, fifth highest in the history of the game. Once asked by a sportswriter how such a small man could hit so well, Keeler replied only, "Keep your eye clear and hit 'em where they ain't." That last phrase became an enduring part of American slang. Wee Willie Keeler played only fourteen games in that first year with the Giants, all at third base. But he hit .321, the best average on the team, and the kranks and writers confidently predicted that Keeler would be the great Giants' star of the future.[23]

The steady stream of new players, while they helped the Giants' record and reduced press criticism, did not bring a needed increase in attendance and revenue. Again the club lost money. The losses were so serious that the club fell three months in arrears on the players' salaries. It came to nearly a thousand dollars a man. Day told his players that the best he could do was give them a quarter on the dollar and notes for the balance. After hearing the grim statistics the players accepted. Serious as the unpaid salaries were, they did not reveal the full measure of the club's insolvency. Salaries had already been slashed twice. In December, 1891 when the two major leagues had merged, the magnates had carried out a general reduction in salaries, regardless of any contracts the players might have signed. On that occasion they had alleged their need to recoup from two financially disastrous seasons, as well as pay for the costs of consolidation. The players, unorganized, caught by surprise, and fearing unemployment if they refused now that the number of major league teams was trimmed to twelve, accepted the magnates' action.

The second salary slash had come in mid-season. On June 13, 1892 the magnates met in New York "...for the purpose of devising some scheme to place all the clubs on an even playing basis."[24] To the magnates, the solution to problems on the field lay in the realm of finance. Costs could be cut by reducing the rosters of each club to thirteen players. Some clubs were carrying, and paying, as many as eighteen men. Over the course of the next few weeks club officials should trim their swollen rosters, and the players released by the better clubs could then be signed by the poorer ones. Thus expenses would be cut, the teams would be more equal, the games would become more interesting, more kranks would come to see them, and the weaker clubs would climb toward solvency with larger crowds and smaller rosters.[25]

The owners also decided, among themselves, to take additional measures to save money. Salaries must go down again. They did not announce this to the press, but they did it anyway. Right after the meeting they cut their players by several hundred dollars a man, informing them that outright release was the alternative to acceptance. Among the Giants, only Tiernan, Rusie, and Fuller refused to take the mid-season reduction, saying that they had signed binding contracts with the club. For the moment Day let it go. But he caught up with the trio at the end of the season. He released them on October 6, thus, in effect, clipping each out of nearly a month's salary. By prior agreement none of the other teams offered them a job, and they had to play out the season free.[26]

The main cause of the magnates' financial woes, aside from poor attendance, was the assessment each club had to pay to the league office in order to retire the collective debt incurred from buying out the Players' League and the American Association. In December 1891 the clubs had agreed to pay the league 10 percent of their income to meet these debts. It was not enough. On June 13, 1892, at their New York meeting, the magnates agreed to go up to 12 1/2 percent. That, too, was insufficient. On September 10 league president Nick Young informed the clubs that the assessment must be raised to 16 percent of their gross receipts.[27] In a good year a slice of that size would have hurt; in a bad one it was catastrophic. But the clubs had to pay. Since the magnates could not duck their assessments, the only way to cut costs was to cut salaries.

Given the increasing distance between the magnates and the players, a rash of salary cuts was not only inevitable, it was, from the magnates' viewpoint, desirable as well.

IV

Toward the middle of February, 1893, the twelve major league clubs were beginning spring training, a meager affair after three seasons during which every club had lost money consistently. There was some apprehension among the magnates about the coming year. They could not afford to lose money indefinitely, and there were sportswriters who predicted the end of professional baseball. No one in the game would admit this, but everyone was worried. A barometer of that concern was the players' salaries. They were slashed again, this time to the level contemplated in the Brush classification plan.

This year, however, the outlook for baseball was clouded even further by a sharp economic depression which began in the middle of February. On February 18 a report of the financial condition of the huge Northern Pacific Railroad was released. It was not reassuring. The document was filled with such phrases as "stupendous and incredible folly," the "deplorable financial condition" of the road, and the present situation being "a menace to stockholders." Rhetoric was supported by statistics. The company owed $9,219,000 in short-term debt alone, and the authors of the report implied that the railroad could not pay.

Bad as this was, it was followed closely by even worse news. On February 18 there was a major run on the stock and mortgage certificates of the Philadelphia and Reading Railroad. Over two and a quarter million in mortgage bonds changed hands at a sharp break in price. The stockholders also unloaded, selling 392,230 shares. The price of the stock dropped sharply, from 47 to 41, a spectacular decline for the nineties. By the 21st of February, when 957,955 shares of Reading were sold at 30 and 4.9 million in mortgage certificates changed hands, the line collapsed. The bankruptcy of the Reading also pulled down an ambitious attempt to control the mining and marketing of anthracite coal, making this the first of the major trusts to go under in the depression of the nineties.[28]

The collapse of the Reading was followed by a steady stream of bad news. Early in March the Pennsylvania Railroad revealed that its profits had fallen substantially in the past year, though the line hastened to add that it was solvent. Similar reports from other major railroads followed, the Missouri Pacific and the Chicago, Burlington and Quincy showing particularly heavy earnings declines. On March 30 the troubles spread to industrial stocks. Wall Street was unnerved by rumors that National Cordage was in financial trouble. There were similar rumors about Distilling and Cattle Feeding (the Whiskey Trust).

Three weeks later the Pennsylvania Steel Company went bankrupt, the first of a long line of failures in this industry that would ultimately lead to the organization of United States Steel. By the middle of April, a week before the new baseball season, it was clear to everyone that the Reading collapse was merely the opening act of a major business crisis.[29]

These business failures were accompanied by a persistent deficit in the balance of payments and a nagging shortage of gold with which to settle accounts. Bankers, stock brokers, and even Treasury officials complained bitterly about the coinage of silver, which had increased considerably as a result of the Sherman Silver Purchase Act of 1890. The conservative businessmen claimed that this extensive coinage of silver had "unsettled" affairs and was responsible for the "unfortunate" series of corporate failures. On April 21 the news from the Treasury confirmed what many astute bankers had suspected. The outflow of gold was so great that the Treasury had fallen below its basic reserves of $100,000,000 in gold. Secretary of the Treasury Carlisle called for the repeal of silver purchase, and he asked bankers to invest gold in the Treasury. This news was not merely unsettling, it was terrifying, and no amount of soothing drivel about conditions being "fundamentally sound" convinced anyone any differently.[30]

On May 3 panic began in earnest. Trading on the Stock Exchange was heavy and prices declined throughout the day. Brokers and their clients surrendered to the months of accumulated bad news.

> Not since 1884 had the stock market had such a break in price as occurred yesterday.... In industrials the general nervousness amounted almost to a panic.[31]

The first victim of the deluge was the National Cordage Trust, which slid right into bankruptcy. It was not alone. Banks and brokers began to call in their margin loans. On May 4 two Wall Street brokerage firms went under, as their clients could not meet the margin calls. Three days later another trio of brokers collapsed. By May 8 the roll call of bank failures had begun. The Chemical National Bank of Chicago was the first, followed closely by the Capital National Bank of Indianapolis and the Columbia National Bank of Chicago. The closure of the Columbia brought a wave of catastrophe to small towns in the mid-west, as its correspondent banks also went under. This was followed by the demise of Whiskey trust, the closing of the first New York banks, bank failures in Denver, Milwaukee, Chicago, and Omaha, the collapse of the Kansas City Grain Company, and the failure of two more railroads, the Little Rock and Memphis and the Toledo, St. Louis, and Kansas City, all within three weeks. It was the classic pattern of nineteenth-century financial deflation.[32]

In the face of the appalling economic disaster, which clearly indicated the onslaught of a major depression, business spokesmen remained outwardly calm and reassuring. The accumulated failures were explained away to the public as mere technical readjustments or the inevitable result of the Sherman Silver Purchase Act. If everyone kept his head things would be fine. The *Commercial and Financial Chronicle* took this soothing tone. There has been

> ...no general panic to disturb confidence; there has been no sudden bringing to light of commercial fraud or weakness: mercantile and banking business is on a conservative basis; and the trade of the country is sound.[33]

Unfortunately, none of these statements was true, and repeating them over and over as a kind of sympathetic magic to ward off disaster had no discernible effect on anything.

Efforts more substantial than incantations were made to halt the catastrophe. On June 5 President Cleveland announced that he would call a special session of Congress to repeal the Sherman Silver Purchase Act. This news shared the front pages with descriptions of a major run on Chicago banks. On June 15 the New York Clearing House issued its first Certificates, which allowed member banks to discharge their debts to each other in paper and save the gold for panicky depositors. The Clearing House's action was both an effort to help and an admission that things had gotten pretty much out of hand.[34]

Issuing Clearing House Certificates and the promise of repeal of the Sherman Act were supposed to add to the supply of confidence, which had run low. The news media did their best to support this campaign, a New York Times article going so far as to claim that the depression was a "...mere spasmodic ripple upon the usually placid stream of American commercial prosperity."[35]

The *Times* may not have been able to find the depression, but it was there, and the respite provided by the Clearing House Certificates was short indeed. Banks continued to fold at a steady rate, and the Central Pacific Railroad defaulted on its loan payments to the government. The Erie Railroad went under, again, and the Northern Pacific also failed. Stocks continued to decline. By the end of July they had fallen to their lowest level since the panic of 1873, a striking measure of the severity of the depression.[36]

Toward the end of August, when the worst was over, it was possible to assess the damage. Almost five hundred banks, mostly small institutions in the south and west, had failed. In the first half of 1893 there had been 6,239 business failures, with a total of over 170 million dollars in liabilities. It was the sharpest national downturn since 1873, and all efforts by the government and the major banks to halt the slide failed. During the summer of 1893 the nation slipped swiftly into a major depression.[37]

The effect of this economic slaughter on Organized Baseball was the exact opposite of what the magnates and their bankers feared. Major League baseball, like the construction of street railways, was a counter-cyclical industry. Instead of going broke like everyone else, baseball prospered. The crowd on opening day at the Polo Grounds was an example of things to come. In spite of the bad season in '92 and the passing of the great heroes of the eighties, a large mob of kranks descended upon the park to see the game. DeWolf Hopper and Nick Engel were there, and so were about 15,000 others. Kranks packed the grandstand and stood around the foul lines and the outfield, and the crush was so great that some who had tickets could not get to the gates. Two bands entertained the crowd, and, when the Giants appeared, the kranks cheered them as if they had been champions. The real champions that day, however, were the Giants' opponents, the Boston Red Stockings, who proceeded to prove it by beating the Giants easily, 9 to 2. But the kranks cheered anyway. Perhaps they did not expect much, perhaps they were just glad to see a baseball game, but the atmosphere of good humor was unmistakable.[38]

The excellent attendance continued, in spite of the fact that the Giants began the 1893 season as they had the previous one, by losing a large number of games. On May 6 nearly 5,000 fans came to see the Giants play the pitiful Washington Senators, and, on May 10, a game with Brooklyn drew over 7,000 persons to the Polo Grounds. The Giants rewarded this loyalty by losing; against Brooklyn the boys blew a nine-run lead. No matter. In spite of such catastrophes, and the press criticism that accompanied them, the kranks continued to support the Giants. For a Memorial Day double-header with Cincinnati, the Giants drew the largest crowd in the history of the club; 23,142 kranks watched the Giants lose the afternoon game to the Reds and over 6,000 were there for the morning contest. For most of the season the crowds rarely dipped below 2,000 fans, and mobs of six or seven thousand were not uncommon.[39]

This delightful and unexpected rise in attendance meant that the Giants made money for the first time since 1889. The club had started the 1893 season almost $35,000 in the red, and by the end of the season it had made that up. The Giants' owners also discharged their debts to the players. On the first of June the club presented checks to the men in payment for the salary arrears of 1892. The total amount was over $12,000. A good many players had despaired of ever seeing their money, not an unreasonable attitude considering the propensity of the magnates to cheat them. But John B. Day, now about broke, was an honest man, and he paid the boys off, in full.[40]

Convincing explanations for the sudden resurgence of the Giants' popularity were hard to find, though the return of John Montgomery Ward as manager was certainly one of them. Ward, who had won twenty shares of New York stock on a bet with E. B. Talcott, was brought over from Brooklyn on the hunch that his name would revive interest in the team. Ward himself was delighted to return to the glamour and theater of Manhattan after his exile across the bridge in the city of churches. The Giants gave Brooklyn a percentage of the gate in payment for Ward's services.[41]

Ward made some changes in the team, including the return of Roger Connor from Philadelphia. His biggest trade, certainly, was to ship the legendary

Buck Ewing to Cleveland for infielder George Davis. He also obtained King Kelly, on loan from Boston, whose owners still held their New York stock and wanted to see the attendance increase in the big city. The King was a great disappointment to the Giants; he reported late, badly out of shape and over the hill. He played in only twenty games.

The team was better than it had been in 1892, but the Giants were not yet a contender. The Giants started poorly, and were in tenth place at the end of May. Not until July did the boys begin a winning spurt that carried them to fifth place, which was where they ended the season. Their record was 68 victories and 64 defeats, not bad for a rebuilding year and a major improvement over the previous season. Ward was satisfied. A little additional strength and he would have the team back at the top.[42]

There was also no doubt that the team was fashionable once more, a tribute to the magic of Ward's name and personality. Again, brokers and sporting young men came to the game. Theater parties reappeared, almost as if they had never been gone. On June 2 the Giants were guests, with three other teams, at a special baseball night at DeWolf Hopper's latest hit, *Panjandrum*. The play was reinforced by Digby Bell's recitation of "The Tough Boy on the Right Field Fence," and, of course, by DeWolf Hopper declaiming "Casey at the Bat." It was like the old days.[43]

There was one event of the 1893 season which did not receive universal applause. On July 27 Ward traded Wee Willie Keeler to Brooklyn for $800. There was a great deal of feeling that this was a rotten idea, as, of course, it was. One sportswriter maintained that Keeler was just the kind of young player every club in the league is scouring the country to secure.[44] Condemnation was coupled with bewilderment. Why had the Giants done it? No satisfactory explanations ever appeared. It was not the money; the Giants were doing exceptionally well at the gate. And few could be brought to believe that Keeler's broken leg, suffered in May, had rendered him permanently *hors de combat*. Perhaps it was part of the New York-Brooklyn deal that had brought Ward to the Giants in the first place. No one ever said.

V

The 1894 season was the beginning of the spectacular career of the Baltimore Orioles, one of the most famous teams in the history of baseball. The Orioles were the creation of Ned Hanlon, who had come over to Baltimore from Pittsburgh as manager after the start of the 1892 season. Hanlon acquired ten percent of the club from its owner, a Baltimore brewer named Harry von der Horst, and began to build a powerful team. There was not much he could do in 1892, and his team finished last. The next year Hanlon acquired Hugh Jennings as shortstop and Joe Kelley for the outfield, and the Orioles climbed to eighth place. Over the winter Hanlon completed the reorganization of his team. He obtained outfielder Steve Brodie from St. Louis, purchased second baseman Henry Reitz from the California League, and made a monumental deal with the hapless Brooklyn Bridegrooms. He sent George Treadway and Bill Shindle, two journeymen players, to Brooklyn for Wee Willie Keeler and Dan Brothers, two of the best in the league. It was the best, or worst, trade in the history of baseball, and it turned the Orioles from a good team into a great one.[45]

The Giants were also in the market for new men. George van Haltren, an excellent outfielder, came from the Pittsburgh Pirates, and the Giants purchased the battery of Jouett Meekin and Duke Farrell from Washington for $7,500. The latter deal was the key for New York. Ward knew this as well as anybody, and he hoped that Meekin and Farrell would put the Giants back on top.

New York and Baltimore were the most improved teams in the league, and they met in Baltimore on opening day. Over fifteen thousand fans came out to see Hanlon's new team, and they were well rewarded. The Orioles defeated the Giants, 8 to 3, and played hard, aggressive baseball. It confirmed Ward's fears. He had said that the Orioles were a good team; he could only hope that, over the whole season, his revamped Giants would be a little better.[46]

But the Giants started badly. At the end of May the boys were in sixth place. By the first of July they had climbed only to fifth. But these defeats, though galling to kranks and press, were not indicative of the team's real strength. After two months of play, the Giants began to improve. It happened on the road. On June 24 the Giants started a western swing on which they won thirteen games and lost only four. When the team returned home it was in third place.[47]

The kranks and press greeted the returning heroes with loud hosannas. This was the kind of team they had waited four years to see. When the players arrived in Jersey City to take the ferry to Manhattan, they were met by a large contingent of enthusiastic kranks, a fitting tribute, wrote Harry Wright, for the Giants' "gallant record" in the west. The boys themselves caught the spirit of the thing and pitcher Huyler Westervelt composed a team victory yell reminiscent of the more fatuous college cheers.

> Oscar Wow Wow!
> Skinny Wow Wow!
> Skinny Wow Wow!
> W-o-o-o-o Hurrah!
> New York!

It was a more innocent time.[48]

Attendance, which had been excellent all year, now became even better. Over 8,000 kranks, including the Catholic Protectory Band and a large delegation from the Stock Exchange, turned out on July 17 to see the Giants begin their home stand. They were amply rewarded as the New York ace, Amos Rusie, defeated Washington, 7 to 2. It was a good start, and both the fans and the press were convinced that the Giants were headed toward first place.[49]

The Giants kept on winning, but so did Boston and Baltimore, the two teams still above them. Not until the first week of September did the Giants finally pass the fading Beaneaters and move into second place. But they never did catch Baltimore. The Orioles kept winning at nearly the same pace as the Giants. When the season ended on September 30, the Giants had a record of 88 victories and 44 defeats, their best since 1885. They were three games behind Baltimore. The three losses to the Orioles to start the season were the final margin of defeat.[50]

Since 1890 there had been no world series. Post-season championship play had been one of the victims of the Brotherhood and the collapse of the American Association. In 1892, the year of the split season, the champions of the two halves, Boston and Cleveland, played a series which had evoked no discernible interest. In 1893 there had been nothing. Both the fans and the press wanted a championship series, and a Pittsburgh sportsman, W. C. Temple, came to the rescue. He presented the league with a large silver trophy to be awarded to the winner of a series between the first- and second-place teams. To give the players some incentive to do their best, the receipts of the first four games were to be divided among them — 65 percent to the winners, 35 percent to the losers. The National League officials accepted this proposal with alacrity and enthusiasm. It appeared to be the perfect substitute for the now-dead world series.[51]

But troubles arose almost immediately and from a most unexpected quarter. The Baltimore players refused to play for the 65-35 split, demanding instead an even division of the money. As Baltimore had won the pennant, and might be presumed to have the stronger team, this demand received universal condemnation and contempt, and Temple himself intervened to say that he would not present his cup under those circumstances. John Ward disclaimed all connection with the mess and said that the Giants were willing to play under the original conditions. Under this kind of pressure the Baltimore players gradually conceded, though John McGraw did not give in until five minutes before the first game began. The games began on schedule and ostensibly under the terms demanded by Temple, though the players agreed among themselves to an even split of the money.

The series opened on October 4 in Baltimore, and nearly 12,000 rabid kranks came to the park to see their new heroes demolish the upstart Giants. They consumed huge quantities of Harry von der Horst's beer, hollered the Baltimore war cry "Get at 'em!," and urged their heroes on. The new heroes, however, were not in the best of condition to do this. After winning the pennant they had accepted dozens of invitations to banquets, testimonials, parties, receptions, and festivities in general. This high-octane dissipation had reduced the Orioles to a sad state of flab and exhaustion. As a result, the

Orioles played sloppy and erratic baseball, and Amos Rusie defeated them, 4 to 1. Both the Baltimore fans and players were deeply disappointed by the game, and a riot was narrowly averted in the seventh inning, when John McGraw ran into Ward and started a fight.[52]

The first game set the pattern for the entire series. The Orioles were in no better shape for the second game than they had been the day before, and the Giants won again, 9 to 6. Jouett Meekin pitched for the Giants, and he survived early difficulties to benefit from a four-run New York rally in the ninth inning. The scene shifted to New York for the next two games, and the Giants' fans, scenting victory, came out to roar for the boys. In the third game, played before nearly 20,000 fans, Amos Rusie won an easy victory for New York, 4 to 1. That victory really decided the issue. Everyone, including the Orioles, expected the Giants to win the next game easily. A baseball night at the Broadway Theater before the fourth game was an early celebration of victory. As the Catholic Protectory Band led the teams onto the field before the fourth game, the crowd of 12,000 sang a ditty composed for the event:

> The Giants' heels are on thy neck,
> Baltimore, my Baltimore.
> Your Orioles are in the wreck,
> Baltimore, my Baltimore.
> They play quite well at cornered cat,
> But when they meet the New York bat,
> Poor Orioles, where are they at?
> Baltimore, my Baltimore.

The game was not much better than the song, but the New York kranks were not disappointed. The Giants scored early and often, and Jouett Meekin defeated the Orioles, 16 to 3. The Giants had won four straight games from the demoralized Orioles and were the guests of honor at a benefit organized by DeWolf Hopper. It was like the old days.[53]

For John Ward, victory in the Temple Cup series was an appropriate climax to his long baseball career. He had done what he promised he would. The Giants were back on top, again the champions of the baseball world. Ward was also aware that he was near the end of his playing days. He decided to retire while he was still a success.

> After this Temple Cup series is over, I do not expect to touch another ball.... I have made up my mind that I have got to retire whether or no in a year or so, and think it best to retire now when I can do so with a good record as a player and a manager.[54]

So John Montgomery Ward, the last of the original Giants, the "...glass of fashion and the mould of form, th' observ'd of all observers...," retired from baseball to practice law.

CHAPTER SEVEN
ANDREW FREEDMAN

The Temple Cup victory, though a shabby substitute for a world series, had nonetheless restored much of the Giants' lost glamour. There was a victory celebration for Ward and the boys, staged by DeWolf Hopper, replete with celebrities of stage and politics. While the benefit lacked some of the exuberance of 1888, it still reflected a comfortable feeling that the upstart Baltimore Orioles had been put in their place. New York, the leading city of the Republic, certainly deserved the best in baseball, and now it had it.

The victory also provided a suitable opportunity for E. B. Talcott, the managing partner of the Giants, to retire from baseball. Talcott had come into the club after the Brotherhood settlement, and he had done so more for cash than for fun. He looked upon the club as a business, and in his first two years that business had been sour indeed. But the profits of 1893 and 1894 had redeemed all that, and Talcott saw a perfect opportunity to get out with his investment intact, something that many capitalists were unable to do in that depression year. In December 1894 the rumors of Talcott's resignation became public knowledge and were accompanied by the hope that Ward might be induced to return to baseball by the offer of Talcott's old position as treasurer of the Giants. But Talcott was not interested in financing Ward's fling at baseball management; he wanted to sell out. By January, 1895, he had found his buyer. It was the financier and Tammany politician, Andrew Freedman.

Andrew Freedman had been born in New York in 1860 into a middle-class family. After a modest education, which included some study of law, Freedman went into the real estate business. Here he showed an exceptional talent for administration and manipulation. He also entered New York politics, on the side of Tammany Hall, and formed a close friendship with a rising Irish politician, Richard Croker. When Croker succeeded John Kelly in 1886 as Tammany chief, he brought his friend Andrew Freedman into the ruling circles of New York City.

This combination of native talent and extraordinary political connections insured the success of Freedman's real estate business. By the mid-nineties Freedman had accumulated a substantial fortune and had begun to branch out from real estate. In 1898 he organized the Maryland Fidelity and Guarantee Company, which sold bonds for the city of Baltimore. In 1903 he sold his holdings and formed the Casualty Company of America. So successful was this venture into insurance capitalism that by 1908, when Freedman sold it, the company had a premium income of over one and a half million dollars a year.

Freedman's most successful and important venture, however, was his participation in the financing and construction of the first New York subway. Although building a subway had been discussed for about a decade, it was not until late in 1900, when Freedman helped put together the IRT (Interborough Rapid Transit) that work actually began. It was a stupendous deal, involving several years of effort, numerous construction companies, the Morgan-Belmont financial interests, over two *billion* (real) dollars in capital, enormous political influence, and considerable graft. The details of this monumental deal are now lost, and efforts by Mayor Seth Low and the New York Legislature failed to unravel Freedman's connection with the various subway companies.

In January 1895 these mammoth deals were still in the future. Freedman, in fact, was somewhat at loose ends. Tammany had just been defeated in the 1894 municipal election by the "reform" administration of Mayor William Strong, largely as a result of the Lexow Committee's exposure of graft, vice, and corruption within the Democratic city machine. The Lexow Committee of the State Senate of New York, chaired by Clarence Lexow, had been formed to investigate the numerous and sensational charges against the municipal police in particular and Tammany Hall in general raised by Dr. Charles Parkhurst, a patrician reformer and the president of New York's Society for the Prevention of Crime. Dr. Parkhurst had started his crusade via sermons in 1892, and he had raised so much noise and suspicion that the Republican state government decided to accede to a request by the city Chamber of Commerce and investigate. The Lexow Committee began work in March 1894 and ran through December. It uncovered enough graft, collusion between saloons, politicians and police, and ordinary outright stealing that both Tammany and the police were seriously embarrassed. Some untoward things occurred during the hearings. Several saloon keepers were so incautious as to tell the truth, while police Captain Miltenberger abandoned all reason and exposed the entire structure of police and political graft, along with, of course, the spectacular career of Inspector Clubber Williams. Although ably defended by lawyer De Lancey Nicoll, the police were shown to be brutal, grasping, crooked, inefficient and ineffective; indeed, it almost appeared that the cops created as much crime as they combatted. Naturally, the cry for reform increased majestically. Tammany was thrown out, Inspector Clubber Williams retired, and reform laws were passed.

The most immediate reform, and one that was designed to strike at the heart of the saloon-Tammany alliance, was the Raines liquor tax law of 1896, which transferred control of saloon licenses from local officials to the state. The State Department of Excise was to enforce the law, including a ban on Sunday liquor sales except to hotels, a limit to hours of sale in saloons, an effort to ensure order in saloons by threat of license revocation, and a rise in the price of licenses to deprive Tammany of both income and control.

The result of the Raines Act was far from what the reformers had expected. All saloons that could transformed themselves into Raines Law Hotels, many with the minimum of ten bedrooms so they could sell booze around the clock every day. The bedrooms came in handy as well, becoming brothels or houses of assignation, thus increasing the income of the saloon (now hotel) owner, increasing the graft to the cops and increasing the mutual interdependence of saloon, police and Tammany Hall. Moreover, Raines Law Hotels were such a lucrative business that many new licenses were applied for, and many were granted as the fees were high, $800 a year in New York, and the State Department of Excise brought in a good income. Reform thus increased instead of diminishing the number of saloons, made them worse not better, added to the graft rather than eliminating it, increased the amount and efficiency of prostitution, and strengthened Tammany instead of weakening it. One would be safe in saying that this was not what the patrician reformers had in mind. Although ardently pursued by the (presumably) high-minded and pure in heart, moral reform was not yet in America an exact science.

Neither was machine rule. As a result of both defeat and exposure, Richard Croker resigned his position as Tammany leader and sailed for England, where he could live in ease, free from the threat of indictment. Out of power and looking for something to do, Freedman decided to purchase the Giants. On January 24, 1895, Andrew Freedman bought 1,200 shares, nine more than an absolute majority, for $45 a share, or a total of $54,000. He assumed control of the club amid expression of general good will from both press and kranks.[1]

In baseball, however, good will is a notoriously fragile commodity, dependent upon continually caressing the sportswriters' sense of importance, giving the fans exciting and winning baseball, and blending in with the other owners. Andrew Freedman, alas, was unable to do any of these things. He rapidly alienated the fraternity of New York sportswriters, who were easy enough for even the most diplomatic to displease. Moreover, the team deteriorated badly, and Freedman's efforts to bolster it were unsuccessful. Still more, Freedman came into serious conflict with his fellow magnates. They lost no opportunity to denounce him in public, while he tried his best to disrupt the league and ruin his enemies. By 1898 Andrew Freedman had thoroughly antagonized everyone, and his role in baseball had degenerated into constant and acrimonious conflict.

For the kranks, the most serious problem of the Freedman era was the decline of the team. To the vast indignation of the New York public, the team went downhill at once. After the Temple cup victory in 1894, most kranks thought that the Giants would win the pennant the next year. Sportswriters encouraged them in this pleasant delusion. "New York unquestionably has the finest baseball team in the League," wrote Sam Crane in *The Press*, and he added that the giants should "stand well up" in the race all season.[92] No one doubted that assessment. The club officials, the new manager, third baseman George Davis, all seemed to feel that this might be the year.

The Giants began the 1895 season at home against Brooklyn. It was an opening day in the style of the Mutrie era. The Seventh Regiment Band played and the stands were decorated with flags and bunting. The Polo Grounds were packed with kranks, who filled the stands and stood around the field. Mayor Strong threw out the first ball, and Brooklyn came to bat. They promptly scored two runs off Amos Rusie and went on to win the game easily. 7 to 4.[3]

Most of the Giants' fans took the defeat lightly, feeling that their team would soon hit its stride and make a run for the pennant. The stride the team hit, however, took it nearer the bottom of the league than the top. By the end of May the Giants were playing exactly .500 baseball and were firmly mired in eighth place. Freedman was as disturbed by this as were the kranks. On June 5 he fired Davis as the manager and replaced him with Dirty Doyle, the team's first baseman. As the team continued to lose, Freedman tried to reassure the fans by announcing that he planned "...to strengthen the team whenever possible," a formula used by new York owners before. When this failed to produce victory, Freedman fired Doyle and replaced him with the club's business manager, Harvey Watkins. It seemed a strange choice to everyone, but Harvey did not do so badly. The team won 18 games and lost 17 for him, which was about what it had done for his two predecessors. But he was not able to move the Giants up in the standings. When the season ended the Giants were in ninth place, with a record of 66 victories and 65 defeats.[4]

The record produced vast discontent in both press and fans. The fans began to desert the Giants for other forms of entertainment, such as booze and bicycles, both then at the height of their popularity. Sportswriters, forced by their professional obligations to continue watching the Giants play, were not compelled to write complimentary articles about the boys. Having shared the general enthusiasm for the Giants pennant chances in April, the sport reporters now reflected the disappointment at the team's performance, as well as resentment at their own failures as prophets. They turned from praise of the players and the new owner to sarcasm and denunciation. After one of their all-too-frequent defeats, did the Giants

> ...come out on the balcony and bow acknowledgements to the frenzied shouts of jubilation by elated thousands?
> No, no, no, we imagine not.[5]

They just slunk away, demoralized and defeated, and Andrew Freedman got most of the blame for it.

All of this got on Freedman's nerves. It was so unjust. Was it his fault that the team was performing so badly in a year when everyone, including Freedman himself, had expected a winner? No. And was he not doing all he could? He bought outfielder Tommy Burns from Brooklyn, and he had his agents scouring the tank towns of the Republic for new talent. He changed managers twice in the same season. What more could anyone expect?

The constant criticism also affronted Freedman's sense of order, deference, and propriety. He was a financial advisor and close personal friend of Richard Croker, the chief of Tammany Hall. Freedman occupied a position of great public power but without much publicity. He was one of the handful of men who ran the party and the city, but he was not exposed to the public scrutiny and criticism that accompanied elective office. His was the politics of executive decisions made in the privacy of back rooms.

Moreover, as a good Tammany man, Freedman was totally committed to the machine and its boss, Richard Croker. Freedman believed in the virtues of personal and political loyalty, and he believed in the hierarchical structure of the Tammany organization. He lived in a world of rank, position, and insulation from public contumely, a world where custom and hierarchy closely governed conduct.

But the Giants, unlike Freedman's political ties, or his real estate holdings, or his financial investments, were genuinely and completely public property. The team belonged to the fans, regardless of the fact that the club was owned by Freedman. He never really understood that, a failure that he shared with most of his fellow magnates during the nineties. With his capitalist's sense of private property and his Tammany understanding of politics, Andrew Freedman thought that he could run the team as he wished, and no one had the right to criticize him for so doing. He expected the journalists, whom he regarded as rather insignificant and unpaid publicists for the club and himself, to be loyal and deferential toward him, just as he was to Croker and the Tammany sachems. Freedman thought of baseball as an extension of Tammany Hall.

When he found out differently, as he did almost at once, Freedman became irritable and then outraged and defiant.[6] He was naturally arrogant, and he had a bad temper at the end of a very short fuse. As the sportswriters' criticisms veered from the team to its owners, Freedman became deeply resentful and looked upon the writers as blatantly, even criminally, insubordinate. He told them so, collectively and individually. When the writers denounced him, he insulted them. In dealing with the press, Freedman's personality as well as his values betrayed him.

The first reporter to drive Freedman beyond his low tolerance for criticism was Sam Crane, who wrote for both the *Commercial Advertiser* and *The*

Press. Crane had written an article in January, 1895, welcoming Freedman to the National league, but by mid-summer he had changed his mind. Now he was one of Freedman's most persistent and caustic critics. On August 18, 1895, Freedman had had enough. He banned Crane from the Polo Grounds. When Crane purchased a ticket, he was still refused admission. Crane got the details of the game from his colleagues, wrote up the story of his banishment from the park, and announced that he had secured John M. Ward as his attorney and was going to sue Freedman and the Giants.[7] The New York sportswriters were behind him in his campaign against Freedman, and so were most of the fans. Freedman's public image sank even further. It was not a good way to end the 1895 season.

The following year no one talked about winning a pennant. In place of the usual hopeful predictions there were dour comments about the team and its management. Baseball produced

> ...less interest ... in the city than has been the case for many years. The manner in which the affairs of the New-York Club have been conducted has caused many of the staunchest friends of baseball in this city to turn to other things.[8]

The reason for all of this hostility was Andrew Freedman, who rapidly assumed the proportions of a major villain in the classic mold.

> The glaring mismanagement last year, which has been repeated this season, has disgusted the intelligent followers of the club, and there is not enough baseball confidence and enthusiasm in this city at present to blow up a toy balloon.[9]

Everything Freedman did was wrong, and his particular sin during the spring of 1896 was the holdout of Amos Rusie. Rusie had won twenty-two games for the Giants in 1895, down from thirty-six the year before, but still enough to make the Hoosier Thunderbolt the best pitcher on the team. At the end of the season Freedman had deducted $200 in fines from Rusie's salary, ostensibly for dissipation and failure to give his best toward the end of the season. Rusie was outraged at this high-handed treatment, and he refused to sign for 1896 until the fines were remitted. Freedman would not budge. Neither would Rusie. When the season opened Rusie was still unsigned, and the pitcher decided to take his case to baseball's supreme court, the National Board of Arbitration.[10]

Most of the fans and the papers strongly condemned Freedman's treatment of Rusie, and not a few argued that he was deliberately trying to ruin the team and kill baseball in New York. Freedman's capacity for resentment was enormous, and he focused his spite and anger on the sportswriters. On April 22, 1896, his antagonisms spilled over, and he punched Edward Hurst of *The Evening World* on the chin to teach him a lesson for writing unfavorably about Freedman's handling of the Rusie case. Freedman followed up his assault by demanding that the paper fire the offending Hurst. *The Evening World* declined, and Hurst announced that he would file both civil and criminal charges, joining Rusie and Crane in challenging Freedman at law.[11] He would not be the last; toward the end of the nineties Freedman was the target of nearly a dozen suits.

This sort of conduct only increased Freedman's reputation for bad temper and bad judgment, and it "...cast more disfavor on the management which has done so much to injure baseball interests in this city during the last year."[12] By and large, the fans agreed with that assessment. What support Freedman did get was confined to those who believed that "discipline" came before winning, and the rebellious workman who was so puffed up as to challenge his employer must be put in his place.[13] Although this was a favorite notion of Gilded Age businessmen, Freedman was personally so unpopular that few could be found who thought it applied to his treatment of Rusie.

Even the few who agreed with Freedman thought that the loss of Amos Rusie would greatly weaken the Giants, who were none too strong in any case. When the season opened the Giants lost no time in confirming this pessimistic diagnosis. The boys lost the opener to Washington, 6 to 3, and were equally inept in their first game at the Polo Grounds. The weather was cold and damp and the crowd was small. Mayor Strong, who was to throw out the first ball, remained at his desk. It was just as well. The Giants lost to Philadelphia, 3 to 1, and the general wisdom was that it would be a long season.[14]

As they frequently did, the Giants played bad baseball during the first month of the season. On the first of June the team was mired firmly in tenth place, and even that was an improvement over its position for most of May. Thereafter, the team did little better, and it was August before the boys staggered up to ninth place. The press and fans, of course, kept up a ceaseless criticism, and the attendance dropped off. Everyone connected with New York baseball was very unhappy.

Andrew Freedman, in spite of a very limited knowledge of baseball, knew that he was going to have to do something. He did what every owner in the history of the game has always done. He fired the manager. On August 8, Arthur Irwin was replaced by Scrappy Bill Joyce, who had recently been traded by Washington to the Giants. Scrappy Billy was a good third baseman, and he was renowned as a "kicker," who complained loudly and profanely at the umpire's decisions. John McGraw and the Orioles were the acknowledged leaders in this sub-art of baseball, and they were also the best team in the league. Perhaps there was a connection; in any case it could not hurt to imitate the leaders. So Scrappy Bill became the new manager, in an effort to shake the boys up and put some "sand" and "ginger" into the team.[15]

Somewhat to everyone's surprise, Scrappy Bill did pretty well. When he took over, the team was in tenth place. The Giants won their first game under

Joyce and most of the others as well. Early in September the team climbed into eighth place, and they finished the season in seventh with a record of 64 victories and 67 defeats.[16] This was a lot better than anyone had had a right to expect in mid-season, and it gave considerable hope for the next year.

But that hope depended in large measure on Amos Rusie, and on this issue Andrew Freedman would not budge. Rusie had defied him, had brought him into court before his fellow magnates, had caused him to be derided in the press, and that could not be forgiven. What had begun as a matter of petty spite had now sunk to a matter of principle, if that word could be applied to a Tammany Tiger. Rusie, one of the few men in the history of the game to hold out for an entire year, could hold out for another if he wished. Freedman was adamant. Rusie must approach him and only then would he pitch again in the National League.

Freedman's fellow magnates generally supported this position; they had, after all, upheld him in the Board of Directors meeting in June, 1896.[17] But the magnates were also businessmen, and they wanted to restore the large crowds in New York that had played so prominent a part in paying for their expenses on the road. The best, the simplest, way to do that was to bring Amos Rusie back to the Giants. In the week before the 1897 season began, several of the magnates began an organized campaign to bring Rusie and Freedman to terms. Freedman's response was simple:

> ...Some of the magnates want to prostitute the game for the sake of a few paltry dollars. They are in dire financial straits and think that Rusie would help them out as a drawing card.[18]

A few days later he made it even clearer: "This club has made no concessions whatever to him [Rusie] and will not do so."[19] It was no deal.

As Rusie was equally adamant, the magnates themselves began the search for a solution. On April 12, 1897, the National League Board of Arbitration met in special session trying to find a way out of the impasse. There was only one. Rusie must sign on Freedman's terms, and a group of the other owners would collect the money to repay him for Freedman's fines, his legal costs, and the "other expenses arising from his regrettable action." The total was estimated at about five thousand dollars. This was certainly the best deal the Hoosier Thunderbolt was going to get, so he rose above principle and signed with the Giants at Freedman's figure: $2400.[20]

On April 22, opening day, Amos Rusie reported to the Giants. This closed the formal breach, but great bitterness remained. Rusie and Freedman never forgave each other, though they both claimed to the press that they were satisfied with each other and things in general. Both had some cause for satisfaction. Rusie had gotten his money, which is always nice, and Freedman had defeated his fellow magnates. But the New York owner had not done so well with the press and public, who thought of him as a petty and vindictive man.

His fellow magnates who had put up the money to pay Rusie felt cheated by Freedman, and the incident rankled. The magnates did not like writing the checks, and they did not like the feeling of having been taken. Gradually, there developed a group of magnates who would oppose Freedman at every turn and would ultimately defeat his efforts to alter the entire structure of Organized Ball.

But that was in the future; for the present the Giants had Rusie back and must be considered a pennant contender. At least the pundits of the press thought so, one of whom wrote that "…of all the teams on the League circuit, none has been strengthened so much in a year as the New-Yorks."[21] The Giants were slow in fulfilling that promise, however. They lost the opening game to Philadelphia and spent most of May in ninth place. Then the team began to move up in the standings. By the second week in June the Giants were in fourth place and were playing steady ball. Toward the end of August, the Giants passed the Cincinnati Reds and moved into third place, raising hopes that the boys would again be playing for the Temple Cup. But the Giants had too far to go to catch the leaders. They finished in third place, nine and one half games behind the new champions from Boston and seven and one half games in back of Baltimore.[22] It was the Giant's best season since 1894, and almost everyone was satisfied. Scrappy Bill Joyce was a hero, second class. Andrew Freedman was tolerable, more or less. As always, victory had its soothing effect on baseball passions.

The winning season of 1897 confirmed what many reporters and fans had long thought: The team was better then its record had shown. At one time the blame for this unfortunate fact had been laid at the door of the players, who were deemed to have "the big head" or to lack "ginger and dash." But that was long ago, in the age of heroes. There was no Buck Ewing, no Tim Keefe, no John Ward now, no one from whom miracles were routinely demanded, and obtained. The players these days were merely human, and no one expected too much. The management, however, was a more inviting target. Freedman's massive arrogance, his capacity for holding a grudge, his inordinate ego, his wealth and power all conspired to make him appear a bit larger than life. Some saw him as an evil genius of baseball, a kind of Councillor Lindorff, who, in his various guises as magnate, politician, and millionaire was ruining the game. And many of his fellow magnates saw him as the one major obstacle to profits.

All of these attitudes hardened during the 1898 season. One of the reasons was the team. The Giants started off well, and for one dizzy day in May they were as high as third place. By the end of June, however, the team had slumped to seventh place, which was where it finished the season.[23] While the fans followed the team, the magnates followed the financial statements. These were particularly unhealthy. As early as June there was bad news at the gate. Several teams, the Giants among them, were losing a lot of money. By the end of the season, league president Nick Young admitted the obvious. Attendance everywhere was down, and Louisville, Baltimore, Washington, St. Louis, Brooklyn, Pittsburgh and Cleveland joined New York in the red. It had been the worst season financially since 1891. The official excuse for the financial disaster was the Spanish-American War, which was supposed to have diverted Americans from their traditional interest in baseball. Most reporters and fans scoffed at this notion, however, asking why other sports retained their popularity. The magnates were also dubious, and several thought that Freedman's mismanagement in New York was a major cause for the decline in attendance and revenues.[24]

The most direct confrontation between Andrew Freedman and the rest of the National League that season came in July and August. It was the Ducky Holmes affair. Ducky Holmes, a journeyman outfielder who had once been with the Giants, was playing with Baltimore when the incident occurred. In the fourth inning of a game at the Polo Grounds he struck out. As he walked back to the Orioles' bench, a krank called him a loser. Holmes shouted back: "Well, I'm damn glad that I don't work for a Sheeny any more!" Freedman heard that and demanded that the umpire remove Holmes from the game. The umpire refused, saying that he had not heard the remark. Freedman then ordered the Giants off the field, and the umpire forfeited the game to Baltimore, which meant an automatic fine of $1,000 against the Giants. Hearing of the forfeit, the fans demanded their money back, and Freedman gave it to them. This provoked a statement from Harry von der Horst, the Orioles' president, that he would appeal to the league for his share of the gate receipts. Finally, Freedman announced that he would report Holmes, who admitted making the remark, to the league Board of Discipline.[25]

Opinion on the incident was mixed. Holmes admitted insulting Freedman, and this was universally condemned. But Freedman was personally so unpopular that many were delighted to see him publicly embarrassed. Furthermore, ethnic and religious slurs were quite common in the Gilded Age, and they were not then viewed as being particularly reprehensible or offensive. So there were many who thought that Freedman had not been sufficiently insulted for him to make such as fuss.

Both Freedman and von der Horst had stated their positions so vigorously and publicly that the incident could not be dropped with a quiet exchange of apologies. In due course, therefore, the Board of Directors of the National League met and made its decision. The forfeiture of the game to Baltimore was sustained, and New York was fined the thousand dollars the league rules demanded. An additional fine of $100 was levied on the Giants, to be paid by the person actually responsible for causing the team to leave the field, and that person was Freedman. Finally, Ducky Holmes was suspended for the remainder of the season.[26]

This effort to find some fault and assess some penalty on both sides satisfied no one. Harry von der Horst, who did not want to lose a regular outfielder when his team still had a chance for the pennant, claimed that "...the board exceeded its authority in suspending Holmes.... Holmes was entitled to a hearing by the board, which he did not get."[27] A number of other magnates, including John Brush of Cincinnati and Frank Robison of Cleveland, agreed with von der Horst. So did the Boston players, who published a protest appealing for a reconsideration of Holmes' suspension and claiming that the whole affair rose from Freedman's "spirit of impatience and intolerance, of arrogance and prejudice toward players, a spirit inimical to the best interests of the game."[28] Considering the nature of Ducky Holmes' remark, this was an incredible complaint, and it testified to the depths of Freedman's unpopularity.

The pressure to reconsider Holmes' suspension went beyond public complaints and the hostility many of the magnates felt for Freedman. Holmes himself secured a court injunction, compelling the Orioles to play him regardless of league suspension. This placed everyone in an impossible position. If the Orioles played Ducky Holmes, as the court said they must, then every game in which Holmes played could, under league rules, be protested, and the pennant race would be fatally compromised. If Baltimore did not play Holmes, the National League would be in court, and baseball, with its peculiar laws and system of justice, had always tried to avoid that. Thus, league president Nick Young telegraphed the club owners to see if they would agree to a reconsideration of Holmes' suspension. Nine magnates responded favorably, and, on August 25, the Board of Directors reversed their previous decision and reinstated Holmes. He had missed two days of baseball.[29]

Naturally, reinstatement of Ducky Holmes did not please Andrew Freedman. Edward McCall, treasurer of the Giants, said that the reversal of Holmes' suspension was illegal. The New York Club would not pay the thousand-dollar fine, and the Giants' management would fight the case to the end. While the New York owners did not wish to hound Ducky Holmes, they did insist on his being punished, and they were "...by no means inclined to abide by the last action of the League directors in rescinding Holmes' suspension."[30] As Freedman himself was in Europe, the New York club did not go to court over the matter, and the issue gradually died down. But Freedman never forgot it. He regarded the Ducky Holmes affair as a personal affront on the part of his fellow magnates, and he could never forgive that. As he was the richest owner in the league, not excepting the Spaldings who were in financial difficulties for most of the nineties, and as he controlled the league's most strategic franchise, his spite and anger were both of major concern. The other magnates might have abandoned and humiliated him now, but let them beware! Later it would be his turn.

Freedman began his campaign for revenge with the new season. He cut players' salaries, alleging poor gate receipts and players' poor performance in 1898 as the reason. Much of the pitching staff became holdouts as a result.

Amos Rusie refused to sign and retired from baseball, to no one's surprise; he had had troubles with Freedman before. Now, however, Cy Seymour, a twenty-five game winner and the ace of the staff, also held out, and did not sign a contract until May 11, almost a month after the season began. This sort of team could not be a winner, but Freedman did not care. Before the season began he announced "...his entire satisfaction with the condition of his team and the prospects for the coming season."[31]

If Freedman was satisfied, he was the only one. The team was terrible, and spent only one day (May 10) out of the second division. For most of June the Giants were in eighth place; in July they were in ninth; by August they had sunk to tenth place, where they ended the season with a record of 60 victories and 90 defeats.[32] It was the worst record in the club's history.

The fans reacted to the Giants' dismal play in the appropriate manner. They stayed away from the Polo Grounds in even greater numbers than they had in 1898. The Giants' attendance then had been about 206,700, a far cry from the better than 121,384 fans who paid their way into the Polo Grounds in 1899.[33] Those who did come were there mostly to boo and hiss the home team. But it was all perfectly satisfactory to Freedman.

> Baseball affairs in New York have been going just as I wished and expected them to go. I have given the club little attention and I would not now give five cents for the best ball player in the world to strengthen it.[34]

And why should he? Things were going well for Andrew Freedman. Tammany was back in power after a brief hiatus for an ineffective and unpopular "reform" administration. He was making huge sums from his bonding company and from real estate, and the enormously complicated and profitable subway negotiations were nearing completion. The money he lost in baseball was insignificant. But the same sum, lost by the other owners, was a great deal of money, which they could ill afford to lose. The weakness of the New York club was hurting them badly. Without the profits from large crowds in New York, many of the marginal franchises were slowly going under. Freedman was delighted. He was succeeding in his threats to ruin his enemies. He boasted openly that he had the league by the throat and that few clubs could make money because of their losses in New York. He predicted that the magnates would beg him to take charge of baseball and put it on a paying basis.[35]

This general attack on the solvency of major league baseball was supplemented by selective and vindictive *attentats* against his particular enemies. Baltimore was the first victim. The Orioles were in the habit of issuing a large number of cards of invitation (free passes) to the opening game, and in 1899 they opened the season against New York. Freedman refused to go along with the Baltimore custom, and the Orioles were forced to pay the Giants the visitor's share based on total attendance, whether paid or not. Later in the season Freedman had a similar opportunity to hurt the Philadelphia owners, Al

Reach and Col. John Rogers, in spite of the fact that they had been among his staunchest allies in league politics. Philadelphia, plagued by exceptionally poor attendance, wished to draw fans by reducing the ticket price from fifty cents to a quarter. Reach and Rogers needed the agreement of each visiting club to make such a reduction, and they got it from most of them. But not from New York. Freedman refused. Reach and Rogers had voted against him in the Ducky Holmes affair, and now he was going to get even. Col. Rogers even went to New York to see Freedman, but the Giants' owner stood firm. No deal.[36]

New York was not the only trouble spot in the National League in 1899, although Freedman's spite and intransigence made it one of the worst. Elsewhere, attendance was also low. In spite of the encouraging statements issued periodically by Nick Young, the game was not recovering from the disastrous season of 1898. The total attendance for 1899 was approximately 2,541,485, a gain of only about 230,000 over the abysmal figures of the previous year. Things were bad in Baltimore, Cincinnati, and Louisville, and appalling in Cleveland. Frank Robison, who owned both the Cleveland and St. Louis clubs, had transferred the cream of the Cleveland team to St. Louis in an effort to build a winner, and the hapless remnants left in Cleveland were playing to crowds of thirty and fifty people. Robison tried shifting Cleveland's games out of town, but fans around the rest of the league were no more anxious than those in Cleveland to see a team that won only 20 games all season and played .130 baseball. The dying franchise badly hurt the entire National League.[37] So serious was the financial crisis that most of the National League magnates began to think about reducing the circuit from twelve clubs to eight, cutting off those franchises that were losing the most money. Baltimore, Louisville, Cleveland and Washington were the candidates most often mentioned for execution, though Freedman wanted Brooklyn to be dropped, giving him exclusive possession of the New York area. Throughout the 1899 season the talk about reorganization of the National League grew in intensity and seriousness, in spite of denials that anything of the sort was being considered, or pious assurances that all was well. By the league meeting in December, 1899, when the magnates had counted their losses, a reduction of the National League to eight clubs had become a certainty. The only question remaining was which clubs would have to go.[38]

Cleveland was a certain casualty; huge losses and a refusal to play home games condemned the franchise in the eyes of both the fans and the magnates. Louisville was another prime candidate for extinction. Here a succession of poor teams and a small population base made profitable management almost impossible. Added to this was the recent purchase of the entire Louisville team, including the immortal Honus Wagner, by Pittsburgh. The cost of this coup was $25,000, and it left the Colonels even more bereft than usual, since Barney Dreyfuss, who now owned both clubs, planned to consolidate the two teams into a winner in Pittsburgh. A third possibility for liquidation was

Washington, which had a poor team, had always had a poor team, was not making money and had never made money. Moreover, there was no Congressional pressure in those innocent days for major league baseball in the nation's capital, and the magnates were free to follow their best commercial judgment in the matter.

The last franchise scheduled to be lopped off was something of a surprise: the Baltimore Orioles. Several factors made Baltimore vulnerable. The club had lost a good deal of money in 1898 and had made only a small profit of about $6,000 in 1899. The Baltimore owners also held the Brooklyn franchise, where they were concentrating their energies, their best players, and their hopes for large profits. Finally, with Cleveland and Louisville leaving the league, a second eastern franchise would have to go. Baltimore was the choice.[39]

Once the necessity for reduction of the league had been accepted, and the damned distinguished from the saved, all that remained was to do it. This was not so easy, as the National League was ripped apart by feuds, both personal and commercial. The first step toward reconciling these feuds sufficiently to reform the league was a meeting in New York early in October, 1899, between Freedman and John Brush, the owner of the Cincinnati Reds. Brush and Freedman had been bitter foes for years, their worst and most recent fight having come in 1898 in the Ducky Holmes affair. Now, with Arthur Soden, the Boston owner and a stockholder in the New York Giants, acting as mediator, Brush and Freedman composed their differences.[40] This was a sensational development, for it ended a breach that few thought could ever heal, and it opened the way for a majority of the league magnates to agree on circuit reduction.

The only obstacle remaining was money, but as the entire history of the National League had shown, this was a substantial problem. At the league meeting in December, 1899, the magnates agreed to cut Baltimore, Cleveland, Louisville, and Washington, but they could not agree on the price to be paid the departing clubs for their franchises. A second meeting was needed, from January 22 to 24, 1900, to get sale terms from the affected clubs. Only the Louisville bid was accepted; it was for $10,000, not an unreasonable figure for a club more or less without players. The other offers were "held for future consideration."

The pressure to complete the amputation was intense, however. It was clearly impossible to cut Louisville alone, or to keep a dead franchise like Cleveland. Finally, in March, 1900, the parties came to terms. Cleveland was bought out for $25,000, an excellent price for such a moribund club, and one that testified to the power of Frank Robison in league councils. Washington went for $39,000, which included the franchise, the park, and the players, such as they were. Baltimore got the best deal, not unexpectedly since the Orioles had a pretty good team and they were owned by the same men who held the

Brooklyn franchise. After vast haggling and squabbling, the Brooklyn owners, Harry von der Horst, Ned Hanlon, Charles Ebbets, and Ferdinand Abell, accepted $30,000 for the Baltimore franchise and park. But they kept control of the players. All in all, it was an expensive transaction. The total cost to the National League was $104,000, and it had to be paid by imposing a 5 percent levy on gate receipts. Thus, the magnates were back where they had been in 1890, with a depressed business and a large collective debt. But they saw no choice. It was either that or go out of business.[41]

This settled the National League for the coming season, but there was one additional piece of business that remained. It was part of the terms of reconciliation between Brush and Freedman. Freedman had always insisted that the thousand-dollar fine levied against the Giants for the Ducky Holmes affair was both illegal and immoral. He wanted his money back. Now he got it. Under the heading of miscellaneous business the National League refunded Freedman his thousand dollars, at 6 percent interest.

Ultimate victory in the Ducky Holmes mess improved Freedman's temper somewhat. During the 1900 and 1901 seasons he refrained from overt wrangles with the league or the owners. He more or less ignored the press, although he and the Giants were continually criticized. Preoccupied with the great subway deal, his interest in baseball waned. He was, relatively speaking, on his best behavior.

If Freedman caused little trouble during the first two seasons of the new century, neither did he move to strengthen his team. Buck Ewing was named manager to start the 1900 season, but there was not much he could do with men as demoralized as the Giants. He had some good players, including Dirty Doyle, George van Haltren, and George Davis, all left over from the Temple Cup victors of 1894, but the pitching was generally atrocious. In July, with the season about half over and the Giants in last place, Buck was replaced by George Davis, who had been the manager in 1895. Davis was a decided improvement, and the Giants won more games than they lost under his regime. But it was too late to save the season, and the Giants finished in the cellar with a record of 60 victories and 78 defeats.[42]

The club lost money, of course. With such a record, losses were inevitable. But not only the Giants suffered; the entire National League, except Pittsburgh, did poorly at the gate.

> The year 1900 must be sadly recorded in base ball history as ... an off year.... There was a decided decline in public interest, and a diminution of press support, and a very material falling off in gross attendance.[43]

Even the pennant-winning Brooklyn club could do no better than break about even. A better team in New York would certainly help the situation, but Freedman would not retreat from his refusal to strengthen the Giants, and the other owners were powerless to move him.

Things were little different in 1901. If anything, the Giants were even weaker, even more demoralized, even less of an attraction than before. Again, George Davis was the manager, and again Freedman paid little attention to his team. This year the Giants began well but collapsed after the second week in July. Pitching was again a major problem, as it usually is with bad teams. The Giants tried nineteen pitchers, but only Christy Mathewson, who won twenty games while losing sixteen, and Dummy Taylor, who won seventeen games and lost twenty-seven, were at all effective. Mathewson, of course, was so great a pitcher that he could win on the worst team in baseball, and the Giants came pretty close. They finished the season in seventh place, one game ahead of Cincinnati. Their record was 52 victories and 85 defeats, the worst in the team's history.[44]

As in previous years, the Giants' weakness affected the entire league. National League attendance for 1901 fell below two million, to about 1,920,000, almost 400,000 below the crisis year of 1898. But attendance was not the only problem. The National League was threatened by the rise of a formidable competitor, the new American League. In October, 1899, the Western League, strongest of the minor circuits, had changed its name to the American League. In 1900 the American League had placed clubs in both Cleveland and Chicago. Before the 1901 season the American League had not renewed its status as a minor league within the framework of the National Agreement and had moved clubs into Boston, Philadelphia, Washington, and Baltimore without the permission of the National League. Moreover, it was enticing players from the National League by paying higher salaries than the older circuit and by refusing to recognize the validity of the National League's reserve rule. A good many men were moving to the new league, including one of the better New York players, pitcher and outfield Cy Seymour. By 1901 it was obvious even to the dullest and smuggest magnate that the American League was serious competition.

And there was even more. After a decade of embittered quiescence, the players were organizing again. The Brotherhood had failed; perhaps the new Protective Association of Professional Baseball Players would not. Organized on June 10, 1900 in New York, the Protective Association raised traditional player grievances at the National League meeting in December, 1900. The players wanted limitations on the reserve clause, prohibition on the sale of a player without his consent, limits on the power of management to fine or suspend players, payment of medical bills by the club, and a Board of Arbitration to hear grievances. The National League refused to meet these terms, but the American League did not. The conciliatory attitude of Ban Johnson, president of the American League, was a major factor in the drift of National League players, such as Cy Young and Wee Willie Keeler, to the new circuit. In 1901, 111 men in the American League had once played in the older league. Next year, if some agreement could not be reached with the American League, the number would be higher. And those who did not go would have to be given higher salaries to stay.[45]

Andrew Freedman watched all of these developments with interest. He had the money to fight indefinitely, and he had the political connections to keep an American League franchise out of New York. But his fellow National League owners, most of whom he hated, lacked both. They had almost gone under in 1898, and they were about to do so again. In 1898 they had been his enemies, as the Ducky Holmes affair had so clearly shown, but now it might be different. Now, when he alone had the resources to survive, his fellow magnates might wish to reconsider their attitude toward him, and accept his leadership in saving the National League. And Freedman had a plan. He would reorganize the National League, placing it under his personal control. He would abolish separate ownership of the different clubs. He would turn the entire National League into a syndicate.

CHAPTER EIGHT
THE BASEBALL TRUST

It began in 1890, during the sustained crisis of the Brotherhood war. In July, 1890, several of the more important National League moguls, including Albert Spalding, Arthur Soden of Boston, Albert Reach of Philadelphia, John Brush of Indianapolis, and Charles Byrne of Brooklyn, were called to New York for an emergency conference. The assembled owners heard very bad news. John B. Day informed them that the Giants were virtually bankrupt and would have to suspend play unless they received immediate financial aid. The sum needed was $80,000. The magnates all agreed that if the Giants collapsed the National League was finished, so they apportioned the New York deficit among themselves. Soden, Brush, and Spalding each put up $20,000, and the remaining $20,000 was divided among the other owners.

> It was pretty costly, but that prompt act saved the National League, and, by saving it, the future of professional baseball in this country was ... also saved.[1]

Whether or not this "prompt act" saved professional baseball, it certainly, for the short run at least, determined its future. For this was the beginning of syndicate baseball.

For most of the nineties, syndicate ball remained a relatively unimportant part of the game. It continued to exist, but it did not dominate the management of the league. Spalding, Brush, and Soden held their stock in the Giants, but they did not try to run the club. When Talcott and McAlphin sold out to Andrew Freedman in 1895, the syndicate stockholders did not object nor try to increase their holdings. They remained silent partners in the New York club, even when Freedman's tactics and temper were costing them money.

During the winter of 1898-1899, however, the full implications of syndicate ownership emerged. The St. Louis Browns, which had become one of the league's doormat teams and franchises, slipped out of the bankrupt hands of Chris von der Ahe. Harassed by creditors, sued by his son for property and

St. Louis Browns: 1888. Chris von der Ahe's championship nine. This was the Browns' fourth consecutive American Association pennant.

by his wife for divorce and alimony, Chris lost control of his club during the 1898 season. A St. Louis court appointed a receiver. The club did not make any money under interim management, and by the spring of 1899 it had become the property of Frank Robison, owner of the Cleveland Spiders. The Cleveland mogul, unhappy over declining attendance in 1898, had transferred many of the Spiders' home games to the visiting park, and now he proposed to make the St. Louis team, newly nicknamed the Perfectos, into one of the strongest in the National League, perhaps even a pennant winner. So the Perfectos were graced by the incomparable Cy Young, the best pitcher in baseball, and outfielder Jesse Burkett, a solid .380 hitter. A team with players like that ought to win games and draw fans, Robison reasoned. Attendance should be particularly good in St. Louis, which had Sunday baseball, which was still banned in Cleveland, the result of the baneful influence of the "church element." In Cleveland, stocked with the dregs of both teams, Robison expected little and cared less.[2]

While the Cleveland/St. Louis merger was arranged, a second syndicate scheme was hatched, involving one of the premier teams in baseball, the Baltimore Orioles. In 1898 attendance had fallen off sharply in Baltimore, in spite of the fact that the Orioles finished in second place and continued to play exciting, colorful baseball. The club was losing money, and the owners, Harry von der Horst and Ned Hanlon, looked around for a way out. Their opportunity came with the death of Charles Byrne, president of the Brooklyn club. Byrne's death left the Brooklyn situation somewhat murky and disorganized, and Hanlon persuaded the remaining major stockholder, Ferdinand Abell, to enter a syndicate with the Baltimore owners. Abell took 40 percent of the stock in both Brooklyn and Baltimore, as did von der Horst. Ned Hanlon took 10 percent of the stock in each club, and Charles Ebbets, a minority stockholder in the Brooklyn franchise, took the remaining 10 percent of each club. As part of the deal, Hanlon agreed to put the best players in Brooklyn, thus forming a superb team which would easily compete successfully with Freedman's deteriorated Giants. Hanlon left John McGraw in Baltimore to manage what was left of the Orioles and Wilbert Robinson stayed to assist him, but the rest of the great Orioles' stars, including Wee Willie Keeler, Hugh Jennings and Joe Kelley, joined the new Brooklyn "Superbas." It was clearly the best team in baseball, and there seemed to be an excellent chance that it would make money as well.[3]

This cynical wheeling and dealing drew roars of outrage from the rest of the league and much of the press, to say nothing of the jilted kranks in Cleveland and Baltimore. But the deals went through; there was no league rule against syndicate management and financial problems prevented any serious attempts to undo a scheme that might make money. Still, the emergence of syndicate baseball left many people convinced that the National League was fundamentally dishonest and unsound. The syndicate deals had

> ...given the public a horrifying view of the utterly antagonistic interests pervading the League ... [and] of the irrepressible, frightful feuds that are rending the organization. No organization can prosper, or even sustain life long, under conditions such as prevail in the National League.[4]

That opinion was reinforced during the 1889 season as the syndicate owners manipulated their clubs to win games and make a profit. Early in August, Freedman sold one of his few good pitchers, Jouett Meekin, to Boston, one of whose owners, Arthur Soden, was a New York stockholder. The price, $5,000, seemed small for a pitcher of Meekin's reputation and ability. Moreover, Boston was the only team with a chance to catch the Superbas, and the sale seemed to be a blatant attempt to help a syndicate stockholder and hurt the Brooklyn magnates, with whom Freedman was feuding. In the opinion of many in the press and public, the deal had "...the taint of that new evil, syndicate ball, and is therefore not calculated to allay the growing distrust of the public of the methods now in vogue."[5] In spite of the criticism, largely accurate, the deal stood and Meekin went to Boston.

The loudest complaints were made against a trade within the Brooklyn-Baltimore syndicate. Although the Superbas were leading the league in August, Hanlon felt that his team needed to be strengthened for the stretch run. Boston, Philadelphia, and Baltimore were too close for comfort. So he sent Hugh Jennings from Brooklyn to Baltimore in exchange for a pitcher, Jerry Nops, and an infielder, Gene DeMontreville. There was immense and immediate indignation at this deal, which seemed to the public, and to Baltimore manager John

McGraw, to be an open fraud. So intense was the fans' dissatisfaction with the trade that Hanlon, who genuinely cared for the good of the game, cancelled it within a week.[6] But it still left a residue of suspicion that next time such a sweetheart deal would stand, and that the game was no longer honest.

Public antagonism to syndicate management, and the unexpectedly low profits the syndicates earned, were major reasons for the reduction of the National League to eight clubs during the winter of 1899–1900. This decision eliminated altogether one of the syndicates, as Cleveland was dropped, leaving the Robison brothers in possession of St. Louis alone. But the remnants of the other syndicate remained. Although the league had bought out the Orioles, the Baltimore-Brooklyn moguls still retained control of the Orioles' players. Once again, Hanlon had the choice of players from two teams, and he used his opportunity to strengthen the Superbas, in particular the transfer of the pitcher, Iron Man Joe McGinnity, from Baltimore to Brooklyn. Again, syndicate ball paid off on the field, though not in the treasury, as Hanlon came up with his second Brooklyn pennant winner. However, 1900 was the last year this could be done, and the evils of syndicate management, while still denounced, definitely took second place to the threat from the new American League.

The presence of the American League, while it shoved denunciations of syndicate management off the front page, merely magnified the evils and inadequacies of the present system. The elimination of the twelve-club league after the 1899 season had been the first major effort to meet the challenge of the new league, but the continuation of syndicate baseball, the loss of patronage, and the hostility of the press proved that still more changes were needed. The new major league, run in the traditional way with effective and honest leadership, without the scandalous and corrupt haggling which stained the National League, presenting an excellent brand of baseball might well win over the patrons of the National Game. The National League moguls certainly thought so. They had to do something. As Willy Loman was to say, attention must be paid.

Within National League councils there developed gradually two views on what that attention should be. One came from Albert Spalding, who by the summer of 1901 had come to the conclusion that there must be peace with the American League. Fearing that the present management of the National League could not bring itself to accept a settlement, Spalding tried to obtain options on the eight National League clubs so that he could talk to Ban Johnson, president of the American League, and bring all of baseball back under a single government. The exact nature of the Spalding proposal to the National League owners was never clear, though it did seem suspiciously like the bicycle trust that Spalding had put together a couple of years before. Only two things about the Spalding plan were obvious: peace with the American League and the elimination of Freedman from baseball. But nothing came of it. Spalding could not get the necessary options, largely because of the opposition of John T. Brush, owner of the Cincinnati Reds. By the end of July, 1901, Spalding had given up the attempt.[7]

Spalding's failure did not end the emergency nor increase attendance at National League games, but it did open the way for a second attempt to reorganize the wounded circuit. This emerged from a meeting held in August, 1901, at the Red Bank, New Jersey, estate of Andrew Freedman. The idea for a baseball trust came from John Brush, now Freedman's closest baseball friend and ally, and he had no trouble in selling the idea to the invited magnates. Not all of the owners were there. Brush (Cincinnati), Freedman (New York), Soden (Boston), and Robison (St. Louis) attended, but the owners of the Pittsburgh, Brooklyn, Chicago, and Philadelphia clubs were not invited. They were either the personal or professional enemies of Freedman.

The reorganization scheme approved at Red Bank was complete and detailed, a far cry from the hazy and tentative ideas previously advanced by Spalding. According to the Brush/Freedman trust scheme, the National League would undergo a total reorganization. The clubs would surrender their autonomy and be merged into a trust, with common and preferred stock, which the individual clubs would receive in exchange for their assets and players. Under the plan,

> New York would hold 30 percent of the trust stock
> Cincinnati would hold 12 percent
> St. Louis would hold 12 percent
> Boston would hold 12 percent
> Philadelphia would hold 10 percent
> Chicago would hold 10 percent
> Pittsburgh would hold 8 percent
> Brooklyn would hold 6 percent

The whole thing would be managed by a Board of Regents chosen by the stockholders, and, given the distribution of stock, this meant Freedman and Brush.[8]

The trust scheme carried Hulbert's idea of limiting competition in baseball to its logical conclusion. Now, with the clubs merged into a single legal entity, baseball would become merely a theatrical enterprise. Baseball would be an exhibition only, similar to modern wrestling. Profits alone would count. Players and managers would be shifted from city to city in an endless search for large crowds. The Board of Regents would determine everything; the clubs would become mere administrative units; the fans and the players would count for nothing.

The idea for an entertainment trust did not come to Brush and Freedman out of the air. Such a thing already existed — the theater trust organized in 1896 by Charles Frohman, A. L. Erlanger, Marc Klaw, and Al Hayman. This Syndicate, which had originated in a casual conversation over lunch, was rapidly transformed from idea into reality. By 1897 it was generally effective, in spite of the opposition of such major stars as Joseph Jefferson (Rip Van Winkle), the Shakespearean actor Richard Mansfield, and Minnie Maddern Fiske, whose husband, Harrison Fiske, was the editor of *The Dramatic Mirror*. Gradually, the others dropped away, and by 1898 Mrs. Fiske stood alone against the Syndicate. Denied the use of Syndicate theaters everywhere, she toured anyway playing in barns, taverns and churches. By 1900 she had acquired allies, the Shubert brothers. During the 1901–1902 season, when the baseball trust issue was at its height, a fierce theater war was being fought with the Syndicate on one side and Mrs. Fiske and the Shuberts on the other. In 1902 it looked as if the Syndicate would win. After all, trusts and combines were part of every aspect of American life. The theater could hardly be different.[9]

Confident that in entertainment as in oil, trust and syndicate was the American way, the baseball magnates anticipated no difficulties and major advantages from the Brush plan. By placating Freedman, he and his massive political influence and growing wealth would be tied to the National League. In effect, this would deny the American League a franchise in New York, and by 1901 it was abundantly clear that no circuit could pretend to be a major league without a team in New York. Moreover, trust organization seemed to promise the owners complete control over the players, who had just formed the Protective Association of Professional Baseball Players. The National League had refused to take this seriously, but the American League had recognized the new group and had acceded to several of its demands. As a result, dozens of National League players jumped to the new circuit, raising considerably the caliber of baseball played there and strengthening the American League's claim to major league status. Legal efforts to stop this had failed; perhaps the trust scheme would do so.

Finally, the trust plan seemed to offer the owners financial security and a guarantee of profits. For four years, many of them had been losing money, and they badly wanted that to end. Not all of the magnates were persuaded by the baseball papers, *The Sporting News* and *Sporting Life*, that syndicate management was killing baseball. Several thought just the opposite. Syndicate management, with its diversification of risk, had enabled them to survive the lean years, and trust management, which was the syndicate carried to its logical extreme, would help them survive the even leaner years that competition with the American League seemed to promise. The magnates, many of them, were for the trust.

There were obvious disadvantages to the trust scheme, of course, though the men assembled at Red Bank tended to ignore them. Baseball reporters had been condemning syndicate management for several years, and they had turned public opinion against it. *Sporting Life*, in particular, had claimed that syndicate ownership was crooked and destroyed the honest competition that made the game great. It argued that much of the popularity of the new

American League arose from public disgust with syndicate collusion in the older circuit. In general, the fans believed this. The National League moguls, however, had not been paying much attention to the fans for the past decade, and they did not intend to start now.

Beyond adverse public reaction, there was another important aspect to baseball that the owners ignored. The fans' loyalty to the game was based in large measure on tradition, on years of rooting for their team and players. Fans endlessly compared this year's team to the rest of the league, this year's players to the heroes of yesterday. Owners and reporters might call an aging veteran a "back number," but the fans remained loyal. This loyalty and support, however, rested on continuity, on seeing players throughout much of their careers, on seeing teams built into contenders, on seeing new men break into the league. The fans' interest in baseball was as much personal as sporting; they went to see their team and players, not just to watch a game. But the magnates, most of whom were not baseball fans, did not know this.

The Red Bank plan could not be carried to completion without one important preliminary step — securing the support of a majority of the club owners. John T. Brush tried to obtain this by a visit to Pittsburgh during the week of December 1 to see Barney Dreyfuss, the owner of the pennant-winning Pirates. He explained the trust scheme briefly and tried to persuade Dreyfuss to support it. Dreyfuss was interested, but he cautiously refused to make a final commitment.[10] Thus, when the annual National League meeting began on December 10, 1901, the proponents of the trust plan did not have their majority.

Failure to win Dreyfuss' support was the crucial blunder for the Red Bank group. On December 11, the magnates voted on a preliminary step to the establishment of a baseball trust. In order to adopt the Brush plan the magnates had to agree to the expiration of the ten-year National Agreement signed in December, 1891, when the twelve-club league was formed. This interpretation of the National Agreement would dissolve the league completely. The National League would have to be reorganized anew, a necessary measure for the Red Bank group since a reconstitution as radical as the trust scheme could not be made within the existing league constitutions. On December 11, therefore, John Brush introduced a resolution declaring the National League terminated as of December 19, thus clearing the way for consideration of the trust plan. Brush's resolution met with a great deal of discussion and criticism. Brush did his best, defending his view of the league constitution vigorously, but he could not carry the day. A majority of the magnates saw the National League as a perpetual body which did not cease to exist merely because the ten-year agreement of 1891 had expired. After several speeches the moguls rejected Brush's resolution, 5 to 1. Only Frank Robison of St. Louis voted yea; Boston, Brooklyn, Philadelphia, Chicago and Pittsburgh voted against it, while Freedman and Brush abstained.[11]

While the defeat of Brush's resolution did not mean that the trust plan was irrevocably dead, it did demonstrate that the owners were unlikely to support it without substantial persuasion. But the rest of the session saw just the opposite. Albert Spalding addressed the magnates. He told them that he had been present at the birth of the National League and now claimed the right to speak at a time when the newspapers said the league was dying. While not mentioning the trust plan nor its authors by name, Spalding told the club owners that the National League could not survive as it was going now. He mentioned his own candidacy for league president, saying that he had not sought the office nor campaigned for it, but he was willing to help the league survive. He asked the owners to vote on his candidacy; up or down, it did not matter to him. By implication, by what he did not say as well as what he had said, Spalding told the magnates that he would kill the trust plan.[12]

Spalding's speech and his attendance at the meeting solidified the ranks of the magnates opposed to the Brush trust plan. Refusing to abandon their support of Spalding or accept oral arguments for the trust, the owners of the Chicago, Brooklyn, Philadelphia, and Pittsburgh clubs forced Brush to provide them with detailed written plans for the proposed baseball trust. While the suspicious magnates were studying Brush's scheme, Spalding called the press to his room on the evening of December 12 and explained his position. His election to the presidency of the National League, Spalding told the reporters, was a matter of personal indifference, but it was an issue of supreme importance to the National League. If elected, Spalding promised to kill the trust plan for good, and govern the league according to the principles laid down by Hulbert and Mills. Spalding stated that the National League as it stood today was discredited. After talking about the trust plan, Spalding turned to Andrew Freedman "My fight is on Freedman's record in baseball. Of him personally I say nothing.... But Freedman — he must go."[13] Finally, Spalding claimed that the whole mess was the result of a conspiracy hatched by Brush and Freedman, a conspiracy which if permitted to succeed would destroy the National League.[14]

Spalding had considerably more skill in handling the press than either Brush or Freedman. While Spalding denounced the already unpopular trust scheme, Brush fumed petulantly and complained that the press was against him. Freedman claimed that Spalding was the true author of the trust scheme, and he accused the sporting goods mogul of returning to baseball for personal profit. But Spalding already had his opponents on the defensive. He had the better case. A decade of muckraking had convinced most Americans that trusts were a serious menace to consumers and even to democracy, and the first years of the new century were the height of that public concern. Moreover, Spalding had been in baseball for thirty years and was generally respected, while Freedman was cordially hated by nearly every sports reporter and krank in the land. Still more, the secrecy that surrounded the trust plan and the reluctance of its authors to explain it contrasted unfavorably with Spalding's willingness to talk. Finally, the trust plan would bring syndicate management to the entire league, and both the press and the fans were hostile to that. After having maintained for years that syndicate management was inherently dishonest, the sportswriters could hardly retract it all and support Brush and Freedman. And they did not. When the stories were printed, Spalding became a hero, and Brush and Freedman became bums.

The climax of the winter meeting came on December 13. The afternoon session began with Brush announcing that the Chicago, Brooklyn, Philadelphia, and Pittsburgh clubs had rejected totally the trust plan. Then came a motion by Brush to postpone the election of a league president until January 7, 1902. The motion failed. Freedman then stated that he could not possibly attend the evening session, and Ferdinand Abell, one of the Brooklyn owners, retorted: "Don't bother! We can do without you!"[15]

When the voting for league president began on the evening of December 13, the lines between the two factions were drawn firmly, and the magnates were angry and embittered. They had been talking to the press and saying some unpleasant things. Abell had remarked that Freedman would "not whip any more magnates into line." Freedman claimed that Spalding was a "trifle hysterical." Spalding himself, carried away by the spirit of the meeting, defied Arthur Soden, the Boston owner, to vote against him for president. "Boston sentiment would not allow Soden to vote against me!"[16] It was all duly reported in the papers.

The voting for president, therefore, was the crucial show of strength for each faction. There were two candidates, Nick Young and Albert Spalding. Each received four votes. New York, Cincinnati, Boston, and St. Louis voted for Young, while Chicago, Brooklyn, Philadelphia, and Pittsburgh supported Spalding. Neither side would budge. The election went on for twenty-five ballots, and the results were always the same. By one o'clock in the morning of the 14th, Arthur Soden, exhausted by the bitter and fruitless conflict, left Parlor F in the Fifth Avenue Hotel and retired for the evening. He was followed shortly by Freedman, Robison, and Brush. Nick Young, who was still president of the league, declared that a quorum no longer existed and no further business could be transacted. Col. John Rogers, one of the Philadelphia owners, argued that the rules of Congress should apply to the meeting. The four missing club owners had left the meeting without reason, notice, or permission, and they had done so while the meeting was in progress and no recess had been taken. Therefore, they should be considered "constructively" present, which meant that a quorum still existed. Nick Young refused to accept this view, and shortly left the meeting.[17]

The Philadelphia, Chicago, Brooklyn, and Pittsburgh owners were not at all reluctant to accept Col. Roger's view of a quorum so they continued with business. Col. Rogers was elected temporary chairman and a twenty-sixth ballot was taken. The owners present, representing four clubs, voted unanimously for Spalding. The roll of the remaining clubs was called, but, of course, they did not vote nor give proxies. Arguing from Congressional practice, Rogers ruled them constructively present, and declared that Spalding had been unanimously elected.[18]

Having "elected" him president, the delegates of the four clubs opposed to the trust went to Spalding's room and woke him up to give him the news. Although not convinced of the legality of his election, Spalding decided to use the situation to his advantage. He dressed, went to Nick Young's suite, and explained the situation to Young and his son, who also were not convinced that Spalding was really president of the National League. During the discussion with the Youngs, Spalding had a porter carry out a large trunk which contained the archives and papers of the National League. By five o'clock in the morning Spalding was in possession of half of the office of league president, and all of the league documents.[19]

The next day Spalding and his supporters completed their efforts to gain control of the National League. When the meeting reconvened at two o'clock in the afternoon of December 14, Spalding took the chair as league president. The Freedman faction was not present, but Spalding noticed the secretary of the New York Giants, Fred Knowles, standing at the door keeping his eye on the proceedings. When Knowles stuck his head in the room to get a better view, Spalding at once counted him present, declared that a quorum existed and business could begin. Spalding called for election of a new Board of Arbitration and a Board of Directors of the league. In an obvious effort at reconciliation, Arthur Soden of Boston was elected to both. Spalding then appointed the three standing committees, and John Brush was named to both the committee on the National Agreement and the league constitution. Reconciliation was balanced by threat, as the four clubs present voted to give Spalding full power to draw up the playing schedule for 1902. Should the Freedman faction refuse to recognize his authority, Spalding could discriminate against them in the choice of playing dates. Finally, the owners who had elected him listened to Spalding's platform. Though general in language, it was clear in intent. Spalding promised

> To promote, foster, elevate and perpetuate the game of baseball....
> To eliminate all objectionable features that may tend to degrade or demoralize the sport.
> To inculcate in the governors of the game, club officials, umpires, players ... a realization of what true sportsmanship is and to subordinate the financial side of the game.
> To establish a central governing body in which all professional baseball interests shall be represented.
> This body to be clothed with ample power ... to maintain the integrity ... of the game.[20]

After approving Spalding's program, the magnates adjourned the winter meeting, and moved to the lobby to give interviews to the press.[21]

Spalding began his press conference by thanking the reporters for helping put him into office and announcing that future National League meetings would be open to the press. This tactful compliment was followed by some premature boasting:

> Now that I'm here, I propose to be the boss from top to bottom. I will do all that lies in my power to win back the public confidence to the National League. As I have declared, Andrew Freedman must get out of baseball. I am going to try all I know to put him out. Either he or I must go.[22]

The next day he went even further. He announced that the fight against Freedman was over and Spalding had won. Further, within twenty-four hours Freedman would be out of baseball, though details of how this might be done were scanty. In any case, it was all over, "water that has passed over the wheel," and Spalding promised to "introduce new issues into the baseball campaign looking toward improved conditions in our great national sport."[23] The assembled reporters presumed that he meant a settlement of differences with the American League.

Andrew Freedman also issued statements. He accused Spalding of coming back into baseball for selfish reasons. Spalding's interest in the National League, Freedman charged, "only awakens when he sees another opportunity for supplying baseballs to the League." However, Spalding, not Brush or Freedman, was the true author of the baseball trust scheme, and Freedman published the letters and sample contracts by which Spalding had hoped to obtain options on all of the National League clubs. Beyond that, Spalding's election as league president was patently illegal, and no "action of Mr. Spalding's private league will be binding." Freedman warned that the New York club was "not worrying over Mr. Spalding's threats. All will be attended to at the proper time and place."[24]

Freedman's statement, though defensive in tone with its disavowal of the unpopular trust plan, made two significant points. Spalding's election, if not illegal, was certainly questionable, and the New York owner was not going to let him get away with it. Freedman wasted no more time in public statements; instead, he went to the courts. On December 16, 1901, Judge Leventritt of the Supreme Court granted Freedman a temporary injunction restraining Spalding from acting as president, secretary, or treasurer of the National League and from taking possession of any of the league papers, and from doing anything that might injure the property rights of the plaintiffs — in this case, the New York, Boston, St. Louis, and Cincinnati clubs. The injunction further restrained Nick Young from giving Spalding any of the books and papers of the league. Finally, the defendants were ordered to appear before Judge Scott on December 19, "to show cause why the injunction should not be made permanent."[25]

The papers were served on Spalding during a press conference in which he claimed his election as league president had been legal and proper. Spalding also challenged Freedman to debate the leading baseball issues and concluded his performance with this grandiloquent announcement.

> "I am the president of the National League. I openly denounce Freedman as a coward as well as a marplot in baseball. I shall be present to preside at the future meetings of the National League. In view of his actions I defy Andrew Freedman to come to the meetings of the National League. I therefore declare him out of baseball."[26]

Receipt of Freedman's injunction took the bloom off the affair. The injunction froze conditions in baseball, with both sides seeking legal advice. Spalding went to see Thomas Reed, the former speaker of the House of Representatives and asked his advice about the contested election. Reed was interested in the contest and sympathetic to Spalding, but he was forced to tell him that the use made of the "constructive presence" was illegal, and so was his election. Reed's opinion turned out to be correct. On December 20, after a day's delay to allow Freedman's lawyer, De Lancey Nicoll, to attend the funeral of a friend, Judge Scott made the injunction against Spalding permanent. Spalding and his lawyer made no objection to the decision.[27]

A permanent injunction paralyzed the National League. It could not hire umpires, approve player contracts, draw up a playing schedule, nor conduct any business at all. Nick Young was still president, but he could do nothing. Everything now waited on the law's delay.

The inability of the National League moguls to settle their problems gave rise to numberless comments and rumors from the press. Most observers were confident that one

> ...way or another the difficulty will be adjusted long before the playing season opens. There is no danger of the National League being so tied up as has been intimated, that its teams will be unable to take the field in April. There is too much at stake for that.[28]

If there was confidence that there would be a baseball season, there was considerable uncertainty as to the form that season might take. One persistent rumor held that the four Spalding clubs would join the American League if Freedman won the fight. Another was that Spalding would form a new National League, putting new teams in the cities of his enemies. A third rumor involved the sale of the Cincinnati Reds to a consortium of local businessmen and the sale of the Giants to their former owner, E. B. Talcott.[29]

All of the rumors seemed somewhat improbable, and the last was promptly and categorically denied. But, by 1901, after more than a decade of baseball wars, shifting franchises, syndicate deals, and sleazy "baseball diplomacy," both the fans and the press were half prepared to believe that anything was possible in baseball.

While the rumors and rumors of rumors circulated, both factions settled in for the real struggle. They both issued periodic propaganda bulletins designed to blacken their opponents and present themselves to the baseball public as statesmen of moderation and good will. Their lawyers also prepared their briefs and exhibits for the day when the case should come to trial. Finally, each faction tried to pry a club loose from the other to end the impasse politically instead of in the courts.

Spalding, who had some experience in public relations, began the propaganda campaign at once. On December 21, 1901, he sent a public letter to the eight club owners, outlining what he had done, which was almost nothing, and assuring the owners that he had not affected their property rights nor involved the National League in any financial engagements. He also wrote that he had had many plans to strengthen the league. But now, with the injunction in force, Spalding wrote sadly that he could do nothing.[30] Spalding also received support from *The Sporting News* and *Sporting Life*, both of which denounced the trust scheme and its authors. Although enjoined from acting as league president, Spalding was clearly winning the war of words.[31]

Having assured himself of a sympathetic audience, Spalding moved to solidify his position as a disinterested and generous advocate of unity and clean management in baseball. On January 7, 1902, he wrote a public letter to John Brush, offering to retire from baseball if Freedman, Robison, and Brush did likewise.[32] There was, of course, no real possibility that this would happen. The Freedman four were confident that their legal position was correct, and Brush, at least, thoroughly enjoyed owning a baseball club and had no desire to leave the game. Nonetheless, Spalding's offer could not fail to seem fair and disinterested, and throw his opponents on the defensive.

Freedman and Brush, seeing their public support wane alarmingly, launched a campaign of their own. They repeated their earlier charge that Spalding's main interest in the National League was a contract to sell baseballs. They argued further that Spalding's methods were exceptionally high-handed and arrogant. Spalding had declared that Andrew Freedman was "out of baseball," ignoring the fact that Freedman owned a majority interest in the most valuable club in the league. If Spalding could drive Freedman out of baseball in this cavalier manner, where was any protection for the property rights of the club owners?[33]

These two new charges failed to impress the public any more than the others had, though there was a great deal of truth in both. So Brush and Freedman tried another tack. The baseball trust was extraordinarily unpopular, and Brush and Freedman suffered from the public belief that they had invented it. They now tried to shift that burden to Spalding. Brush gave the press a letter written in July, 1901, to Frank Robison, describing the trust scheme as Spalding had presented it to him. Brush wrote that Spalding had illustrated his plan by

> ...using the Bicycle Trust, and that illustration simply took all power out of the hands of the individual club ... to have any voice or control whatever.[34]

Brush warned Robison that the plan was a poor one, not to have anything to do with it, and that he was against it. Brush then issued a further statement that the trust plan was not discussed at the December meeting of the National League.

> No measure or plan or code of laws for the reorganization of baseball or for the control and management of the game ... was ever presented to the League or was even discussed during a League session.[35]

Therefore, the trust plan was Spalding's and no one else's, and Spalding's claim that the recent National League meeting had been spent discussing the Brush trust plan was utterly false.

Driven on the defensive, Spalding struck back. He could hardly deny that he had contemplated some sort of syndicate reorganization of the National League during the summer of 1901, so he ignored the matter completely. But he knew that Brush had lied about not discussing the trust scheme in the December meeting, so Spalding called for the publication of the league minutes at his own expense. He wrote to Nick Young that the "welfare of baseball" demanded publication of "a true account of the entire proceedings of this annual meeting."[36] Young agreed. When the transcriptions were published in the February 8, 1902, edition of *Sporting Life* Spalding was vindicated. The magnates had talked about a trust plan at the meeting. Indeed, they had talked about nothing else. And it was the Brush/Freedman plan they had discussed.[37]

Spalding also moved in another direction to validate his claim in the public mind to control the National League. He held a conference in Chicago with Ban Johnson, president of the American League, to discuss baseball matters in general. The two agreed that baseball needed two major leagues, that there must be peace between the leagues and a new National Agreement, and that the four Spalding clubs would not join the American League. They agreed further that there ought to be a joint conference on the playing rules, which would be held in Buffalo on February 10. The Spalding clubs would meet then with the American League delegates to create a unified set of rules.[38] If Johnson were meeting and talking with Spalding, and not with Brush and Freedman, could the public think that Spalding would not eventually win the fight?

But the war of words was not the only war. By the middle of February, 1902, adverse public opinion had made a baseball trust unlikely, no matter who won, but this did not mean that Spalding would become undisputed league president. There was the distinct possibility that one of the clubs would change sides, thus bringing the deadlock to an end. This political solution would end the struggle quickly and decisively, and Spalding moved to seize the initiative. On January 2, 1902, he sent a public letter to the club owners. In this epistle, Spalding informed the moguls that he had talked to E. B. Talcott, a former owner of the Giants, about the possibility of buying the club, should the stockholders be persuaded to sell. Spalding also commented on a Washington meeting with Nick Young, during which Young had informed him of the league's several unpaid obligations. Finally, Spalding asked the owners for their opinions on the stalemate within the National League and for "such information and suggestions as may have a bearing on the future conduct of this baseball campaign."[39]

In due course replies came in from the Spalding four and from Arthur Soden in Boston. Spalding held back the Soden letter, but gave the others to the papers. They were notes of support, though the one from Barney Dreyfuss, the Pittsburgh owner, was noticeably lukewarm. Barney wanted peace.[40]

The letter from Soden was not published for another three days, when Spalding, harassed and bedeviled by the reporters, released the entire file of correspondence with the Boston owners. The letters revealed that Soden had doubts about the legality of Spalding's election, wanted to see what the courts said about it, and opposed only the methods Spalding had used in the election, not the candidate himself. Moreover, Soden revealed that he was quite prepared to sell his interest in the New York club and even to sell his share of the Boston stock and retire from baseball. Further, in a letter to Spalding on January 8, 1902, asking that previous correspondence not be published, Soden wrote that

> ...the Boston club never endorsed the trust scheme, and discouraged the plan as not feasible and sure to be a failure. Mr. Freedman invited me to Red Bank ... and, when it [the trust scheme] was outlined to me, I opposed it strenuously.[41]

Lest this letter seem too friendly to the Spalding faction, however, Soden called Freedman on January 9 and assured him of continued support.[42]

The exchange of letters showed that both factions had a weak point. For the Freedman four it was Boston. Arthur Soden, the dominant Boston partner, was placating both sides, trying to work both sides of the street. In a quarrel this sharp, with the issues defined in court, such waffling could lead nowhere. So Soden, prompted by his partners who were opposed to Spalding, and the superior legal position of the Freedman group, returned his original alliance:

> There is no condition or circumstance that can arise in the National League under which the vote of the Boston Club will ever be cast for A. G. Spalding for any office in it.[43]

That communication, extracted from Soden by Andrew Freedman, settled it. Soden stuck with his side.

The Spalding faction faced possible desertion from Barney Dreyfuss, owner of the champion Pittsburgh Pirates. Having a good team, which made a lot of money, Dreyfuss wanted to play baseball much more than he wanted Spalding to be president of the National League. By the end of January, Dreyfuss had admitted to the press that he would stick with Spalding until the court decision, but, if the courts favored Freedman, the Pittsburgh club would vote for someone else as league president.[44]

Although the Spalding faction was holding its side together and winning the struggle for public opinion, it was far less confident of winning in court. But if negotiation could not succeed, the law must. The case moved fairly rapidly, considering the usual pace of things in court. On January 27, 1902, Spalding's lawyers filed a demurrer in the New York Supreme Court, alleging that the state court did not have proper jurisdiction in the case. Therefore, the injunction it had granted was null and void and had been from the beginning. Moreover, the demurrer questioned the legal capacity of the plaintiffs to sue.[45] The demurrer did nothing to change the legal position of either faction, as it did not deal with the merits of the case. It merely dealt with procedure, thus adding another step to the legal process and pushing the final decision further into the spring.

The case was heard on March 11 by Judge Truax of the New York Supreme Court. Attorneys for the Spalding faction, including John M. Ward, repeated their previous arguments. De Lancey Nicoll, Freedman's lawyer, made a strong presentation of the issues in both the demurrer and the case itself. Efforts had been made, in New York, to damage Freedman's property, and Freedman had the right to sue. Moreover, Spalding's election to the league presidency had been fraudulent. Four votes was not a majority, and the presiding officer at the meeting in question, Nick Young had given the four absent clubs permission to leave. The opposing group had made no protest at this. The doctrine of constructive presence did not apply to this situation. Thus, the action brought by plaintiffs was both legal and proper. Judge Truax took the papers in the case and reserved his decision.[46]

The final decision came on March 29. Judge Truax overruled Spalding's demurrer on both counts, the jurisdiction of the court and the sufficiency of the complaint. Thus the legal situation reverted to the point when Freedman had obtained his injunction. Judge Truax did not prevent Spalding from answering Freedman's original charge, that four votes for league presidency was not a majority and four clubs in a meeting was not a quorum. But a hearing on the merits of this issue was months away. The baseball season must begin in three weeks.[47]

For all practical purposes Judge Truax's decision on the demurrer settled the case completely. All of the clubs which had backed Spalding's candidacy were ready to settle, agree on a schedule, and begin the season. Secret negotiations for peace, which had been going on fitfully for most of March, now came into the open, and a league meeting was called for April 1 in New York. Everyone came, and the talk in the corridors of the Fifth Avenue Hotel was harmony, playing dates, and ways to keep the American League from signing all the best players.

On April 1 the main business was the presentation of three proposed schedules, all of which were referred to a committee for consideration. No public reference was made to the deadlock over league officers. The next day was devoted to the election of a league president. The session began with the reading of Spalding's letter of resignation from an office he had never really held. In his letter, dated March 8, 1902, Spalding repeated the platform on which he had run for office. He then wrote that conditions had arisen "which in my opinion make it impossible at this time to carry out all the principles embodied in the above platform." Spalding also stated that his resignation was the result of his belief that the political deadlock in the league should not be extended into the playing season, as that "would be distasteful to the public, injurious to the National League in particular, and to professional baseball in general." No one could argue with that, and Spalding's letter was gratefully received.[48]

The magnates then turned gingerly to the task of finding their new president. No one wanted a new rupture, so provocative nominations were avoided. Several names were mentioned, among them John M. Ward, and finally William C. Temple, the Pittsburgh millionaire who had donated the Temple Cup, was a neutral and unanimous choice. Informed of his election, Temple promptly declined the burden, and the magnates went back to the drawing board. This time there was no single candidate who could satisfy both factions, so the magnates came up with a three-man executive board, consisting of Brush, Soden, and James Hart (president of the Chicago club). Both factions had a man on the board, and the swing man, Arthur Soden, though a Freedmanite, was the most neutral man available.[49]

After this exercise in diplomacy the magnates adjourned to prepare for the season, a mere three weeks away. Aside from adopting a playing schedule, no further business was transacted or even attempted. No one wanted to take a chance of disrupting the fragile truce. Divisive issues, and there were many, could wait. The time to fight had passed. The time to play had come. The war had ended with an apparent victory for Freedman and Brush, and their allies were both enthusiastic and reluctant. Freedman had won his case in court and had denied Spalding the office of league president. Moreover, the Freedman four had the preponderance of votes within the new executive board and would, presumably, control the affairs of the league. Freedman and Brush had won the legal and political battles.

But they had lost the war. Spalding had capitalized on a press and public already hostile to syndicate baseball, to the arrogance of the feuding magnates, and the casual contempt the National League had shown for the past decade to both the fans and the players. The trust scheme seemed to be the last straw, the final seamy grab for power and profits, the final insult to the fans. That is what Spalding said it was, over and over and over again. He managed to stick Freedman and Brush with the authorship of this outrageous scheme, and he successfully evaded responsibility for his own trust plans. Try as they might, Brush and Freedman could never escape from the public impression that the trust plan was theirs, nor could they convince the fans and press that the trust plan was either harmless or unimportant. Spalding understood, as Freedman and Brush did not, that the fans were the reason for baseball. The magnates owned the clubs, but the fans owned the game.

There was another, more general, reason why the public was unremittingly hostile to the trust plans. Freedman and Brush had had the poor judgment to launch their plans during the high tide of the public revulsion to trusts. It was the Progressive Era, a time of alarums and excursions, of vast enthusiasms for various forms of uplift and reform. There were campaigns for women suffrage laws, efforts to outlaw child labor, attempts to abolish vice and introduce prohibition, and a renewed interest in Christian revivalism. In such a fervent time, of course, there were also demons. Chief among them were those forms of business combination generally, though not always accurately, known as Trusts. Trusts, the Progressives said, were the main Corruptor of American Democracy. They debased the National Character. They stripped away from the Average Man his Self-Reliance, his Control over his own Destiny. They made the Common Man a Slave to the Interests. They possessed all of the immense power of Capital and Political Pull. They controlled state governments; indeed, their insidious influence dominated the Congress of the United States. They were Evil Incarnate, the very quintessence of social callousness and irresponsibility.

Now was the time to stop these wicked and depraved trusts, said the Progressives, now, while we still could. The Progressives demanded trust reform with roar and bellow. They radiated righteous indignation. They glowed with religious fervor. They knew that they were on the side of right and the Trusts were instruments of the devil. William Jennings Bryan struck the right tone on this, as he so often did in his crusades: "Is God or Nature responsible for the trust? Is God or Nature responsible for private monopolies?"[50] No. It was irresponsible men, and it was the duty of God-fearing citizens to stop them.

These opinions on the trusts, because they were vastly oversimplified and endlessly repeated, became tremendously popular. Businessmen might claim that trusts posed no threat to American institutions or character, but almost no one believed them. Large numbers of books and articles appeared on the trust problem. Popular magazines such as *McClure's* and *Colliers* published dozens of articles on the trust menace. Sober and exact tomes appeared, such as Ida Tarbell's *History of the Standard Oil Company*. There were also alarmist, even apocalyptic, books: Thomas Lawson, *Frenzied Finance*; "The Impending Crisis," by B. Bournoff; and "To What Are the Trusts Leading," by J. B. Smiley. By 1900 books and articles on the trust were running at nearly two hundred a year and the tide was rising.[51]

Politicians, always anxious to hitch a ride on the prevailing bandwagon, began to regard trusts as inappropriate, even undesirable. William McKinley liked trusts, by and large, but even he was obliged to have the United States Industrial Commission hold months of hearings and issue a nineteen-volume report on them. When Teddy Roosevelt became president, the situation changed. Teddy loved activity, and he was not altogether out of sympathy with those who claimed that trusts were a menace. So he had Attorney General Philander Knox issue a statement that the government was going to prosecute J. P. Morgan's latest railroad trust, the Northern Securities Company. That was on February 18, 1902, right in the middle of the fight over the baseball trust. Morgan, of course, was shocked and appalled at the idea that the government was going to try and enforce the Sherman Anti-Trust Act, but the public and the press overwhelmingly applauded Roosevelt. By 1902, trusts were definitely in bad odor.

Public opposition to the baseball trust was unquestionably part of its opposition to trusts in general. Freedman and Brush overlooked that; Spalding did not. Spalding was speaking to an audience already largely converted to his viewpoint, an audience so hostile to trusts that it was not impressed by the irony of seeing a monopolist denouncing monopoly. All Spalding had to do was convince the fans that Freedman and Brush were indeed the authors of the trust scheme and that they were trying to foist this baneful and monstrous practice on baseball. Spalding did both, brilliantly. There were local as well as national reasons for the demise of the trust plan. The progressive movement went well beyond an assault on trusts, though that was a national mark of progressive identity. Progressives also engaged in a major effort to clean up politics, particularly local politics, an unfinished task bequeathed to them by the patrician reformers of the previous century. In part this meant the continuing effort to elect reform mayors, such as Hazen Pingree in Detroit, Tom Johnson in Cleveland, or Seth Low in the recently consolidated New York. But the new century also saw new ideas concerning municipal reform. The old notions, characteristic of patrician reformers of the Tweed era, contemplated a total cleansing, mostly moral in nature, that would eliminate the evils of the saloon, graft and crime, and bring the city decent rule by the best men.[52] The new style, which emerged after 1900, meant a narrower attack on a specific social problem, such as tenement houses, and omitted a condemnation of urban government in general. The progressive reformers argued for such things as

>...better utility services and regulation, health, housing and factory laws, zoning and city planning, the renovation of government ... and an improved educational system....[53]

In this manner the city could be improved without alienating the machine.

Efforts to ameliorate urban life took several forms. There was in the first place research, as progressive reformers sought to establish how bad things really were. Such agencies as the Bureau of Municipal Research in New York carried out continuous investigations on current social problems. The results of this research were made available to municipal officials, who found that their interest was served better by accepting rather than denying reality.[54] Added to research efforts was the work of private reform groups. An example in New York was the Charity Organization Society, a group that gathered evidence and lobbied for change. One of its notable successes was the tenement house report, presented in 1900, which was sufficiently compelling that Governor Roosevelt persuaded the legislature to create New York's Tenement House Commission. A year later came an improved tenement house law, and with it the Municipal Tenement House Department, whose secretary, Lawrence Veiller, had been the author of the Charity Organization Society's initial report.[55] The third element in progressive era municipal reform was the establishment of city agencies and bureaus. This was the key to the success of the entire progressive urban reform movement. For municipal agencies gave reform permanence, transforming it from moral outrage and private charities into bureaucratic jobs and functions which every administration, whether machine or reform, felt obliged to protect and expand.[56]

The impact of administrative reform on the city was clear and momentous. Where previously important social issues had been ignored or dealt with by ward bosses on an ad hoc basis, they were now addressed in an increasingly professional and continuous manner. System replaced caprice; routine insured that social problems were never lost from view. Measurement replaced judgment, as statistical criteria for progress were established. None of this was perfect, of course, and the moral and decent government by the best men, the patrician dream, was never realized. Nonetheless, over the short run, New York made undeniable and important progress in dealing with serious social problems.

There was also a profound irony in the success of the progressive era administrative reformers. The ward leaders and machine bosses were gradually losing administrative power at the same time as they consolidated their hold on urban party organization.[57] Richard Croker and his successor, Charles Murphy, controlled Tammany to an extent that Honest John Kelly could only dream of, yet the use of that power was daily being curtailed by the new urban social services bureaus. The irony of this development was frequently lost on contemporaries, who, used to the style and symbols of the Gilded Age, continued to swear by Tammany or rant against it. Indeed, it was the politicians who caught on to the ironic reality first, as increasingly the ward healers themselves went to the bureaus in their ceaseless effort to exchange favors for votes.

Finally, the administrative reformers like Lawrence Veiller had an impact on the press. Newspapers might support or oppose Tammany, but it was impossible to favor slums, vice, disease, filth, ignorance and early death. A salubrious city was not a partisan issue. So the papers could only quibble with "methods" while perforce supporting ends and reform in general. In the baseball issues, then, the New York papers tended to take an anti-trust, anti–Freedman tone. Even *The Press*, rabidly pro–Freedman in general, was cautious this time. The general climate of reform, both local and national, demanded it. The reformers had seized the moral high ground and newspaper comment reflected it.

Thus Spalding won the war of words, which as it turned out was a more important victory than any which might have been won in court. In effect, Spalding's prolonged denunciation of Freedman, Brush, and the trust scheme made any baseball trust an impossibility. No one would stand for it. At the spring meeting, after their victory in court, Freedman and Brush did not even bring the trust plan up. They dominated the league, but they could not use their power. Indeed, for Freedman, victory in court was virtually his last act in baseball. Ninety days after the Truax decision, Andrew Freedman sold the Giants and was out of baseball.

CHAPTER NINE

UNDER NEW MANAGEMENT

I

A lot of men in baseball are tugging in different directions. Some of them will win. Others will lose out.
Who will lose out?
Those who haven't played baseball, or those who forgot it's a game first, then a business. The game first and the entertainment, the competition, and the fight-all that comes first. Without it, there's no game, and certainly no business to battle over.[1]

That was how Blanche Sindall remembered a conversation in July, 1901, with her fiancé, John J. McGraw. She was worried. Would her man lose out? It was not likely. Already, in 1901, the playing manager of the Baltimore Orioles in the new American League, McGraw had demonstrated plenty of toughness, will to survive, love of baseball, and business shrewdness necessary to avoid losing out.

John McGraw was born in Truxton, New York, a hard-scrabble town south of Syracuse. The year was 1873. His parents were poor; his father was a section hand on the railroad for a dollar a day, and there were nine children. There was never enough of anything, and the children were expected to earn their way from an early age. That was fine with young John. He was a resourceful boy, who worked hard and kept his wits about him, but he did not want to work at trades that his father considered suitable. John wanted to play baseball, and his father opposed it bitterly. The boy would come to no good, he said. He was frittering away his time in silly games. He was costing the family money every time he broke a window. Money needed for food and clothes was going for baseballs. It had to stop. John was the eldest son. He must settle down and take up a trade.

But to John McGraw, baseball was not a game. It was his life's passion.

He thought about it constantly. He read the current baseball guides until he knew them by heart. He practiced baseball constantly, with the same terrible intensity that W. C. Fields possessed in learning to juggle. Hour after hour, day after day, John McGraw played baseball. He learned to bunt. He learned to run the bases. He learned to hit to the opposite field. He became the best player in Truxton, then the best player in the entire area.

This went on until the winter of 1884. John McGraw, the little Irish kid, earned money as a butcher boy on the railroad, as a newsboy for the *Elmira Telegram*, as a casual laborer in the village, and spent as much time as he could learning baseball. But that winter the McGraw family was struck by diphtheria. John's mother and four of the children died within a week of a savage disease which no one could understand, cure, or prevent. A dirt-poor widower with five young children, John's father would no longer tolerate baseball. John must become a breadwinner in earnest. But the boy could not give baseball up, and, after a ferocious beating from his father for breaking another window, young John left home. He moved across the street, to the Truxton House Inn, where a neighbor family took him in. He was already mature and responsible, and he earned his keep by doing chores. As always, he worked at becoming a baseball player. He was eleven.

William "Cap" Anson: 1888. The most celebrated player of the Chicago players, Anson was the last active player who played in 1876, the National League's first season, and was by 1890 a genuine national celebrity.

In the spring of 1890, when he was seventeen, John McGraw became a professional baseball player, a goal he had cherished as long as he could remember. He played hard, with the same total determination that had marked his years of preparation. He knew the rules by heart and took every advantage of them he could think of. These were numerous, because John McGraw thought about baseball constantly, trying to understand the strategy of the game as well as merely how to play it.

He was a fresh kid. He taunted his opponents unmercifully, including the legendary Cap Anson, whom he first played against in an exhibition game in the spring of 1891. Anson was impressed with the wise kid who got two hits and told him that he was a good player who might want to play with Chicago some day. Anson was right. McGraw was good enough to play in the majors.

When he came up to the Baltimore Orioles toward the end of the 1891 season, he was already a polished fielder and base runner. His hitting was adequate, though improving rapidly, and his confidence and enthusiasm were enormous, almost monstrous. He knew he would make it. He told everyone he would become a regular, would lead the team to glory and triumph beyond imagining. The Oriole veterans were both amused and irritated with the brash kid, and many tried their best to ignore him. But he was right and they were wrong. By 1893 he was the acknowledged leader of the legendary Baltimore Orioles, the most notorious, and best, baseball team of the nineties. In 1899, when the bulk of the Baltimore stars were transferred to Brooklyn in the syndicate deal, McGraw, now half owner of the prosperous Diamond Cafe, remained behind as the manager of what was left of the Oriole team. To the astonishment of everyone but himself, McGraw brought his collection of castoffs and rookies home in fourth place and even challenged for the lead in a September spurt. Two years later he managed an even more ragged group of players for Baltimore in the new American League and finished fifth. He was already a good manager. He knew baseball and he knew men, and he had an uncanny ability to get the best his players had to give.[2]

In 1902 John McGraw returned as manager of the Baltimore Orioles. But things were not going well between McGraw and Ban Johnson, the autocratic and capable president of the American League. The suspicions were mutual, and the recriminations, *sotto voce* at first, grew steadily louder and more public. The story first appeared in July, 1901. The papers declared that Ban Johnson had information that McGraw was planning to jump to the Giants, taking several American League players with him. McGraw's reply was a demand that Johnson produce evidence. All that emerged from several weeks of columns and stories was that McGraw had talked several times with officials of the New York club, including Freedman himself. It was not much, but it was enough. Although McGraw kept in close touch with Ban Johnson, neither really trusted the other. Johnson thought McGraw really was going to the Giants, in spite of the fact that there was no hard evidence of a deal. McGraw thought Ban Johnson was going to junk the Baltimore franchise, in which McGraw had invested seven thousand dollars, and move it to New York. Indeed, McGraw was willing to assist in such a move, which was vital to the prestige of the American League, but only if he himself would not "lose out." And that was the point. If Johnson made the move, and McGraw did not have another position for himself, he could then be out of baseball. For John McGraw that was impossible.[3]

McGraw moved cautiously through the maze of baseball politics in the spring of 1902. He remained as manager and part owner of the Orioles, but he increased the tempo of his negotiations with Andrew Freedman. As the spring wore on, the size of the deal increased dramatically. Instead of involving the shift of a player-manager from one warring league to the other, it had now grown to include the sale and shift of entire franchises. By June, 1902, John McGraw's move from Baltimore to New York included the sale of the Cincinnati Reds to the "Yeast Kings," Max and Julius Fleischmann, Freedman's sale of the Giants to John Brush, and the move of the Baltimore Orioles to New York.

News of the deal broke on July 2, the day after McGraw had signed a tentative contract with Freedman, but the entire transaction was not completed until July 16, 1902. The next day the details became public. New York fans were less interested in the complicated shifts in franchises and management than in the changes in the hapless Giants, who were languishing in last place, as usual. John McGraw, as it turned out, did not come alone. He brought some players with him. There were six of them, including Iron Man Joe McGinnity, one of the great pitchers in the history of baseball, and a young catcher, Roger Bresnahan, who, like McGinnity, is now in the Baseball Hall of Fame. The new men took the field for the first time on July 19, before a large and enthusiastic New York crowd. The Giants lost to Philadelphia, 4 to 3, but the crowd did not seem to mind.[4] They had seen the Giants do that a lot lately, and they were looking for improvement, not perfection. The fans wanted hustle and excitement, and McGraw promised both. One fan was heard to comment that it looked like a new era for the Giants. It was.

II

By 1902, baseball had settled into stable patterns of management, play, and patronage. The owners' control over the structure of the game was now tempered by a sharp rise in salaries caused by the appearance of a second major league. Once Andrew Freedman disappeared from the scene, the players completely filled the public eye to such an extent that some became cultural paradigms of virtue and skill. Christy Mathewson, the Giants' great pitcher, fell into both categories; he was without a peer on the mound and he refused to play baseball on Sunday. It was also alleged (falsely) that he never smoked, drank, or swore. Ty Cobb and Honus Wagner, who escaped transfiguration though they were the greatest players of their era, also became the idols of a generation of boys who hoped in vain to emulate them.

The first years of the new century also saw baseball emerge as a ritual act of public celebration. The National Game, of course, celebrated the United States itself, every bit as much as the parades, races, fireworks and church suppers of Independence Day. The game reinforced the sense of being an American, and was a ready path of psychological entry for immigrants into the arcane mysteries of the new world.[5] As was appropriate in a mobile society, baseball was a public celebration, a civic ritual, open to all, whether a participant, a spectator, or a fan who followed the game in the newspapers. All were included, for the game stretched beyond the place of celebration as any public ritual must. Much of the ritual character of baseball came from the rules. By 1900 the rules of play were wondrously complex and precise. For every possible event on the field there was a rule, usually several. Every interpretation of play that could suggest itself to the official scorer was also meticulously prescribed by law or custom. This scrupulousness extended to superstition, which in baseball developed into a minor art form. Fielders were careful not to touch the baselines at the end of an inning. Pitchers tugged at their hats the same way every time, whether there was a foreign substance on the bill or not. Bat boys never crossed the bats; it would choke off the supply of hits. The game was a miracle of order.

For a ritual to succeed in its ceremonial and liturgical functions it must embody not only order but right order. The rules and rubrics of ritual must be ratified by God or the people, the only possible sources of authority great enough to endow a ceremony with a general significance and meaning that transcends both person and time.[6] In baseball, this general meaning can be seen in the adoption of the infield fly rule in 1895. The rule itself is as precise and arcane as probabilist theology.[7] But the need that called it into being was both clear and pressing. The Baltimore Orioles were deliberately muffing short pop flies. If the base runners ran the fly would be caught so the runner doubled off base. If the base runners stayed, the fly would be dropped and the fielder would throw to the lead base and begin a double play. None of this was illegal. In their defense the Orioles argued that they were merely playing hard and aggressive ball. They employed as well the lawyers' contribution to American ethics: if anything is legal it is also moral. No one was persuaded by this. The lawyers' ethics might be fine for such depraved institutions as corporations, universities or municipal governments, but they were utterly unacceptable in an essentially liturgical setting. The Orioles' play was a violation of the spirit of baseball. It was an abuse of the game.

Abuse of the game was the worst charge that could be made because abuse destroyed the correct order of the ritual, carrying the game outside the realm of the sacred and into the realm of the everyday and the ordinary.[8] Thus the game ceased to be a game at all but became instead a mere occasion for commerce. It was no longer a *dromenon*, a thing acted out. And, of course, having lost its status and function as a rite, baseball could not include the whole community. Such a thing was impossible. The correct order must be restored, even at a time when everything else in baseball was in decline and disarray. The infield fly rule fixed all that and restored to baseball the deeply-felt and appropriate balance amongst hitting, base running and fielding. The ritual was made whole and beautiful. Baseball was, once again, perfect.[9]

Finally, the new century also saw baseball attain its marked historical dimension, which is now so integral a part of the game and its appeal. By 1902 there were second-generation, even third-generation, baseball fans who had been brought up in the game and saw it from the perspective of maturity as well as youth. Young people whose fathers had rooted for Buck Ewing or Cap Anson, now cheered for Christy Mathewson or Ty Cobb. No matter how good Mathewson or Cobb might be, there were always older fans who swore that Tim Keefe or Cap Anson were better, while the true graybeards claimed superiority for Albert Spalding or George Wright. All such statements were met with scorn and ridicule by the many unbelievers, which inevitably led to argument. Everyone produced supporting statistics, along with appropriate samples of anecdote, myth, and legend. These arguments were endless and insoluble, but they were not pointless, for they fixed the historical character of baseball. They helped create life-long fans who forever compared the heroes of their youth with the inevitably inferior players of a degraded present. It was an attitude *amer-douce*, with an element of nostalgia, of lost youth, of an awareness of time:

> Time is of the essence. The crowd and players
> Are the same age always, but the man in the crowd
> Is older every season. Come on, play ball![10]

NOTES

Chapter One

1. Quoted in a long, front page article in the *New York Daily Tribune*, April 9, 1889. See also description in *The New York Clipper*, Vol. XXXVIII, #5, April 13, 1889, pp. 79–80. The banquet also received a long description in Adrian C. Anson, *A Ball Player's Career* (Chicago, 1900), pp. 274–280. See also the superb and scholarly book by Harold Seymour, *Baseball: The Early Years* (New York, 1960), pp. 8–9. A description of the banquet can also be found in Seymour's doctoral dissertation from Cornell University, *The Rise of Major League Baseball to 1891* (University Microfilms, Ann Arbor, Michigan, 1956), pp. 2–3. This thesis is of great use to the serious historian, largely because of Seymour's meticulous and exhaustive research, which is recorded in thousands of footnotes. These have, alas, been omitted from the published book. See also the important books by Peter Levine, *A.G. Spalding and the Rise of Baseball: The Promise of American Sport* (New York, 1988), particularly Chapters 3 and 4. See also Steven Riess, *Touching Base: Professional Baseball and American Culture in the Progressive Era* (Westport, Connecticut, 1980), and *City Games: The Evolution of American Urban Society and the Rise of Sports* (Urbana, 1989), two essential books for understanding the history and cultural setting of baseball. See also Allen Guttmann, *A Whole New Ball Game: An Interpretation of American Sports* (Chapel Hill, 1988), particularly Chapter 5. For the background of sports in New York City, the essential book is Melvin Adelman, *A Sporting Time: New York City and the Rise of Modern Athletics 1820–70* (Urbana, 1986). See also as background to the rise of professional baseball and the social and sporting context in which it expanded, George B. Kirsch, *The Creation of American Team Sports: Baseball and Cricket. 1838–72* (Urbana, 1989), particularly Chapters 1, 6 and 9. The different levels of popular success between baseball and cricket are an important indicator of the direction of American social change in the Gilded Age, particularly the impact of immigration upon the cities and the democratization of American social assumptions. In this respect, one must recall both Mark Twain and Horatio Alger. See also David Q. Voigt, *America Through Baseball* (Chicago, 1976), particularly pp. 1–106. Voigt treats baseball as a whole, concentrating on the interconnections between the sport and society at large. This is an essential book for understanding baseball. See also Douglas Noverr and Lawrence Ziewacz, *The Games They Played: They Played Sports in American History, 1865–1980* (Chicago, 1983), Chapter 1. This book helps set baseball in a sporting context, considering it in comparison with other games. Finally, see George Will, *Men at Work: The Craft of Baseball* (New York, 1990), particularly the introduction. Finally, no one should overlook Mr. Dooley on

baseball. See Finley Peter Dunne, "The Higher Baseball" in *Mr. Dooley at His Best*, ed. E. Ellis (New York, 1943), pp. 170–174. This last says all there is to be known or imagined about the art, mystery and science of the game.

2. *New York Daily Tribune*, April 9, 1889.

3. See Seymour, *Baseball...*, Chapters 1–12; Seymour, *The Rise of Major League Baseball...*, Chapters 1–10. See also the curious book published privately by Preston D. Orem, *Baseball (1845–1881): From the Newspaper Accounts* (Altadena, California, 1961). This book contains little commentary by the author, being instead abstracts from newspaper stories. See also Albert G. Spalding, *America's National Game: Historic Facts Concerning the Beginning, Evolution, Development, and Popularity of Baseball with Personal Reminiscences of its Vicissitudes, its Victories and its Votaries* (New York, 1911), pp. 47–269, which carries the story up to the banquet of 1889. Spalding's book contains some mythology, including the Doubleday story. See also Anson, *A Ball Player's Career*, pp. 32–144, covering the years up to 1890. See also David Quentin Voigt, *American Baseball: From Gentleman's Sport to the Commissioner System* (Norman, Oklahoma, 1966), pp. 3–99. This is the first volume of a three-volume study. Voigt's book is an important scholarly work and is beautifully written, with numerous anecdotes that amuse and enlighten. It presents the thesis that baseball was a crucial part of the development of professional spectator activities for leisure time in a mass, urbanized, industrial society. No one could argue with that.

4. On the color line in baseball, see Art Rust, Jr., *Get That Nigger Off the Field!* (New York, 1976), pp. 11–18.

5. Quoted from an unidentified number of the *Baseball Magazine*, in Douglas Wallop, *Baseball: An Informal History* (New York, 1969), p. 52.

6. *Spalding's Official Base Ball Guide: 1885*, pp. 96–97.

7. The details of this episode can be found in Spalding's *America's National Game...*, pp. 523–26; see also the *New York Sun*, June 6 and August 5, 1886, for information on Spalding's scheme for the creation of a detective agency to watch the salient boozers in the National League. For the text of Spalding's temperance pledge in 1888, see the *New York Clipper*, vol. XXXVI, #7, April 28, 1888, p. 109.

8. *Spalding's Official Base Ball Guide: 1889*, p. 58.

9. Preston D. Orem, *Baseball (1884): From the Newspaper Accounts* (privately published, Altadena, California, 1967), p. 169. These pamphlets cover the years from 1882 through 1891, and have been printed in separate, yearly segments. They are numbered consecutively, from pages 1 through 629. The pamphlets are a continuation of Orem's book on baseball from 1845 through 1881.

10. *New York Daily Tribune*, July 16, 1883. For the official statistical record of the career of Mike Dorgan, or of any other major league player or manager, see *The Baseball Encyclopedia: The Complete and Official Record of Major League Baseball* (lst edition, New York, 1969; 2nd edition, New York, 1974). Dorgan's record is on pp. 404 and 1027 of the second (1974) edition, to which all citations refer unless otherwise indicated. This encyclopedia is the result of a generally successful effort to obtain accurate statistical information on everyone who played major league ball, and to reconcile practices in scoring and record keeping that existed before 1920 with the modern ones. Thus, this book supercedes previous efforts to produce a complete statistical record of baseball. In particular, Hy Turkin and S. C. Thompson, *The Official Encyclopedia of Baseball* (New York, 1951, 1956, 1959, 1963, 1968). Other, earlier attempts at a statistical record, which were incorporated into Turkin and Thompson, are now also outdated. See, as examples, A. H. Spink, *The National Game* (St. Louis, 1910), or Francis C. Richter, *Richter's History and Records of Base Ball. The American Nation's Chief Sport*

(Philadelphia, 1914), or Ernest J. Lanigan, *The Baseball Cyclopedia* (New York, 1922, with annual supplements through 1933), or George Moreland, *Balldom: The Britannica of Baseball* (New York, 1914 and 1927).

11. *New York Daily Tribune*, April 27, 29, 1888.
12. *New York Times*, May 19, 1888.
13. *New York Times*, May 19, 1888.
14. Preston D. Orem, *Baseball (1888): From the Newspaper Accounts*, pp. 366–67.
15. On Billy Sunday see two excellent and informative books by William G. McLoughlin, Jr., *Billy Sunday Was His Real Name* (Chicago, 1955), and *Modern Revivalism. Charles Grandison Finney to Billy Graham* (New York, 1959), pp. 400–55. McLoughlin presents a balanced and sensitive account of revivalism as both a religious and social phenomenon. See also Elijah "Ram's Horn" Brown, *The Real Billy Sunday* (New York, 1914), written by a man who participated with Sunday in his dismal trade. See also William Ellis, *Billy Sunday: The Man and His Message* (Philadelphia, 1914, reissued in 1936). See also Theodore Thomas Frankenburg, *The Spectacular Career of Rev. Billy Sunday* (Columbus, Ohio, 1913). Finally, for the flavor of revivalism before the Great War see the little book, *Burning Truths from Billy's Bat: A Graphic Description of the Remarkable Conversion of Rev. "Billy" Sunday Embodying Anecdotes. Terse Sayings. Etc. Compiled from Various Sources* (Philadelphia, 1914).
16. Billy Sunday's recollection of his conversion experience is in Ellis, *Billy Sunday...*, p. 41, Frankenberg, *The Spectacular Career of Rev. Billy Sunday*, p. 65, and *Burning Truths From Billy's Bat:...*, p. 10.
17. For a jaundiced view of the YMCA atmosphere in the nineties, see H. L. Mencken, *Heathen Days* (New York, 1942), Chapter 2.
18. See John Higham, *Strangers in the Land* (New York, 1963, 2nd edition) for a superb and illuminating discussion of nativism and the image of immigrant Americans.
19. Frankenberg, *The Spectacular Career of Rev. Billy Sunday*, pp. 65–70, and *Burning Truths From Billy's Bat:...*, pp. 11–15. For a general description of orthodox American opinion on working men and their leisure time, see Edward C. Kirkland, *Industry Comes of Age: Business, Labor, and Public Policy. 1860–1897* (New York, 1961), pp. 342–45. For a general overview of the social and political thought of American businessmen of the Gilded Age, such as Spalding, see the delightful, imaginative, and provocative little book by Edward C. Kirkland, *Dream and Thought in the Business Community 1860–1900* (Ithaca, New York, 1956).
20. For a discussion of the origin of this myth, see Seymour, *The Rise of Major League Baseball...*, pp. 2–10. See also Frederick G. Lieb, *The Baseball Story* (New York, 1950), p. 325, for a gentle debunking. See also Robert Henderson, *Bat, Ball, and Bishop* (New York, 1947), for an extensive survey into baseball's origins. See also Spalding, *America's National Game...*, pp. 19–26, for a contemporary statement of the myth. The game of baseball, American Style, was invented in 1845 by Alexander Cartwright, who wrote down the rules he thought best, and saw them adopted by the Knickerbockers club, the earliest of the organized baseball teams. The first game played under the Cartwright rules was in 1846 in Hoboken, New Jersey. It is here, and not in Cooperstown, New York, that the Baseball Hall of Fame ought to be located. No one has suggested that it be moved, however, and no one who has ever been to Hoboken would agree to such a scheme.
21. On the general American opinion of the moral superiority of the country over the wicked city, see the interesting and important book by David Grimsted, *Melodrama unveiled: American theater and culture. 1800–1850* (Chicago, 1968).

22. The chorus of the song went as follows:

> Slide, Kelly, Slide!
> Your running's a disgrace!
> Slide, Kelly, Slide!
> Stay there, hold your base!
> If someone doesn't steal you,
> And your batting doesn't fail you, They'll take you to Australia!
> Slide, Kelly, Slide!

The song was the vehicle of the popular music hall singer, Maggie Cline. There was also a painting, though not a very good one, by Frank O. Small, entitled "Slide, Kelly, Slide!" See Voigt, *American Baseball...*, I, pictures between pages 48–49. The painting, interestingly enough, shows Kelly sliding head first instead of using his more famous hook slide. The cover and music of the song "Slide, Kelly, Slide!" are pictured in Joseph Durso, *The Days of Mr. McGraw* (Englewood Cliffs, New Jersey, 1969), between pages 54 and 55.

23. See *Burning Truths from Billy's Bat:...*, pp. 10–11.

24. For the official statistical summary of Mike Kelly's career, see *The Baseball Encyclopedia*, pp. 560, 1136, 1396. On the great trade that sent the King from Chicago to Boston and shook the baseball world, see George Tuohey, *A History of the Boston Baseball Club: Being a Public Testimonial to the Players of the 1897 Team in Recognition of the Magnificent Work of the Past Season* (Boston, 1897), pp. 88–94. For a general appreciation of Kelly's life and the story of the unsuccessful attempt to win him away from the Brotherhood, see Spalding, *America's National Game...*, pp. 295–97. See also the autobiographical material in Alfred Cappio, *Slide, Kelly, Slide!* (Passaic County, New Jersey Historical Society, 1962). See also Voigt, *American Baseball...*, I, pp. 178–79 and 243–45. See also Lee Allen, *The National League Story* (New York, 1948), pp. 56–57 and Harold Kaese, *The Boston Braves* (New York, 1948), pp. 41–49. Kaese's book is probably the best of the team histories written by sportswriters. See also the *New York Times*, November 9, 1894 and the *New York Daily Tribune* of the same date for Kelly's death notices.

25. For the statistical summary of John M. Ward's career, see *The Baseball Encyclopedia...*, pp. 875, 1345, and 1411. Ward's own description of his adventures breaking into baseball can be found in John Montgomery Ward, "Notes of a Base-Ballist," *Lippincott's Magazine*, XXVIII (August, 1886), pp. 212–15. For an appreciation of his later career as a lawyer, baseball magnate, and social figure, see the *New York Times*, March 5, 1925, for the death notice.

26. John M. Ward, *Baseball: How to Become a Player, with the Origin, History, and Explanation of the Game* (Philadelphia, 1889). This charming and informative book traces the origin of the game to Anagalla, a pre-Classical Greek lady of Corcyra. Ward was not a believer in the Doubleday myth.

27. *New York Times*, July 13, 14, 1887.

28. *New York Times*, April 26, 1888.

29. See the delightful and important little book by William L. Riordan, *Plunkitt of Tammany Hall* (New York, 1963).

30. Moses Rischin, ed., *Grandma Never Lived in America: The New Journalism of Abraham Cahan* (Bloomington, Indiana, 1985). In an effort of almost Talmudic scholarship, Professor Rischin has recovered the essentially fugitive English journalism of Abraham Cahan for the *New York Commercial Advertiser* between 1897 and 1903. "The Last American" is from February 14, 1899.

31. All immigration legislation is in Vol. XXXIX of The United States Immigration Commission *Report*, 41 vols. (Washington, 1911–1912). For New York City in particular and immigration in general see Vol. XV of The United States Industrial Commission *Reports*, 19 vols. (Washington, 1901–1902).

32. Thomas Kessner, *The Golden Door: Italian and Jewish Immigrant Mobility in New York City 1880–1915* (New York, 1977), p. 5. See also Philip Taylor, *The Distant Magnet: European Emigration to the USA* (London 1971).

33. See Higham, *Strangers in the Land*, Chapters 3 and 4. See also John Higham, *Send These to Me: Immigrants in Urban America* (Baltimore, 1984), Chapters 1 and 2.

34. William Z. Ripley, *The Races of Europe: A Sociological Study* (New York, 1923, reprint edition). This was still being taught in public schools in New York as late as World War II.

35. On general nativist agitation for restriction see the indispensable Higham, *Strangers in the Land*, Chapters 2 and 3, and particularly pp. 97–105. See also Higham, *Send These to Me*, pp. 29–58; see also Morton White, *Social Thought in America: The Revolt Against Formalism* (Boston, 1957), for a discussion of pluralism in American thought and its position as a formula for minority rights; for specific examples of the rejection of pluralism see Elmer Sandmeyer, *The Anti-Chinese Movement in California* (Urbana, 1939), which examines, among other things, fears of social stratification based on race. On the Chinese again see the more recent books by Stuart Miller, *The Unwelcome Immigrant: The American Image of the Chinese. 1785–1882* (Berkeley, 1969), and Alexander Saxton, *The Indispensable Enemy: Labor and the Anti-Chinese Movement in California* (Berkeley, 1971). Though the last three citations are tangential to this study, they give a specific focus to anti-immigrant feeling in the United States and provide concrete examples often lacking in the generalizations made about nativism.

36. On Abraham Cahan see Higham, *Send These to Me*, Chapter 4 (devoted entirely to Cahan); see the absolutely indispensable book by Moses Rischin, *The Promised City: New York's Jews 1817–1914* (Cambridge, Massachusetts, 1962), particularly Part III. Cahan left a large memoir in Yiddish *Bletter fun mayn lebn* (New York, 1926–1931), the first two volumes of which were translated into English as *The Education of Abraham Cahan* (Philadelphia, 1969), introduction by Leon Stein. See also Lilian Wald, *The House on Henry Street* (New York, 1915); see also Ronald Sanders, *The Downtown Jews: Portraits of an Immigrant Generation* (New York, 1969), largely about Abraham Cahan, and Jules Chametzky, *From the Ghetto: The Fiction of Abraham Cahan* (Amherst, 1977); see also Gregory Weinstein, *The Ardent Eighties* (New York, 1928).

37. On this see Isaac Metzker, ed., *A Bintel Brief* (New York, 1972) and the selection of the bintel briefen in Allen Schoener, ed., *Portal to America: The Lower East Side 1870–1925* (New York, 1967), pp. 245–56.

38. H. L. Mencken, *Newspaper Days 1899–1906* (New York, 1941), pp. 262–63.

39. Mencken, *Newspaper Days*, pp. 264–66.

40. Richard Harding Davis was at the height of a substantial popularity in the decade around the turn of the century. This was based both on reporting and fiction, which were then not so far apart as journalists now like to pretend. On journalism, Davis wrote, among other things, *Cuba in War Time* (New York, 1898), illustrated by Remington, as well as adventure stories, such as *Gallegher and Other Stories* (New York, 1891), the title story being about the newspaper business.

41. See the important book by Charles Brown, *The Correspondent's War: Journalists in the Spanish-American War* (New York, 1967), particularly pp. 100-21, 80–82. This is the basic book on Spanish-American War journalism. See also Marcus Wilkerson, *Public Opinion and the Spanish-American War* (Baton Rouge, 1932).

42. On the war itself one might start with the delightful and profusely illustrated book by Frank Freidel, *The Splendid Little War* (Boston, 1958); on the effect of the war on baseball and sport, see Levine, *A. G. Spalding and the Rise of Baseball*, p. 98; on the war see also Theodore Roosevelt, *The Rough Riders* (New York, 1899) and Richard Harding Davis, *Cuba in War Time*. A more distant view can be obtained from Walter Millis, *The Martial Spirit* (New York, 1931).

43. Sidney A. Witherbee, ed., *Spanish-American War Songs: A Complete Collection of Newspaper Verse During the Recent War with Spain* (Detroit, 1898), p. 30. This book is 984 pages long, including a *lot* of newspaper verse.

44. Witherbee, *Spanish-American War Songs*, p. 505. This was by Eugene Wane (Ironquill) in the Topeka *Capital*.

45. Witherbee, *Spanish-American War Songs*, p. 440. This effort, a bit cynical for the enthusiasm of the times, was by G. V. Hobart.

46. One of the most important writers in America in the generation before the Great War, Finley Peter Dunne, the creator of Mr. Dooley, had a knack of giving truth a humorous twist which lessened the hurt. On Roosevelt and his history of the Rough Riders see "A Book Review" in Finley Peter Dunne, *Mr. Dooley at His Best*, pp. 99–103. On the war in general, see Finley Peter Dunne, *Mr. Dooley in Peace and War* (Boston, 1898).

47. Lincoln Steffens, *The Autobiography of Lincoln Steffens* (New York, 1931), pp. 311-27.

48. See, for example, Eugene Sue, *Les Mysteres de Paris* (Paris, 1848), or later, *Paris Spleen of Charles Baudelaire*. The genre goes back to Restif de la Bretonne, *Oeuvnes*, ed. H. Bachelin, 9 vols. (Paris, 1930–1932, Geneva, 1971), particularly vols. 1, 7 and 8.

50. Rischin, *Grandma Never Lived in America*, pp. 4–5, from February 22, 1893.

51. Rischin, *Grandma Never Lived in America*, p. 73, from January 24, 1901.

52. Rischin, *Grandma Never Lived in America*, pp. 364-65, from October 21, 1901.

53. Rischin, *Grandma Never Lived in America*, p. 60, from September, October, 1899. All of the above incidents, typical yet highly individual, were part of the fabric of daily survival in immigrant New York. But there was more than survival; there was also success. Here again, we turn to Abraham Cahan, *The Rise of David Levinsky* (New York, 1917). This is the major novel on immigrant adjustment to success and to loss. A final word on the lower east side must be said with pictures. See Schoener, *Portal to America*, a book one cannot fail to consult.

54. Abraham Cahan, *Yekl* (New York, 1896), p. 10. See the comments on *Yekl* in Allen Guttmann, *A Whole New Ball Game*, p. 58.

55. See Joy Jackson, *New Orleans in the Gilded Age: Politics and Urban Progress 1880–1896* (Baton Rouge, 1969).

56. Colonel Sartoris is a creation of William Faulkner and is familiar to all, but Louise-Clarke Pyrnelle, *Diddie, Dumps and Tot* (New York, 1882, 1916) may be new to some. A book about old south plantation life, written for girls in a time when there was a sharp distinction between what was thought suitable for girls and suitable for boys, *Diddie, Dumps and Tot* contains ideas and language that were politically correct for that time. Times change. See also W. J. Cash, *The Mind of the South*.

57. On mining towns and immigration, see the excellent book by Victor Greene, *The Slavic Community on Strike: Immigrant Labor in Pennsylvania Anthracite* (Notre Dame, 1968). This is an essential complement to the *feuilletons* of Abraham Cahan.

58. Mark Sullivan, *Our Times: The United States 1900–1925*, 6 vols. (New York, 1926–1935), vol. 1, *The Turn of the Century* (1927), p. 2, has the map.

59. On Tammany and Bryan, see Riordan, *Plunkitt of Tammany Hall*.

60. Booth Tarkington and Harry Leon Wilson, "The Man From Home," quoted in Mark Sullivan, *The Turn of the Century*, p. 3.
61. Rischin, *Grandma Never Lived in America*, pp. 70–71, from December 30, 1899.
62. On both Jewish and Italian life on the lower east side see Thomas Kessner, *The Golden Door: Italian and Jewish Mobility in New York City 1880–1915* (New York, 1977), pp. 3–44.
63. See Moses Rischin, *The Promised City*, pp. 115–70.
64. Abraham Cahan, *The Rise of David Levinsky* (1951 edition), p. 61.
65. Rischin, *The Promised City*, p. 127.
66. Incidentally, the article in the *Jewish Daily Forward* was not immediately dependent on local success. The Giants did not win the pennant in 1909, nor had they won in 1906, 1907 or 1908, nor were they to win in 1910.

An excellent source for the inter-relationships of the city to baseball is Riess, *City Games*, particularly Chapters 2, 3, 6 and 7.

67. *New York Daily Tribune*, July 29, 1888.
68. John Montgomery Ward, "Notes of a Base-Ballist:, *Lippincott's Magazine*, XXVIII (August, 1886), p. 214.
69. This little poem from the eighties has been widely reprinted. A convenient modern reference is Lawrence S. Ritter, *The Glory of Their Times: The Story of the Early Days of Baseball Told by the Men Who Played It* (New York, 1966), p. 20.
70. This story was related by the Giants' center fielder in those years, Fred Snodgrass, in Ritter, *The Glory of Their Times...*, pp. 93–97.
71. Stanley Coveleski, the Hall of Fame pitcher for Cleveland, in Ritter, *The Glory of Their Times...*, p. 115.
72. An extended examination of the early management of baseball can be found in Seymour, *Baseball: The Early Years*, pp. 75–359. The structure and organization of baseball are the main themes of this excellent book. See also Levine, *A. G. Spalding and the Rise of Baseball*, pp. 21–29.
73. Fifty cents was a lot of money. To get the approximate purchasing power in today's terms (1996), multiply by 25.
74. For the final standings of 1882, see *The Baseball Encyclopedia...*, pp. 58–59.
75. For the text of the National Agreement see Spalding, *America's National Game...*, pp. 244–48; *Spalding's Official Base Ball Guide: 1884*, pp. 47–51.
76. *New York Clipper*, vol. XXX, #39, December 16, 1882, p. 629.
77. For the official records of Clapp's career, see *The Baseball Encyclopedia...*, pp. 209, 346, 1385.
78. For the official records of Buck Ewing's career, see *The Baseball Encyclopedia...*, pp. 424, 1042, 1389.
79. For Mickey Welch's official records, see *The Baseball Encyclopedia...*, p. 1351.
80. Quoted in Voigt, *American Baseball...*, I, p. 116.
81. For Roger Connor's official records, see *The Baseball Encyclopedia...*, pp. 361–62, 1386; see also the important column by Arthur O. Schott, "A Schott from the Bleachers," *New Orleans States-Item*, May 15, 1974, on Connor's home run record.
82. For Pat Gillespie's official records, see *The Baseball Encyclopedia...*, p. 462.
83. For Tim Keefe's official records , see *The Baseball Encyclopedia...*, pp. 1133–4.
84. For John Troy's official records, see *The Baseball Encyclopedia...*, p. 855, for Mike Dorgan, pp. 404, 1027; for Ed Caskin, p. 337; for Frank Hankinson, pp. 491, 1088; for J. H. Humphries, p. 531: for James "Tip" O'Neill, pp. 701, 1231; for Grayson Pearce, p. 711. For the Giants roster of 1883 or any other year see S. C. Thompson,

All-Time Rosters of Major League Baseball Clubs (New York, 1967), p. 229.

85. *New York Times*, April 14, 1883. See also the *New York Clipper*, vol. XXXI, #5, April 21, 1883, p. 66, for an excellent box score of the game, including the "At Bat" column, which was not always included in nineteenth-century box scores. Generally, the *Clipper* and the *New York Daily Tribune* had the best box scores, although the *Clipper* was a bit skimpy on the summary.

86. *New York Times*, April 14, 19, 20, 25, 26, 27, 28, 1883; *New York Clipper*, vol. XXXI, #6, April 28, 1883, p. 85 and vol. XXXI, #7, May 5, 1883, pp. 98, 101.

87. *New York Times*, April 16, 1883.

Chapter Two

1. *New York Times*, May 2, 1883.

2. *New York Times*, May 2, 1883. See also the *New York Daily Tribune*, May 2, 1883, for a story that dealt almost exclusively with the size and behavior of the crowd, with the band, and with the betting. The game itself was dismissed in a couple of sentences at the end of the story. Except as an unusual and somewhat surprising spectacle, baseball had not yet assumed the status of real news at the dignified and staid *Tribune*. See also the *New York Clipper*, vol. XXXI, #7, May 5, 1883, p. 98; *Spalding's Official Base Ball Guide: 1884*, pp. 12–13: George Tuohey. *A History of the Boston Baseball Club...*, p. 80. The casual reader may also consult Frank Graham, *The New York Giants* (New York, 1952), pp. 3–6. The line score and the New York lineup are as follows:

| New York | 3 | 1 | 2 | 1 | 0 | 0 | 0 | 0 | 0 | 7 |
| Boston | 0 | 0 | 2 | 1 | 1 | 1 | 0 | 0 | 0 | 5 |

		Runs	Hits	Errors
Ewing	C	0	1	0
Connor	1B	1	2	0
Ward	CF	1	1	0
Gillespie	LF	1	2	0
Dorgan	RF	1	2	0
Caskin	2B	1	2	1
Welch	P			
Troy	SS	0	0	5
Hankinson	3B	1	1	0

3. *New York Clipper*, vol. XXXI, #8, May 12, 1883, p. 117; *New York Times*, May 3, 1883.

4. *New York Clipper*, vol. XXXI, #8, May 12, 1883, p. 117, *New York Times*, May 4, 1883 and the *New York Daily Tribune* of the same date.

5. *New York Daily Tribune*, May 4, 1883.

6. For Old Hoss Radbourne's official records, see *The Baseball Encyclopedia...*, pp. 731, 1259. In 1883 Radbourne won 49, lost 25, and had an earned run average of 2.05.

7. *Chicago Tribune*, May 6, 1883; *New York Clipper*, vol. XXXI, #8. May 12, 1883, p. 115; *New York Times*, May 5, 6, 8, 1883; *New York Daily Tribune*, May 5,6,8, 1883.

8. *New York Times*, May 5, 1883.

9. Quoted from Abram S. Hewitt's oration at the opening of the Brooklyn Bridge. See the *New York Times*, May 24, 25, 1883; Opening Ceremonies of the New York and

Brooklyn Bridge (Brooklyn, 1883); Alan Trachtenberg, *Brooklyn Bridge: Fact and Symbol* (New York. 1965). See also Allan Nevins, *Abram S. Hewitt with Some Account of Peter Cooper* (New York, 1935), pp. 447–50; see also Allan Nevins, ed., *Selected Writings of Abram S. Hewitt* (New York, 1937), pp. 295–311, for Hewitt's Brooklyn Bridge speech.

10. Romans 8:28 (KJV)

11. *New York Times*, May 24, 25, 26, 1883; see also Trachtenberg, op. cit., pp. 93–129; on this general topic of reactions to industrialization in America, see Leo Marx, *The Machine in the Garden* (New York, 1964).

12. For comments on the White Stockings of the eighties, see Voigt, *American Baseball...*, I, pp. 99–121; Seymour, *Baseball: The Early Years*, pp. 172–89; Anson, *A Ball Player's Career*, pp. 100–144. There is no use at all in looking at Warren Brown, *The Chicago Cubs* (New York, 1946). This book is breathtakingly bad. It is so confused, so incoherent, so full of errors, so badly written that it boggles and flabbergasts the reader.

13. *Chicago Tribune*, May 16, 17, 18, 1883; *New York Clipper*, vol. XXXI, #10, May 26, 1883, pp. 154–55; *New York Times*, May 16, 17, 18, 1883.

14. *New York Times*, June 1,2, 1883; *New York Clipper*, vol. XXXI, #12, June 9, 1883, pp. 188–189, and #13, June 16, 1883, p. 202.

15. *Chicago Tribune*, June 3, 1883; *New York Clipper*, vol. XXXI, #12, June 9, 1883, p. 186; *New York Times*, June 3, 1883; *New York Daily Tribune*, June 3, 1883.

16. *Chicago Tribune*, June 5, 6, 8, 1883; *New York Clipper*, vol. XXXI, #12, June 9, 1883, p. 186 and #13, June 16, 1883, p. 204; *New York Times*, June 5, 6, 8, 1883; *New York Daily Tribune*, June 5, 6, 8, 1883.

17. *New York Daily Tribune*, June 9, 1883; see also the *New York Clipper*, vol. XXXI, #13, June 16, 1883, p. 205, for a description of the anger of betters who had lost their wagers.

18. This poem is a "classic," if that is the word, of the anti-umpire genre that was popular in the eighties. It is quoted in Voigt, *American Baseball...*, I, p. 189, and is traced by him to the *Chicago Tribune*, August 15, 1886. It is also quoted in Seymour, *The Rise of Major League Baseball...*, p. 577, and is traced by him to the Washington *Critic*, in the *Official Base Ball Record*, August 20, 1886. See also the song by Monroe H. Rosenfeld, "Finnegan the Umpire," the title page of which is pictured in Durso, *The Days of Mr. McGraw*, between pp. 54 and 55. The title page of the song shows the umpire Finnegan, depicted as an oaf in a dress suit, being assaulted by bats and balls heaved by righteously indignant players. The whole question of umpire baiting and the reasons for it are covered admirably in Voigt, *American Baseball...*, I, pp. 183–92. See particularly Voigt, *America Through Baseball*, Chapter 11. Voigt's work on umpires and their role as "status abusers and arrogators" within the mythology of baseball fans is definitive.

19. *New York Daily Tribune*, June 10, 1883.

20. *New York Daily Tribune*, June 25, 1883.

21. *New York Clipper*, vol. XXXI, #17, July 14, 1883, pp. 268–69; *New York Times*, July 5. 1883; *New York Daily Tribune*, July 5, 1883.

22. *New York Times*, July 6, 1883; *New York Daily Tribune*, July 6, 9, 16, 1883.

23. *New York Daily Tribune*, July 19, 1883.

24. The Giants' record at the end of the road trip was 28 and 37. The team was five games behind fifth place Buffalo and only one game ahead of seventh place Detroit. See the *New York Times*, August 6, 1883.

25. *New York Daily Tribune*, August 6, 1883.

26. See the *New York Daily Tribune* for August 9, 13, 14, 20, 27, 29, 31, and September 1, 12, 15, 17, 19, 29, 1883, for games where even the box score has been omitted.

27. *Chicago Tribune*, September 30, 1883; *New York Clipper* vol. XXXI, #29, October 6, 1883, p. 468; *New York Times*, October 1, 1883; *Spalding's Official Base Ball Guide, 1884*, pp. 14 and 17; *The Baseball Encyclopedia...*, p. 60

28. *The Baseball Encyclopedia...*, p. 424.

29. *The Baseball Encyclopedia...*, p. 1351.

30. *The Baseball Encyclopedia...*, p. 361.

31. See Preston D. Orem, *Baseball (1845–1881)*.

32. *New York Daily Tribune*, July 9, 1883.

33. *New York Sun*, October 11, 1885; *New York Daily Tribune*, November 3, 1889.

Chapter Three

1. Alfred, Lord Tennyson, "Ulysses" (1842), lines 65-67.

2. On Fernando Wood, see Leonard Chalmers, "Tammany Hall, Fernando Wood, and the Struggle to Control New York City, 1857–1859," *The New-York Historical Quarterly*, Vol. LIII (January, 1969), #1, pp. 7–33; see also Edward K. Spann, *The New Metropolis. New York City. 1840–1857* (New York, 1981), chapters 12 through 15. See George Templeton Strong, *Diary*, eds. Allan Nevins and Milton H. Thomas (New York, 1952), 4 vols., vol. 2, pp. 343–45: see also Herbert Asbury, *The Gangs of New York: An Informal History* (New York, 1927), pp. 112–17.

3. Adrian Cook, *The Armies of the Streets: The New York City Draft Riots of 1863* (Lexington, Kentucky, 1974), is an excellent, careful and detailed book. See also Irving Werstein, *The Draft Riots. July 1863* (New York, 1971). See also James F. Richardson, *The New York Police. Colonial Times to 1901* (New York, 1970), chapter 6.

4. The tunnel, under Park Avenue, was the Fourth Street street railway access to Vanderbilt's Grand Central Terminal on 42nd Street.

5. Mark D. Hirsch, "Richard Croker: An Interim Report on the Early Career of a 'Boss' of Tammany Hall," in Irwin Yellowitz, ed., *Essays in the History of New York City: A Memorial to Sidney Pomerantz* (Port Washington, New York, 1978), pp. 106–107. See also Alfred Connable and Edward Silberfarb, *Tigers of Tammany: Nine Men Who Ran New York* (New York, 1967), Chapter 7 for a balanced and substantial account of Croker's leadership of Tammany and political career. See also Lincoln Steffens, *Autobiography*, pp. 234–38 for an account of an illuminating interview with Richard Croker.

6. Asbury, *The Gangs of New York...*, pp. 225–38.

7. Richardson, *The New York Police...*, particularly chapters 8, 9 and 12. See also A. E. Costello, *Our Police Protectors: History of the New York Police from the Earliest Period to the Present Time* (New York, 1885). The two books are quite different. Costello, a *New York Herald* police reporter, saw the cops as a strong force for decency, safety and order, at least until the Lexow Committee. Richardson, an ernest liberal writing in the sixties, emphasized violations of civil liberties, particularly among the poor. Asbury, *The Gangs of New York...*, p. 237.

8. On the general career of Inspector Williams up to 1885 see Costello, *Our Police Protectors*, pp. 364–69. For the rest, the Lexow Committee report will provide all that is needed.

9. James D. McCabe, Jr., *Lights and Shadows of New York Life: or, the Sights and Sensations of the Great City* (Philadelphia 1872).

10. Richard L. McCormick, *From Realignment to Reform, Political Change in New York State, 1893–1910* (Ithaca, New York, 1981), p. 21.

11. On this point see Leo Hershkowitz, *Tweed's New York* (New York, 1977), for a sympathetic view of Tweed; see also Lyle W. Dorsett, "Bosses and Machines in Urban America," in *Forums in History, FA 029* (1974), quoted in Mark D. Hirsch, "Richard Croker...," p. 103. See also Richard L. McCormick, *From Realignment to Reform...*, particularly chapter 1; see also Edward K. Spann, *The New Metropolis...*, particularly chapters 12 through 15. For an absolutely indispensable view of the institutions of city government in New York, see David T. Valentine, ed., *Manual of the Corporation of the City of New York* (New York, 1865). The Valentine manuals cover the years 1841–1866. See also the previously cited "memoirs" of George Washington Plunkitt.

12. On the Tweed era see Leo Hershkowitz, *Tweed's New York*, for the most detailed and scholarly review of the "Ring." A shorter recent work is Seymour Mandelbaum, *Boss Tweed's New York* (New York, 1965); for the traditional view see Denis Lynch, *"Boss" Tweed: The Story of a Grim Generation* (New York, 1927). See also Morton Keller, *The Art and Politics of Thomas Nast* (New York, 1968); see also, from a participant, Samuel J. Tilden, *The New York City "Ring": Its Origin, Maturity and Fall Discussed in a Reply to the* New York Times (New York, 1873); see also, *The Record of a Four Years' Campaign against Official Malversation in the City of New York. A.D. 1871 to 1875* (New York, 1875), a collection of the legal documents in the litigation against the Tweed "ring."

13. Allan Nevins, *Abram S. Hewitt...*, pp. 460–69.

14. Henry George was famous in advanced circles for his single tax treatise, *Progress and Poverty* (San Francisco, 1879).

15. See the little book by Louis F. Post and Fred C. Leubuscher, *Henry George's 1886 Campaign: An Account of the George-Hewitt Campaign in the New York Municipal Election of 1886* (New York, 1887) (1961 reprint). Assuming that no more than 20 percent of the Tammany votes were fraudulent, a reasonable figure for nineteenth century municipal elections, Hewitt really was the People's Choice.

16. Giuseppe di Tomasi di Lampedusa, *Il Gattopardo* (Milano, 1958), p. 21.

17. This favorable view of machine government is taken from the previously cited "memoirs" of George Washington Plunkitt, in *Plunkitt of Tammany Hall*.

18. John G. Sproat, *"The Best Men": Liberal Reformers in the Gilded Age* (New York, 1968), p. 275. This is an important book which presents an accurate and balanced view of patrician reform in Victorian America.

19. *Brooklyn Daily Union*, July 11, 1865, quoted in Harold Coffin Syrett, *The City of Brooklyn, 1865–1898: A Political History* (New York, 1944), p. 33.

20. Quoted in Syrett, *The City of Brooklyn...*, p. 106.

21. Syrett, *The City of Brooklyn...*, chapters 7,8,9. On the issues of efficiency, see the important book by Martin J. Schiesl, *The Politics of Efficiency, Municipal Administration and Reform in America. 1800–1920* (Berkeley, California, 1977). See also the previously cited Richard L. McCormick, *From Realignment to Reform...*, particularly chapter 1. See also Paul Boyer, *Urban Masses and Moral Order in America, 1820–1920* (Cambridge, Mass, 1978), particularly Part III.

22. Quoted in Morton Keller, ed., *Problems of Modern Democracy, Political and Economic Essays by Edwin Lawrence Godkin* (Cambridge, Mass., 1966), p. XXXI.

23. E. L. Godkin, "Business Administration," *The Nation*, LXI (October 24, 1985), p. 287.

24. Quoted from Boyer, *Urban Masses and Moral Order...*, p. 129. This important book is a key source for this paragraph and the one following. See also, Robert

Wiebe *The Search for Order* (New York, 1967), as well as, for example, Edward K. Spann, *Ideals and Politics: New York Intellectuals and Liberal Democracy, 1820–1880* (Albany, New York, 1972); see also David C. Hammack, *Power and Society: Greater New York at the Turn of the Century* (New York, 1982), particularly parts I and II. On the physical move uptown, see Charles Lockwood, *Manhattan Moves Uptown: An Illustrated History* (Boston, 1976). For the view of a participant in the struggle for genteel reform, see Rev. Charles Henry Parkhurst, *Our Fight with Tammany* (New York, 1895), dealing mainly with the Lexow Committee (1894) and its aftermath. There are, of course, many accounts by patrician reformers, both male and female, interested in charity, social uplift, education, crime, sanitation, housing, or all of the above. For another view of the drift of patrician opinion see also James Bryce, *The American Commonwealth* (New York, 1887), 2 vols., particularly vol. 2, see also E. L. Godkin, *Problems of Modern Democracy*, ed. Morton Keller (Cambridge, Mass., 1966); John Tomisich, *A Genteel Endeavor. American Culture and Politics in the Gilded Age* (Stanford, Calif., 1971); Moisei Ostrogorski, *Democracy and the Organization of Political Parties*, vol. 2: "The United States," (New York, 1905), pp. 94 forward; David Hammack, "Elite Perceptions of Power in the Cities of the United States, 1880–1900: The Evidence of James Bryce, Moisei Ostrogorski, and Their American Informants," *Journal of Urban History* 4 (1978), pp. 363–96.

25. *The Baseball Encyclopedia*..., pp. 531, 701.

26. Turkin and Thompson, *The Official Encyclopedia of Baseball*, p. 585; *The Baseball Encyclopedia*..., appendix C, p. 1525.

27. *Chicago Tribune*, May 2, 1884; *New York Times*, May 2, 1884; See also the *New York Daily Tribune*, May 2, 1884 for a restrained story that gave full credit for the victory to "...the bad play of the Chicago men." The line score was as follows:

Chicago	0	2	0	0	0	0	0	0	1	3
New York	1	3	0	1	2	0	4	4	x	15

The lineups were:

Chicago:			New York:		
	Dalrymple	LF		Ewing	C
	Gore	CF		Ward	CF
	Kelly	C/3B		Connor	2B
	Anson	1B		Gillespie	LF
	Williamson	3B/C		Dorgan	RF
	Burns	SS		McKinnon	1B
	Pfeiffer	2B		Welch	P
	Corcoran	P		Caskin	SS
	Sunday	RF		Hankinson	3B

28. *Chicago Tribune*, May 3, 1884; see also the *New York Times*. May 2, 3, 4, 6, 9, 10, 11, 14, 15, 16, 17, 1884 for comments and box scores on the Giants' twelve victories.

29. For Welch's record in 1884, see *The Baseball Encyclopedia*..., p. 1351; for Ward's record, p. 1345; for Begley's, p. 946; for Dorgan's p. 1027. See the *New York Times*, September 7, 1884 for Ewing's game as pitcher.

30. *Spalding's Official Base Ball Guide: 1885*, p. 21; *New York Times*, October 20, 1884; *The Baseball Encyclopedia*..., pp. 61–62.

31. For Radbourne's 1884 record, see *The Baseball Encyclopedia*..., p. 1259.

32. *New York Times*, October 21, 1884.

33. Robert Lewis Taylor, *W. C. Fields: His Follies and Fortunes* (New York, 1967), pp. 44–46.

34. Voigt, *American Baseball...* I, pp. 130–37; see also Seymour, *Baseball: The Early Years*, pp. 148–61.
35. Voigt, *American Baseball...*, I, p. 137; Seymour, *The Rise of Major League Baseball...*, pp. 350–51.
36. For Gerhardt's and O'Rourke's records, see *The Baseball Encyclopedia...*, pp. 457, 702.
37. Seymour, *The Rise of Major League Baseball...*, p. 230.
38. *New York Times*. May 3, 1885; *New York Daily Tribune*, May 3, 1885. The New York lineup was as follows:

O'Rourke	CF	Gillespie	LF	Richardson	RF
Connor	1B	Ward	SS	Welch	P
Ewing	C	Esterbrook	3B	Gerhardt	2B

39. The standings were tied on June 15, with both teams at 24 and 6. On June 22 the White Stockings had a two-and-one-half game lead; Chicago was 30 and 6 while New York was 27 and 8. See the *Chicago Tribune*, July 6, 1885; *New York Times*, June 15, 22, 1885.
40. *Chicago Tribune*, July 4, 5, 7, 1885; *New York Times*, July 4, 5, 7, 1885.
41. *New York Times*, September 2, 1885.
42. *New York Times*, July 19, 21, 1885.
43. *New York Times*, July 23, 1885.
44. *New York Times*, August 2, 3, 1885.
45. *Chicago Tribune*, August 2, 1885. The *New York Times* August 2, 1885 gave this game almost two full columns. See also the *New York Daily Tribune*, August 2, 1885.
46. *New York Times*, August 11, 1885.
47. *New York Daily Tribune*, August 31, 1885.
48. *New York Times*, October 1, 1885.
49. *New York Times*, August 31, 1885.
50. *Spalding's Official Base Ball Guide: 1886*, pp. 65–66; *Chicago Tribune*, September 27, 30, October 1, 2, 4, 1885; *New York Sun*, October 2, 3, 1885; *New York Clipper*, vol. XXXIII, #30, October 10, 1885, pp. 473, 478; *New York Times*, September 30, October 1, 2, 3, 4, 1885.
51. "The Song of the Chicagos" was reprinted from the *Chicago Tribune* in the *New York Clipper*, vol. XXXIII, #32, October 24, 1885, p. 505.
52. *Chicago Tribune*, October 4, 1885. This was in a front page advertisement.
53. *New York Times*, October 12, 1885.
54. *New York Daily Tribune*, May 18, August 31, 1885.
55. *New York Daily Tribune*, October 11, 1885.
56. *New York Clipper*, vol. XXXIII, #31, October 17, 1885, p. 489; *New York Sun*, October 11, 1885; *The Baseball Encyclopedia...*, p. 64.
57. *New York Daily Tribune*, October 11, 1885.
58. *Spalding's Official Base Ball Guide: 1885*, pp. 97–98.
59. *The Sporting News*, vol. 1 #9, May 10, 1886, p. 2; *New York Clipper*, vol. XXXIV, #8, May 8, 1886, p. 116; *New York Times*, April 30, 1886. The line score and the New York lineup are as follows (see also the *New York Sun*, April 30, 1886):

Boston	0	2	0	0	0	0	0	0	0	1	1	0	4
New York	0	0	2	1	0	0	0	0	0	0	1	1	5

O'Rourke	CF	Gillespie	LF	Welch	P
Connor	1B	Dorgan	RF	Ward	SS
Ewing	C	Esterbrook	3B	Gerhardt	2B

60. *New York Daily Tribune*, May 16, 1886: *New York Sun*, May 14, 16, 21, June 3, 1886.

61. *The Sporting News*, vol. 1, #13, June 7, 1886, p. 2;
New York Clipper, vol. XXXIV, #12, June 5, 1886, p. 179; *New York Times*, May 31, June 1, 1886: *New York Sun*, June 1, 1886.

62. *Spalding's Official Base Ball Guide: 1887*, p. 20; *New York Clipper*, vol. XXXIV, #31, October 16, 1886, p. 490; *The Baseball Encyclopedia...*, p. 66.

63. *New York Daily Tribune*, July 20, 1886. See also the *New York Sun*, May 6, 1886.

64. On the Gore trade see *The Sporting News*, vol. 2, #15, November 27, 1886, p. 1; for Tiernan's official records, see *The Baseball Encyclopedia...*, p. 848.

65. *The Baseball Encyclopedia...*, p. 1526.

66. *The Sporting News*, vol. 3, #8, April 30, 1887, p. 2; *New York Clipper*, vol. XXXV, #8, May 7, 1887, p. 121; *New York Times*, April 29, 1887. The Giants' lineup was as follows:

Ewing	2B	O'Rourke	C	Richardson	3B
Ward	SS	Gillespie	LF	Keefe	P
Connor	1B	Dorgan	RF	Tiernan	CF

67. *New York Times*, May 11, 1887.

68. *New York Daily Tribune*, May 15, 1887.

69. *New York Daily Tribune*, July 13, 1887.

70. The full text of Ward's statement is in the *New York Times* and the *New York Daily Tribune* of July 14, 1887. See also *The Sporting News*, vol. 3, #19, July 16, 1887, p. 1.

71. *New York Daily Tribune*, July 14, 1887.

72. *Spalding's Official Base Ball Guide: 1888*, p. 25; *New York Clipper*, vol. XXXV, #31, October 15, 1887; *New York Times*, October 10, 1887; *The Baseball Encyclopedia...*, p. 67.

73. *New York Clipper*, vol. XXXV, #32, October 22, 1887, p. 509; *New York Times*, June 7, 1887; see *Spalding's Official Base Ball Guide: 1888*, pp. 58–60, for the inflated batting averages under the 1887 scoring rules; see *The Baseball Encyclopedia...*, p. 875, for Ward's average recomputed according to the modern standards.

74. See the *New York Times*, May 21, 31, 1887 for George's efforts in the box. For George's official records, see *The Baseball Encyclopedia...*, p. 1067; for Ledell Titcomb's records, p. 1331; for Mickey Welch's records, p. 1351; for Tim Keefe's records, p. 1134.

75. *New York Daily Tribune*, October 9, 1887.

Chapter Four

1. Clarkson, a rather irritable and unpleasant man, was one of the best pitchers in baseball, one of the few players in the history of the game to win over 300 games. For Clarkson's official records, see *The Baseball Encyclopedia...*, p. 994. Like Kelly before

him, Clarkson was sold to Boston for $10,000, a move that Cap Anson deeply regretted. See A. C. Anson, *A Ball Player's Career*, pp. 139–40. On preseason speculation about the pennant race, see *New York Clipper*, vol. XXXVI, #7, April 28, 1888, p. 109. See also *The Press* (New York), March 25, 1888, for one of the rare articles that took an optimistic view of he Giants' chances to win.

2. See Charles Lockwood *Manhattan Moves Uptown*, particularly Chapter 14.
3. *The Press* (New York), April 20, 1888; *New York Daily Tribune*, April 22, 1888.
4. *New York Clipper*, vol. XXXVI, #9, May 12, 1888, pp. 141–42; *The Press* (New York), April 28, 1888; *New York Times*, April 28, 1888. Keefe's first game was a victory over Boston, 6 to 1. See *New York Times* and *The Press* (New York), May 2, 1888.
5. *New York Times* and *New York Daily Tribune*, March 13–18, 1888.
6. *The Baseball Encyclopedia...*, p. 1526.
7. *New York Daily Tribune*, September 2, 1888.
8. *New York Clipper*, vol. XXXVI, #7, April 28, 1888, p. 111, *New York Times*, April 21, 1888; *The Press* (New York), April 21, 1888. Only 2647 spectators saw the game, far fewer than New York's standard opening day crowd. The Giants' lineup follows:

Gore	LF	Ewing	3B	Foster	CF
Tiernan	RF	Ward	SS	Murphy	C
Connor	1B	Richardson	2B	Titcomb	P

9. *New York Clipper*, vol. XXXVI, #8, May 5, 1888, p. 126; *The Press* (New York), April 26, 1888; *New York Times*, April 26, 1888.
10. *New York Daily Tribune*, April 26, 1888.
11. DeWolf Hopper and W. W. Stout, *The Reminiscences of DeWolf Hopper: Once A Clown Always A Clown* (Garden City, New York, 1925), pp. 72–98. Hopper placed the date of this great event on May 13, 1888. The Giants and Chicago were indeed playing each other on that date, but they were doing it in Chicago. On August 13, however, the Giants and White Stockings were in New York, and boxes were reserved for the players at Wallach's Theater, while McCaull's Opera Company, which included Hopper, was invited to the game. See the *New York Times*, August 12, 1888. Hopper was very clear on the May date, however, linking it with something he was not likely to forget, the illness of a child. I have no explanation for the inconsistencies aforementioned. See also Martin Gardner, *The Annotated Casey at the Bat* (New York, 1967), pp. 3–5.
12. *The Press* (New York), May 5, 1888; *New York Daily Tribune*, May 6, 1888.
13. *The Press* (New York), May 25, 1888; *New York Daily Tribune*, May 27, 1888.
14. *New York Times*, May 19, 1888.
15. *New York Daily Tribune*, April 29, 1888.
16. *The Sporting News*, Vol. 5, #18, July 14, 1888, p. 4; *New York Times*, June 5, 1888; *The Press* (New York), June 5, 1888.
17. *New York Times*, June 17, 1888; *The Press* (New York), June 17, 1888; for Whitney's official records, see *The Baseball Encyclopedia...*, p.889.
18. *New York Times*, June 24, 1888; *The Press* (New York), June 24, 1888; for an overview of Keefe's winning streak, see Turkin and Thompson, *Official Encyclopedia of Baseball...*, p. 502.
19. *New York Times*, July 5, 1888; *The Press* (New York), July 5, 1888; *The Sporting News*, vol. 5, #19, July 21, 1888, p. 2; *The Press* (New York), July 15, 17, 18, 22, 1888; *New York Times*, July 15, 17, 18, 22, 1888.
20. *The Sporting News*, vol. 5 #20, July 28, 1888, p. 1.
21. *New York Daily Tribune*, July 29, 1888.
22. *The Sporting News*, vol. 5, #20, July 28, 1888, p. 3; *New York Clipper*, vol.

XXXVI, #20, July 28, 1888, p. 318; *The Press* (New York), July 24, 1888; *New York Times*, July 24, 1888.

23. *The Sporting News*, vol. 5, #21, August 4, 1888, p. 1; *The Press* (New York), July 29, 1888; *New York Times*, July 29, 1888.

24. *New York Clipper*, vol. XXXVI, #21, August 4, 1888, p. 333, #22, August 11, 1888, pp. 349–50; *The Sporting News*, vol. 5, #21, August 4, 1888, pp. 3, 6; *New York Daily Tribune*, August 1, 1888; *The Press* (New York), July 29, August 1, 1888; *New York Times*, August 1, 1888.

25. *New York Clipper*, vol. XXXVI, #23, August 18, 1888, p. 366; *The Press* (New York), August 12, 1888; *New York Times* August 1, 2, 3, 4, 5, 7, 8, 9, 10, 11, 12, 1888; *The Sporting News*, vol. 4, #22, August 11, 1888, p. 3, #23, August 18, 1888, p. 3.

26. *New York Clipper*, vol. XXXVI, #31, October 13, 1888, p. 498; The *Chicago Tribune*, October 5, 1888, *New York Daily Tribune*, October 5, 1888.

27. *Spirit of the Times*, vol. 116, #12, October 13, 1888, p. 450, #13, October 20, 1888, p. 488; *New York Clipper*, vol. XXXVI, #32, October 20, 1888, p. 513; *New York Daily Tribune*, October 15, 1888: *The Press* (New York), October 15, 1888.

28. *The Baseball Encyclopedia...*, pp. 68–69, 361–62, 424, 1134.

29. On the evolution of Spalding's career, see Arthur Bartlett, *Baseball and Mr. Spalding: The History and Romance of Baseball* (New York, 1951), pp. 200–284.

30. *St. Louis Post-Dispatch*, October 1, 5, 8, 13, 1888; The *Chicago Tribune*, October 5, 1888; *The Press* (New York), October 5, 1888; *New York Clipper* vol. XXXVI, #31, October 13, 1888, p. 497; *The Sporting News*, vol. 5 #26, September 8, 1888, p. 1, vol. 6, #1, September 15, 1888, p. 1, #2, September 22, 1888, p. 1, #3, September 29, 1888, p. 3. The above sources deal with the negotiations for the series. The letter from Chris von der Ahe to A. H. Spink authorizing the train expenditure, and Spink's description of the trip can be found in A. H. Spink, *The National Game* (St. Louis, 1910), pp. 298–300.

31. *New York Clipper*, vol. XXXVI, #33, October 27, 1888, pp. 529–30; *The Sporting News*, vol. 6, #6, October 20, p. 1; *New York Times*, October 17, 1888; *New York Daily Tribune*, October 17, 1888; *The Press* (New York), October 17, 1888; see also John C. Tattersall, *The Early World Series, 1884–1890* (privately printed in Havertown, Pennsylvania, 1976), p. 44. Tattersall has published Xerox copies of the stories and box scores of the world series games, appending a statistical summary of the teams and players. Most of the stories are by Tim Murnane and were printed in the *Boston Herald*. The batting orders were as follows:

New York		St. Louis	
Tiernan	RF	Latham	3B
Ewing	C	Robinson	2B
Richardson	2B	O'Neill	LF
Connor	1B	Comiskey	1B
Ward	SS	McCarthy	RF
Slattery	CF	Lyons	CF
O'Rourke	LF	White	SS
Whitney	3B	Boyle	C
Keefe	P	King	P

See also the more recent book on early baseball championships by Jerry Lansche, *The Forgotten Championships: Postseason Baseball. 1882-1981* (Jefferson, North Carolina, 1989), p. 28. The championship trophy, incidentally, was called the Dauvray Cup, after Helen Dauvray, wife of John Montgomery Ward, who had thought of the idea of a large silver trophy.

32. *New York Clipper*, vol. XXXVI, #33, October 27, 1888, pp. 529–30; *St. Louis Post-Dispatch*, October 17, 1888; *The Press* (New York), October 18, 1888; *New York Times*, October 18, 1888; *The Sporting News*, vol. 6, #6, October 20, 1888, p. 1; Tattersall, *The Early World Series...*, p. 45; on the reaction of the St. Louis kranks to this victory see A. H. Spink, *The National Game*, pp. 298–300. See also Lansche, *The Forgotten Championships*, p. 28.

33. *St. Louis Post-Dispatch*, October 18, 19, 20, 21, 22, 1888; *New York Times*, October 19, 20, 21, 23, 1888; *The Sporting News*, vol. 6, #6, October 20, 1888, p. 1; *New York Clipper*, vol. XXXVI, #33, October 27, 1888, pp. 529–30; *The Press* (New York), October 19, 20, 21, 23, 1888; Tattersall, *The Early World Series...*, pp. 46–51. See also Lansche, *The Forgotten Championships*, pp. 29–30.

34. *St. Louis Post-Dispatch*, October 24, 25, 1888; The *New York Times*, October 25, 26, 1888; *The Press* (New York), October 25, 26, 1888; *New York Clipper*, vol. XXXVI, 334, November 3, 1888, p. 545. There were two scheduled series games left and both were played. St. Louis won them, 14 to 11 and 18 to 7. Ward, Keefe, Ewing, and Crane did not play for the Giants. See the *New York Times*, October 27, 28, 1888. For the end of the series see Tattersall, *The Early World Series...*, pp. 52–56. In the 1888 series Ward hit .379 and stole six bases, while Ewing hit .346, Tiernan .310, and Connor .304. Keefe won four games without a loss, and had an earned run average of 0.51. See Tattersall, *The Early World Series...*, p. 56. The Series brought in revenues of $24,362.10, with expenses running at $8,000. Each New York player received $200 for the series. See *Spalding's Official Base Ball Guide: 1889*, p. 84. See also Lansche, *The Forgotten Championships*, pp. 31–32.

35. For an exhaustive description of that tour see A. C. Anson, *A Ball Player's Career*, pp. 144–273; see also *The Press* April 7, 1889; Henry Clay Palmer, J. A. Fynes, Frank Richter, W. I. Harris, *Athletic Sports in America, England, and Australia* (Philadelphia, 1889), pp. 151–460. *The Sporting News* took a hostile view of the great tour. See, for example, the article entitled: "The Grand Laugh: That is What Spalding and His Fakirs are Getting," in vol. 6, #21, February 2, 1889, p. 3.

36. *New York Times*, June 17, July 15, 1888; *The Press* (New York), July 16, 1888; *The Sporting News*, vol. , #19, July 21, 1888, p. 4.

37. *New York Times*, February 9, March 22, 28, 31, 1889; *New York Daily Tribune*, February 9, 1889; *The Press* (New York), February 8, 10, March 22, 28, 31, 1889; *The Sporting News*, vol. 7, #5, April 13, 1889, p. 1.

38. *New York Daily Tribune*, April 24, May 9, 10, 12, 1889; *New York Times*, April 25, May 10, 1889; *The Sporting News*, vol. 6, #10, November 17, 1888, pp. 1, 4; see vol. 7, #4, April 6, 1889, p. 2 for statements that Ward was going to Boston for $15,000. See *The Sporting News*, vol. 6, #11, November 24, 1888, p. 2, #22, February 9, 1889, p. 1, #26, March 9, 1889, p. 1, vol. 7, #2, March 23, 1889, p. 1, #3, March 30, 1889, p. 1; see #4, April 6, 1889, p. 1, for stories on Washington's efforts to get Ward as manager. See *The Press* (New York), March 25, 31, April 1, 2, 1889, for Ward's final refusal to go to Washington. On Tim Keefe see *The Sporting News*, vol. 7, #6, April 30, 1889, p. 5, #10, May 18, 1889, p. 1; *The Press* (New York), May 10, 1889. For Ward's signing, see *The Press* (New York), April 25, 1889.

39. *New York Clipper*, vol. XXXVII, 38, May 4, 1889, p. 128; *The Sporting News*, vol. 7, #7, April 27, 1889, p. 3; See *The Press* (New York), April 25, 1889, for a front-page article on the game. See also the *New York Times*, April 25, 1889; *New York Daily Tribune*, April 25, 1889.

40. *New York Daily Tribune*, June 2, 1889; see also David Voigt, *American Baseball...*, I, p. 119.

41. *New York Times*, June 1-8, 1889; See the *New York Daily Tribune*, June 1-8, 1889, for extensive coverage of the flood. Stories on the flood continued in both papers for the rest of the month. See also Herman Dieck, *The Johnstown Flood* (n. p., 1889), as an example of the numerous books written immediately after the flood to satisfy the public's demand for material on the disaster. See the horrible book by Duke Bailie, *Through Mighty Waters Saved: A Romance of the Johnstown Destruction* (Chicago, 1889), an example of Victorian sentimentality at its worst. An excellent modern monograph on the flood is David G. McCullough, *The Johnstown Flood* (New York, 1968). McCullough assembled all of the available records, including the Pennsylvania Railroad inquiry, which had not been previously consulted. He also talked with the few survivors of the flood. This is a comprehensive and well-written book. See also Tom L. Johnson, *My Story* (New York, 1911), pp. 33-47. The quotation is taken from McCullough, *The Johnstown Flood*, p. 219.

42. The other two are: "Never give a sucker an even break," and "It won't heal if you keep scratching it." This is the opinion of H. L. Mencken.

43. *New York Times*, May 30, June 8, 11, 13, 22, 27, 1889; *The Press* (New York), June 10, 23, 1889; *New York Daily Tribune*, June 22, 23, 30, 1889; *New York Clipper*, vol. XXXVI, #16, June 29, 1889, p. 261.

44. *The Sporting News*, vol. 7, #10, May 18, 1889, pp. 1, 2; *The Baseball Encyclopedia...*, pp. 1042, 1094, 1331; *New York Daily Tribune*, May 16, 1889; *New York Times*, June 26, 27, 28, 29, 30, July 2, 3, 5, 6, 7, 1889.

45. *New York Daily Tribune*, May 19, 1889.

46. *New York Daily Tribune*, June 24, 1889.

47. *New York Clipper*, vol. XXXVI, #18, July 13, 1889, p. 296; *The Press* (New York), July 9, 1889; *New York Daily Tribune*, July 9, 1889.

48. *New York Daily Tribune*, July 22, 1889.

49. *New York Times*, July 23, 24, 25, 26, 27, 28, 30, 31, 1889.

50. *The Sporting News*, vol. 8, #24, August 24, 1889, p. 5; *The Press* (New York), August 20, 21, 22, 1889; *New York Daily Tribune*, August 4, 11, 14, 16, 17, 18, 20, 21, 22, 1889; *New York Times*, August 4, 11, 14, 16, 17, 18, 20, 21, 22, 1889.

51. *Chicago Tribune*, September 15, 1889; *The Press* (New York), September 15, 1889; *New York Times*, September 4, 15, 1889; *The Sporting News*, vol. 9, #2, September 21, 1889, p. 3.

52. *New York Daily Tribune*, July 16, 1889; *New York Times*, August 30, 31, September 1, 3, 15, 1889.

53. *New York Clipper*, vol. XXXVII, #28, September 21, 1889, p. 468; *The Press* (New York), September 17, 27, 1889; *New York Times*, September 17, 19, 20, 21, 22, 24, 25, 26, 27, 1889; *New York Daily Tribune*, September 22, 1889.

54. *The Sporting News*, vol. 9, #4, October 5, 1889, pp. 5, 6; *New York Daily Tribune*, October 3, 1889; *The Press* (New York), October 3, 1889, covered the story on page one.

55. For a recapitulation of the close pennant race, see *Spalding's Official Base Ball Guide: 1890*, pp. 71-74; *New York Times*, October 6, 1889; *The Sporting News*, vol. 9, #5, October 12, 1889, p. 2; *The Press* (New York), October 6, 1889; *New York Daily Tribune*, October 6, 1889; *New York Clipper*, vol. XXXVII, #31, October 12, 1889, pp. 520-21.

56. *New York Times*, October 7, 1889; *The Press* (New York), October 7, 1889; *New York Daily Tribune*, October 7, 1889.

57. *New York Clipper*, vol. XXXVII #33, October 26, 1889, p. 555; see *The Sporting News*, vol. 9, #6, October 19, 1889, p. 1, for details on the format of the series, and

vol. 9, #7, October 26, 1889, p. 3, for information and box scores of the first game. See also *The Press* (New York), October 19, 1889; *New York Times*, October 19, 1889. See also Lansche, *The Forgotten Championships*, pp. 34–35.

58. *New York Clipper*, vol. XXXVII, #33, October 26, 1889, p. 555; *New York Times*, October 20, 1889; *The Press* (New York), October 20, 1889; *The Sporting News*, vol. 9, #7, October 26, 1889, p. 3; *Spalding's Official Base Ball Guide: 1890*, p. 117 gives the attendance at the game as 16,172. See alsoTattersall, *The Early World Series...*, pp. 58–59. See also Lansche, *The Forgotten Championships*, pp. 35–36.

59. *New York Clipper*. vol. XXXVII, #34, November 2, p. 571; Tattersall, *The Early World Series...*, pp. 59–62: *New York Times*, October 23, 24, 1889; *The Press* (New York), October 23, 24, 1889; *The Sporting News*, vol. 9, #7, October 26, 1889, p. 3. See also Lansche, *The Forgotten Championships*, pp. 36–37.

60. *New York Clipper*, vol. XXXVII, #34, November 2, 1889, pp. 571–72, #35, November 9, 1889, p. 587; Tattersall, *The Early World Series...*, pp. 62–75; *The Sporting News*, vol. 9, #7, October 26, 1889, p. 3, #8, November 2, 1889, pp. 4–5; *New York Times*, October 25, 26, 27, 29, 30, 1889; *The Press* (New York), October 25, 26, 27, 29, 30, 1889. See also Lansche, *The Forgotten Championships*, pp. 37–40.

61. Spirit of The Times, vol. 118, #13, October 19, 1889, p. 520; *New York Clipper*, vol. XXXVII, #32, October 19, 1889, p. 539, #33, October 26, 1889, p. 555; *The Press* (New York) October 21, 1889; *New York Times*, October 21, 1889; *New York Daily Tribune*, October 21, 1889; David Voigt, *American Baseball...*, I, pp. 119–120.

Chapter Five

1. *New York Times*, October 29, 1889. The reserve lists were published in the *New York Times*, October 20, 1889.

2. Lee Allen, *The National League Story: The Official History* (New York, 1961), p. 57.

3. Text of the amended National Agreement, which includes the limitation rule is in the *New York Clipper*, vol. XXXIII, #32, October 24, 1885, p. 505.

4. *Spalding's Official Base Ball Guide: 1890*, p. 19.

5. *Spalding's Official Base Ball Guide: 1890*, pp. 19–21; Seymour, *The Rise of Major League Baseball...*, p. 238a.

6. All three quotes are from *Spalding's Official Base Ball Guide: 1884*, pp. 41–44.

7. *New York Clipper*, vol. XXXV, #28, September 24, 1887, p. 442; #30, October 8, 1887, p. 477; #37, November 26, 1887, p. 591.

9. Quoted in Seymour, *The Rise of Major League Baseball...*, pp. 231–32. On matters of baseball law and management Seymour is completely authoritative. See also *The Sporting Life's Official Base Ball Guide and Hand-Book of the National Game for 1891*, ed. Francis Richter (Philadelphia, 1891), pp. 28–29. There has, of course, been no permanent resolution to the problems of institutional and management structure in professional baseball. The owners' views prevailed, generally speaking, until 1975, when the Andy Messersmith arbitration decision by Peter Seitz, the most important man in modern baseball, shifted the balance in favor of the players. Other issues, unknown in the nineteenth century, have emerged, the most important being the medium of television. But, while the specifics have changed, the basic issues seem remarkable similar. The Messersmith arbitration case refought the legal issue in the Brotherhood War, and Seitz's decision changed the results of that conflict. Television has emphasized and reinforced, though it did not invent, the differences between large

markets (New York) and small ones (Louisville or Pittsburgh). In a general way, the issues have remained the same: control of the game, division of the income, allocation of franchises. But the numbers have changed. A lot. The modern problems of baseball are beyond the scope of this essay, but a couple of books, as a beginning, can be cited. See Roger Noll, ed., *Government and the Sports Business* (Washington, D.C., 1974), a Brookings Institution study on the eve of the Seitz decision, and Robert Berry, William Gould IV, and Paul Standohar, *Labor Relations in Professional Sports* (Dover, Massachusetts, 1986).

    10. *The Sporting News*, vol. 3, #26, September 3, 1887, p. 1; vol. 4, #9, November 19, 1887, p. 7; #10, November 26, 1887, p. 4; *New York Clipper*, vol. XXXV, #37, November 26, 1887, p. 591.

    11. *New York Times*, June 11, 1888; *The Press* (New York), June 11, 1888; Seymour, *The Rise of Major League Baseball...*, p. 480.

    12. John Stayton, "Baseball Jurisprudence," *American Law Review*, vol. XLIV (May-June, 1910), pp. 380–81. See also David Voigt, *American Baseball...*, I, p. 155 for a witty comment on Ward's letter.

    13. All preceding quotes are from the *New York Times*, July 17, 1887. This letter is an abstract of the important article by John Montgomery Ward, "Is the Base-Ball Player a Chattel?" *Lippincott's Magazine*, vol. XL (August, 1887), pp. 310–19. This article has remained a living part of the continuing arguments over the reserve clause. See, for example, E. C. Alft, "The Development of Baseball as a Business: 1876–1900," *Study of Monopoly Power: Hearings before the Subcommittee on Study of Monopoly Power of the Committee on the Judiciary. House of Representatives. Eighty-Second Congress. First Session* (Serial I, part 6, Organized Baseball) (United States Government Printing Office, Washington, D. C., 1952), pp. 1432–43. See also comments by Ward in 1886 and 1887 in Palmer et al., *Athletic Sports in America...*, pp. 145, 146; *New York Clipper*, vol. XXXV, #1, March 19, 1887, p. 8 ; #29, October 1, 1887, p. 460.

    14. John Montgomery Ward, "Is the Base-Ball Player a Chattel?" *Lippincott's Magazine*, vol. XL (August, 1887), p. 311.

    15. *New York Times*, September 24, 1888. See also John M. Ward, "Our National Game," *The Cosmopolitan*, vol. V, #6 (October, 1888), pp. 442–55. In this article Ward did say, however, that he did not wish to destroy the reserve clause, merely reform it.

    16. It is not at all clear *why* this test case was not undertaken. It would have settled the problem once and for all, and Ward appeared confident of victory. This confidence was well placed. In 1890, when the Giants sued Ewing to keep him with the club, Buck won his case. See *Metropolitan Exhibition Company v. Ewing*, (Circuit Court, Southern Division, New York, March 25, 1890), *The Federal Reporter*, XLII 205; *New York Clipper*, vol. XXXVIII, #2, March 22, 1890, p. 25; #4, April 5, 1890, p. 57.

    17. *The Sporting Life's Official Base Ball Guide...* for 1891, p. 30; *The Sporting News*, vol. 6, #11, November 24, 1888, p. 2; *The Press* (New York), November 22, 23, 1888; *New York Clipper*, vol. XXXVI, #38, December 1, 1887, p. 609.

    18. *New York Times*, July 18, 1889; *New York Clipper*, vol.. XXXVII, #12, June 1, 1889, p. 195; #13, June 8, 1889, p. 211; Seymour, *The Rise of Major League Baseball...*, p. 482.

    19. *New York Clipper*, vol. XXXVII, #18, July 13, 1889, p. 295. For a contemporary comment on this crucial meeting see O. P. Caylor, "Opening of the Base-Ball Season of 1890," *Harper's Weekly*, vol. XXXIV, #1741 (May 3, 1890), pp. 353–56. See also *The Sporting News*, vol. 7, #15, June 22, 1889, p. 1; #16, June 29, 1889, p. 1; *New York Clipper*, vol. XXXVII, #17, July 6, 1889, p. 277.

    20. Most of the information contained herein came from Tom Johnson, *My Story*,

pp. 9–108. See also the detailed and excellent study by Hoyt Landon Warner, *Progressivism in Ohio, 1897–1917* (Columbus, Ohio, 1964), pp. 54–211, for an examination of Johnson in politics. See also *The Street Railway Journal*, vol. VI (January, 1890), p. 26, for information on the Johnson ownership of the South Side Street Railway Companies in Brooklyn in 1890. See also Eugene C. Murdsock, "Cleveland's Johnson: At Home," *Ohio State Archaeological and Historical Quarterly*, vol. LXIII (October, 1954), pp. 319–35, for information on the career of Albert Johnson.

21. *The Sporting News*, vol. 9, #1, September 14, 1889, p. 1; see #2, September 21, 1889, p. 1, for the Johnson interview; #3, September 28, 1889, pp. 3, 4; *New York Daily Tribune*, September 15, 1889; *The Sporting Life's Official Base Ball Guide ... for 1891*, p. 31; *New York Clipper*, vol. XXXVII, #29, September 28, 1889, p. 485.

22. *The Sporting News*, vol. 9, #7, October 26, 1889, p. 3; *New York Times*, September 20, 1889; *The Press* (New York), September 30, October 27, 1889.

23. *The Sporting News*, vol. 9, #5, October 12, 1889, p. 1; *The Press* (New York), October 10, 1889; *New York Clipper*, vol. XXXVII, #32, October 19, 1889, p. 539.

24. *New York Times*, October 14, 1889; *The Press* (New York), October 27, 1889.

25. There is a certain amount of literature on cooperation, though not a whole lot because cooperation never amounted to much. It remained the dream of middle class reformers, and most cooperative ventures ended as failures. They were victims of the persistent hostility of more orthodox corporations, insufficient capital, and the inability to find a satisfactory role for workers hired after the charter members had started the venture. One contemporary commentary on cooperation is Herbert B. Adams, ed., *History of Co-operation in the United States. The Johns Hopkins University Studies in Historical and Political Science*, vol. VI (Baltimore, 1888). It states, on page nine, that "one of the prime conditions of success of cooperation is the moral integrity of the co-operators. The cause of failure is more frequently ethical than intellectual weakness." For modern works on cooperation see Jonathan Grossman, *William Sylvis. Pioneer of American Labor, Columbia University Studies in History, Economics, and Public Law*, no. 516 (New York, 1945), or the appropriate chapters in John Commons, et al., *History of Labour in the United States*, 4 vols. (New York, 1918–1935), II, pp. 430–39. See also Kirkland, *Industry Comes of Age...*, pp. 356–99; and Norman Ware, *The Labour Movement in the United States 1860–1895: A Study in Democracy* (New York, 1929), pp. 320–34.

26. *New York Times*, September 23, 24, October 14, 22, 24, 29, November 2, 3, 5, 8, 10, 1889; *New York Daily Tribune*, October 30, November 5, 7, 8, 9, 10, 11, 1889; *The Sporting Life's Official Base Ball Guide ... for 1891*, pp. 73–75; *The Press* (New York), October 30, November 2, 3, 5, 7, 8, 1889; *Reach's Official Base Ball Guide ... for 1891*, pp. 15–16; *New York Clipper*, vol. XXXVII, #35, November 9, 1889, p. 588; #36, November 16, 1889, p. 603; *The Sporting News*, vol. 8, #3, September 28, 1889, p. 3.

27. Spalding, *America's National Game...*, pp. 272–73; *New York Times*, November 5, 1889; *New York Daily Tribune*, November 5, 1889; *The Press* (New York), November 5, 1889.

28. *The Sporting News*, vol. 9, #11, November 23, 1889; *Spalding's Official Base Ball Guide: 1890*, p. 25; *New York Times*, November 14, 15, 1889; *New York Daily Tribune*, November 12, 13, 14, 15, 1889; *The Press* (New York), November 13, 14, 15, 16, 1889; *Reach's Official Base Ball Guide: 1890*, p. 14; *New York Clipper*, vol. XXXVII, #36, November 16, 1889, p. 604; #37, November 23, 1889, p. 619; #39, December 7, 1889, p. 651.

29. Spalding, *America's National Game...*, pp. 273–77; *Spalding's Official Base Ball Guide: 1890*, pp. 28–31; *New York Times*, November 22, 1889; *The Press* (New York), November 22, 1889; *New York Clipper*, vol. XXXVII, #38, November 30, 1889, pp. 634–35.

30. Arthur Bartlett, *Baseball and Mr. Spalding...*, p. 146.

31. See the *New York Clipper*, vol. XXXVII, #26, September 7, 1889, p. 431, for the announcement that Spalding had bought out Reach's Philadelphia retail store. This was a fairly typical step in Spalding's drive toward monopoly. See Bartlett, *Baseball and Mr. Spalding...*, pp. 99–101, 110–11, 146–47, 219–39; see Spalding, *America's National Game...*, pp. 217–39, 269–85, 531–42, for Spalding's general outlook on life and baseball. See also Voigt, *American Baseball...*, I, pp. 215–19.

32. *New York Clipper*, vol. XXXVII, #34, November 2, 1889, p. 571; *New York Times*, October 22, 29, 1889; *The Press* (New York), November 2, 1889.

33. *New York Times*, November 2, 1889; *The Press* (New York), November 2, 1889.

34. *New York Times*, November 8, 22, 1889; *The Press* (New York), November 24, 1889; *New York Clipper*, vol. XXXVII, #36, November 16, 1889, p. 603.

35. *New York Clipper*, vol. XXXVII, #37, November 23, 1889, p. 619; #38, November 30, 1889, p. 635; #39, December 7, 1889, p. 651; #40, December 14, 1889, p. 667; #41, December 21, 1889, p. 683; #42, December 28, 1889, p. 699; *New York Times*, November 13, 15, 22, 23, 25, 26, 27, 30, 1889; *The Press* (New York), November 13, 14, 16, December 16, 17, 1889; *New York Daily Tribune*, November 12, 1889.

36. The rosters of the players on the teams in the three leagues can be found in O. P. Caylor, "Opening of the Baseball Season of 1890," *Harper's Weekly*, vol. XXXIV, #1741, May 3, 1890, pp. 353–56.

37. *The Press* (New York), January 19, 1890.

38. *New York Daily Tribune*, November 10, 1889.

39. *New York Clipper*, vol. XXXVII, #36, November 16, 1889, p. 603.

40. *The Press* (New York), November 15, December 22, 1889, *New York Clipper*, vol. XXXVII, #42, December 28, 1889, p. 700.

41. *New York Clipper*, vol. XXXVII, #38, November 30, 1889, p. 635.

42. *New York Times*, November 10, 1889.

43. *New York Clipper*. vol. XXXVII, #38, November 30, 1889, p. 635; #39, December 7, 1889, p. 651; #41, December 21, 1889, p. 683; *New York Times*, November 10, 22, 1889; *The Press* (New York), November 24, 1889; O. P. Caylor, "Opening of the Base-Ball Season of 1890," *Harper's Weekly*, vol. XXXIV, #1741, May 3, 1890, p. 355.

44. 0. P. Caylor, "Opening of the Base-Ball Season of 1890," *Harper's Weekly*, vol. XXXIV, #1741, May 3, 1890, p. 355.

45. *New York Clipper*, vol. XXXVIII, #3, March 29, 1890, p. 41; *The Press* (New York), January 5, February 9, 11, 19, 23, March 18, 22, 23, 1890; O. P. Caylor, "Opening of the Base-Ball Season of 1890," *Harper's Weekly*. vol. XXXIV, #1741, May 3, 1890, p. 355.

46. *New York Clipper*, vol. XXXVII, #38, November 30, 1889, p. 635.

47. *New York Clipper*, vol. XXXVII, #38, November 30, 1889, p. 635.

48. *New York Clipper*, vol. XXXVII, #38, November 30, 1889, p. 635.

49. *The Press* (New York), November 24, December 16, 1889, January 5, 1890.

50. Seymour, *The Rise of Major League Baseball...*, pp. 497–99.

51. *New York Clipper*, vol. XXXVII, #38, November 30, 1889, p. 635.

52. *New York Clipper*, vol. XXXVII, #41, December 21, 1889, p. 653.

53. *The Sporting News*, vol. 9, #3, September 28, 1889, pp.3–4.

54. Seymour, *The Rise of Major League Baseball...*, p. 500.

55. *New York Clipper*, vol. XXXVII, #34, November 2, 1889, p. 571.

56. *The Press* (New York), November 3, 1889; *New York Times*, November 3, 1889.

57. *New York Clipper*, vol. XXXVII, #34, November 2, 1889, p. 571: #42, December 28, 1889, p. 699; for Ward's comment, see #40, December 14, 1889, p. 667.

58. *The Press* (New York), November 16, 1889.
59. *New York Clipper*, vol. XXXVII, #41, December 21, 1889, p. 683; #42, December 28, 1889, p. 699.
60. *New York Clipper*, vol. XXXVII, #42, December 28, 1889, p. 700; #44, January 11, 1890, p. 732.
61. *The Press* (New York), January 10, 1890; *New York Clipper*, vol. XXXVII, #45, January 18, 1890, p. 747.
62. *The Press* (New York), January 17, 1890; *New York Clipper*, vol. XXXVII, #46, January 25, 1890, p. 763.
63. *New York Clipper*, vol. XXXVII, #48, February 8, 1890, pp. 794–95, for the full text of Judge O'Brien's decision. See *The Press* (New York), January 29, 1890, for the significant portions of the document.
64. *New York Clipper*, vol. XXXVII, #48, February 8, 1890, p. 795: #49, February 15, 1890, p. 811; #50, February 22, 1890, p. 827; #51, March 1, 1890, p. 843; *The Press* (New York), January 30, February 2, 19, 24, 1890.
65. *New York Clipper*, vol. XXXVII, #52, March 8, 1890, pp. 858–59; *The Press* (New York), February 27, 1890.
66. *New York Clipper*, vol. XXXVIII, #2, March 22, 1890, p. 25.
67. *The Press* (New York), March 27, 1890; *New York Clipper*, vol. XXXVIII, #4, April 5, 1890, p. 57.
68. *New York Clipper*, vol. XXXVII, #52, March 8, 1890, p. 858; vol. XXXVIII, #1, March 15, 1890, p. 9; #3, March 29, 1890, p. 42; *The Press* (New York), March 4, 5, 6, 1890.
69. *The Press* (New York), April 1, 1890; *New York Clipper*, vol. XXXVIII, #7, April 26, 1890, p. 106. The Giants' lineup was:

Tiernan	CF	Bassett	2B	Clarke	RF
Glasscock	SS	Denny	3B	Buckley	C
Hornung	LF	Crane	1B	Rusie	P

70. *New York Times*, April 20, 1890; *New York Clipper*, vol. xxxviii, #7, April 26, 1890, p. 106.
71. *New York Times*, April 20, 1890; *New York Clipper*, vol. XXXVIII, #7, April 26, 1890, p. 106. The New York Players' League lineup was:

Gore	CF	O'Rourke	LF	Hatfield	SS
Richardson	2B	Ewing	C	Whitney	3B
Connor	1B	Slattery	RF	Keefe	P

72. *Spalding's Official Base Ball Guide: 1891*, pp. 74–77; *New York Clipper*, vol. XXXVIII, #10, May 17, 1890, p. 154; The *New York Times*, May 13, 1890; *The Press* (New York), May 13, 1890.
73. Final standings for 1890 are in *Spalding's Official Base Ball Guide: 1891*, p. 19; *New York Times*, October 4, 1890; *The Baseball Encyclopedia...*, p. 72.
74. *Reach's Official Base Ball Guide: 1891*, pp. 25–26; *The Press* (New York), October 7, 1890.
75. *New York Times*, July 8, 9, 10, 11, 12, August 12, 1890.
76. *Spalding's Official Base Ball Guide: 1895*, p. 123.
77. *The Press* (New York), October 1, 3, 4, 5, 1890; *New York Daily Tribune*, October 3, 5, 1890; *The Sporting Life's Official Base Ball Guide ... for 1891*, pp. 89–90.
78. *The Press* (New York), October 9, 1890.

79. *The Sporting Life's Official Base Ball Guide ... for 1891*, p. 91; *New York Daily Tribune*, October 8, 10, 1890; *The Press* (New York), October 9, 10, 1890.

80. *The Sporting Life's Official Base Ball Guide ... for 1891*, p. 91; *New York Daily Tribune*, October 10, 1890: *The Press* (New York), October 10, 1890.

81. Spalding, *America's National Game...*, p. 288; *New York Daily Tribune*, October 11, 1890; *The Press* (New York), October 11, 1890; *The Sporting Life's Official Base Ball Guide ... for 1891*, pp. 91–92.

82. *New York Daily Tribune*, October 13, 15, 16, 1890; *The Press* (New York), October 15, 1890; *The Sporting News*, vol. 11, #10, November 8, 1890, p. 1.

83. *New York Daily Tribune*, October 22, 1890; *The Press* (New York), October 22, 1890.

84. *The Sporting News*, vol. 11, #9, November 1, 1890, p. 1; *The Sporting Life's Official Base Ball Guide ... for 1891*, p. 92; *The Press* (New York), October 22, 1890; *New York Daily Tribune*, October 22, 1890.

85. Seymour, *The Rise of Major League Baseball...*, p. 526.

86. *The Sporting Life's Base Ball Guide: 1891*, p. 92; *New York Daily Tribune*, October 23 1890; *The Press* (New York), October 23, 1890; Seymour, *The Rise of Major League Baseball...*, pp. 524–27.

87. *The Sporting News*, vol. 11, #11, November 15, 1890, p. 3; *The Sporting Life's Official Base Ball Guide ... for 1891*, pp. 92–93; *The Press* (New York), November 13, 16, 1890.

88. *The Sporting News*, vol. 11, #11, November 15, 1890, p. 3; *The Sporting Life's Official Base Ball Guide ... for 1891*, pp. 92–93; *The Press* (New York), November 13, 16, 1890.

89. *The Sporting News*, vol. 11, #12, November 22, 1890, pp. 1–2; vol. 11, #13, November 29, 1890, p. 1; *The Press* (New York), November 13, 1890; Seymour, *The Rise of Major League Baseball...*, pp. 530–31.

90. *The Sporting Life's Official Base Ball Guide...for 1891*, p. 97; *New York Daily Tribune*, January 7, 11, 1891; Seymour, *The Rise of Major League Baseball...*, pp. 531–34.

91. *New York Daily Tribune*, January 24, 1891.

92. *The Sporting Life's Official Base Ball Guide...for 1891*, p. 91.

93. *Reach's Official Base Ball Guide: 1891*, pp. 7–10; *The Sporting Life's Official Base Ball Guide...for 1891*, pp. 93-103; *The Press* (New York), January 11, 13, 15, 17, 1891; *New York Daily Tribune*, January 8, 11–17, 24, 1891; Seymour, *The Rise of Major League Baseball...*, pp. 534–39.

94. Voigt, *American Baseball...*, I, p. 168. Voigt has an uncanny eye for the single detail that illuminates an entire event.

95. *Spalding's Official Base Ball Guide: 1891*, p. 13.

96. *Spalding's Official Base Ball Guide: 1891*, p. 16.

97. *The Sporting Life's Official Base Ball Guide...for 1891*, pp. 73, 74.

98. *The Sporting Life's Official Base Ball Guide...for 1891*, pp. 76–80.

99. *Reach's Official Base Ball Guide: 1891*, p. 7.

100. This particular analysis came from the National Bureau of Economic Research, in A. F. Burns and W. C. Mitchell, *Measuring Business Cycles* (New York, 1946), p. 78. See also the excellent article by Charles Hoffmann, "The Depression of the Nineties," *The Journal of Economic History*, vol. XVI, June, 1956, p. 138.

101. *Commercial and Financial Chronicle*, vol. 51, August 23, 1890, p. 220.

102. *Commercial and Financial Chronicle*, vol. 51, August 30, 1890, p. 258; September 13, 1890, p. 314; September 20, 1890, p. 358; September 27, 1890, p. 396.

103. *Commercial and Financial Chronicle*, vol. 51, November 8, 1890, p. 624;

November 15, 1890, pp. 654–55; November 22, 1890, pp. 692–93; *The Press* (New York), November 16, 1890.

104. *Spalding's Official Base Ball Guide: 1891*, pp. 4445.

Chapter Six

1. *New York Daily Tribune*, April 19, 22, 23, 1891; *New York Times*, April 23, 1891. The New York Lineup was:

Gore	GF	O'Rourke	LF	Denny	3B
Tiernan	RF	Connor	1B	Buckley	C
Glasscock	SS	Richardson	2B	Rusie	P

2. *New York Times*, May 29, 1891.

3. *Chicago Tribune*, June 13, 14, 16, 17, 1891; *New York Times*, June 13, 14, 16, 17, 1891; *The Sporting News*, vol. 12, #15, June 20, 1891, pp. 1, 5.

4. *New York Daily Tribune*, June 25, July 23, 1891; *New York Times*, June 25, July 11, 12, 14, 23, 1891.

5. *New York Times*, August 11, 13, 19, October 4, 1891; *The Baseball Encyclopedia...*, pp. 73–74; *Spalding's Official Base Ball Guide: 1892*, p. 48.

6. *New York Daily Tribune*, April 26, 1891,

7. *New York Daily Tribune*, August 3, 30, September 10, 27, 1891.

8. *New York Times*, May 27, June 28, 1891. Outlandish cures were common during the Gilded Age. Consider the following endorsement from one David S. Exford. "I have used several bottles of your Kendell's Spavin Cure ... both in my family and for my horse with great success." God alone knows what disorders the Spavin Cure healed. Similar claims were made for a concoction called Gombault's Caustic Balsam. See *Spirit of the Times*, vol. 107, #15, May 10, 1884, p. 439; vol. 111, #14, May 1, 1886, p. 412.

9. See the *New York Daily Tribune*, May 3, 10, 1891, for comments on Gore and O'Rourke and October 4, 1891, for a laudatory comment on the New York career of Tim Keefe. The poem is "Polo Grounds," by Rolfe Humphries, republished in Charles Einstein, ed., *The Fireside Book of Baseball* (New York, 1956), pp. 204–205. This poem is, in my opinion, the greatest single piece ever written on baseball.

10. For Mutrie's records, see *The Baseball Encyclopedia...*, p. 1402.

11. *Chicago Tribune*, October 4, 1891; *New York Times*, October 4, 1891; see *The Sporting News*, vol. 12, # 20, October 3, 1891, p. 1 for comments on this entire question.

12. *The Sporting News*, vol. 12, #20, October 3, 1891, p. 1; #21, October 10, 1891, p. 1; *Chicago Tribune*, October 2, 4, 1891. George Tuohey, *A History of the Boston Base Ball Club...*, makes no mention of the Chicago charges.

13. *Chicago Tribune*, December 13, 15, 16, 17, 18, 19, 20, 22, 1891; *New York Daily Tribune*, December 13, 16, 18, 19, 20, 22, 1891; Harold Seymour, *Baseball: The Early Years*, I, pp. 251–62.

14. For the official records of Boyle, Fuller, Lyons, and King, see *The Baseball Encyclopedia...*, pp. 301, 446, 607–608, 1140–41.

15. *New York Daily Tribune*, April 13, 1892. The New York lineup was:

Gore	CF	D. Lyons	3B	Fields	RF
Ewing	1B	Bassett	2B	Rusie	P
O'Rourke	LF	Boyle	C	Fuller	SS

16. *New York Daily Tribune*, April 24, 1892.
17. *Spalding's Official Base Ball Guide: 1893*, p. 31; *New York Daily Tribune*, July 13, 1892.
18. *Spalding's Official Base Ball Guide: 1893*, pp. 18–19, 31; *New York Daily Tribune*, October 16, 1892.
19. *New York Daily Tribune*, October 6, 7, 1892.
20. *New York Daily Tribune*, August 20, 1892. For an account of the O'Rourke contretemps, see the *New York Times*, September 11, 14, 16, 28, 1892.
21. *New York Times*, June 23, 24, 30, 1892; *New York Daily Tribune*, July 2, 1892; for Doyle's official records, see *The Baseball Encyclopedia...*, pp. 406–407.
22. *New York Times*, September 28, 1892.
23. For Wee Willie Keeler's official records, see *The Baseball Encyclopedia...*, pp. 556–57.
24. *New York Times*, June 13, 1892.
25. *New York Times*, June 13, 14, 1892; *New York Daily Tribune*, June 13, 14, 1892; Seymour, *Baseball: The Early Years*, I, pp. 266–70.
26. *New York Daily Tribune*, October 7, 1892; *New York Times*, October 11, 1892.
27. *New York Times*, June 14, September 10, 1892; Seymour, *Baseball: The Early Years*, I, pp. 268–70.
28. *Commercial and Financial Chronicle*, vol. LVI (February 25, 1893), pp. 308–22; (March 18, 1893), pp. 437–39; *New York Times*, February 18, 19, 20, 21, 22, 1893; Edward Kirkland, *Industry Comes of Age...*, p. 5.
29. *Commercial and Financial Chronicle*, vol. LVI (April 1, 1893), pp. 518–19; (April 22, 1893), pp. 646–47; *New York Times*, March 30, April 22, 1893.
30. *Commercial and Financial Chronicle*, vol. LVI, March 11, 1893), pp. 393–95; (April] 22, 1893), pp. 644–52; *New York Times*, April 21, 22, 23, 24, 1893.
31. *New York Times*, May 4, 1893.
32. On the panic see Charles Hoffman, "The Depression of the Nineties," *Journal of Economic History*, XVI (June, 1956), p. 158; *Commercial and Financial Chronicle*, vol. LVI (May 6, 1893), p. 728; *New York Times*, May 4, 5, 6, 9, 12, 13, 16, 17, 22, 23, June 4, 6, 14, 1893.
33. *Commercial and Financial Chronicle*, vol. LVI (May 6, 1893), p. 728.
34. *Commercial and Financial Chronicle*, vol. LVI (June 17, 1893), pp. 990–91, 1000; vol. LVII (July 29, 1893), pp. 167–68; *New York Times*, June 6, 15, 16, 1893.
35. *New York Times*, June 26, 1893.
36. *Commercial and Financial Chronicle*, vol. LVII (July 1, 1893), p. 2: (July 29, 1893), pp. 162–65; *New York Times*, June 14, 19, 21, 30, July 12, 16, 18, 19, 20, 22, 23, 24, 26, 27, 1893.
37. Hoffmann, "The Depression of the Nineties," *Journal of Economic History* vol. XVI (June, 1956), pp. 137–64; *New York Times*, July 1, 28, 1893; *Commercial and Financial Chronicle*, vol. LVII (August 19, 1893), p. 272.
38. *New York Daily Tribune*, April 29, 1893; *New York Times*, April 29, 1893; George Tuohey, *A History of the Boston Base Ball Club...*, p. 110. The New York lineup was:

Burke	LF	Connor	1B	Doyle	C
Tiernan	RF	Davis	3B	King	P
Ward	2B	Fuller	SS		

39. *New York Daily Tribune*, May 7, 10, 31, 1893.
40. *New York Daily Tribune*, June 2, September 25, 1893.
41. Seymour, *Baseball: The Early Years*, I, pp. 295, 303.

42. On Kelly see the *New York Daily Tribune*, May 1, 20, 21, 26, June 6, 11, 22, 1893. For the Giants' season record see *The Baseball Encyclopedia...*, p. 76; *Spalding's Official Base Ball Guide: 1894*, pp. 22–24.

43. *New York Daily Tribune*, June 3, 11, 1893.

44. *New York Daily Tribune*, July 30, 1893.

45. John H. Lancaster, "Baltimore, a Pioneer in Organized Baseball," *Maryland Historical Magazine*, vol. XXXV, #1 (March, 1940), pp. 36–50; Seymour, *Baseball: The Early Years*, vol. I, pp. 302–304; *The Baseball Encyclopedia...*, pp. 491, 1392; *New York Daily Tribune*, April 20, 1894. Six of the players on the 1894 Orioles are now in the Baseball Hall of Fame: John McGraw, Hugh Jennings, Wilbert Robinson, Joe Kelley, Wee Willie Keeler, and Dan Brouthers.

46. *New York Daily Tribune*, April 20, 1894; Voigt, American Baseball..., I, pp. 256–57; Durso, The Days of Mr. McGraw, pp. 25–26. The lineups for the game were:

New York		Baltimore	
Murphy	SS	McGraw	3B
Ward	2B	Keeler	RF
Van Haltren	CF	Brodie	CF
Tiernan	RF	Brouthers	1B
Davis	3B	Kelley	LF
Connor	1B	Reitz	2B
Burke	LF	Jennings	SS
Farrell	C	Robinson	C
Rusie	P	McMahon	P

47. *New York Daily Tribune*, July 15, 16, 1894.

48. *New York Daily Tribune*, July 15, 16, 1894.

49. *New York Daily Tribune*, May 31, July 18, 1894. The Memorial Day crowd was the largest in the club's history, and the attendance for the season was 340,000, also a club record. See *Reach's Official Base Ball Guide: 1895*, p. 98.

50. *Reach's Official Base Ball Guide: 1895*, p. 12; *New York Daily Tribune*, September 30, 1894.

51. *New York Daily Tribune*, June 3, 1894.

52. See the *New York Herald*, October 5, 1894, for a long and flowery story by one of the leading sportswriters of the era, O. P. Caylor. See also the *Chicago Tribune*, October 5, 1894, for a superior box score of the game. See also *The Press* (New York), October 5, 1894; *Baltimore Sun*, October 5, 1894; *New York Daily Tribune*, October 5, 1894; *New York Times*, October 5, 1894; *Reach's Official Base Ball Guide: 1895*, pp. 31–34. See also Lansche, *The Forgotten Championships*, pp. 49–50.

53. *New York Herald*, October 6, 7, 9, 1894; *Chicago Tribune*, October 6, 7, 9, 1894; *The Press* (New York), October 6, 7, 9, 1894; *Baltimore Sun*, October 6, 7, 9, 1894; *New York Daily Tribune*, October 6, 7, 9, 1894; *New York Times*, October 6, 7, 9, 1894; *Reach's Official Base Ball Guide: 1895*, pp. 31–34; see the *Spirit of the Times*, vol. 128, #13, October 13, 1894, p. 440 for a notice of the Giants' benefit. A complete statistical summary of the 1894 Temple Cup series has been made by Mr. Arthur Schott of New Orleans, and is, as far as I know, the only such summary in existence. See also Lansche, *The Forgotten Championships*, pp. 50–53.

54. *The Press* (New York), October 3, 1894.

Chapter Seven

1. *Spirit of the Times*, vol. 128, #13, October 13, 1894, p. 440; *The Press* (New York), December 6, 1894, January 6, 17, 20, 24, 25, 1895; *New York Times*, January 17, 25, 1895; *New York Daily Tribune*, January 17, 18, 19, 21, 24, 25, 1895; Seymour, *Baseball: The Early Years*, I, p. 296; *Dictionary of American Biography*, vol. IV, p.8; Mrs. John McGraw and Arthur Mann, *The Real McGraw* (New York, 1953), pp. 168–71. The stockholders who sold out to Freedman were E. B. Talcott, E. A. McAlpin, F. B. Robinson, Cornelius van Cott, John M. Ward, and Walter Spalding. John T. Brush, who owned the Cincinnati club, Ferdinand Abell, a Brooklyn owner, Al Reach, one of the Philadelphia partners, and Arthur Soder, the managing partner of the Boston Red Stockings, all held their stock. The Giants thus remained a syndicate club. On Freedman's political connections see *Report of the Special Committee of the Assembly Appointed to Investigate the Public Offices and Departments of the City of New York and of the Counties Therein Included* (Mazet Committee), 5 vols. (Albany 1900), vol. I, pp. 604–34. On the problems Tammany had in the mid-nineties with crime, corruption, saloons and graft, see Charles Parkhurst, *Our Fight with Tammany*, pp. 8–25. See also the *Report and Proceedings of the Senate Committee Appointed to Investigate the Police Department of the City of New York* (The Lexow Committee) (New York, 1895), 5 vols. On the sad results of the Raines Law see Willoughby C. Waterman, *Prostitution and Its Repression in New York City: 1900–1931* (New York, 1932), pp. 30-35. On politics in general and baseball and Freedman in particular, see Steven Riess, *Touching Base*, pp. 66–77.

2. *The Press* (New York), April 21, 1895.

3. *New York Daily Tribune*, April 19, 1895; *New York Times*, April 19, 1895; *The Press* (New York), April 19, 1895. The *Tribune* estimated the crowd at 20,000, while *The Press* had a count of 28,874. If *The Press* count was accurate, opening day, 1895, was the largest crowd in the Giants' history.

4. For the final standings of 1895, see *The Baseball Encyclopedia...*, p. 78. For Freedman's statement on strengthening the team, see *The Press* (New York), July 1, 1895; for Doyle's dismissal and the appointment of Watkins, see *The Press* (New York), August 22, 1895.

5. *The Press* (New York), April 24, 1895.

6. An indication of Freedman's bad temper, his defiance of public criticism, his arrogance, and his sense of what belonged in the private, not public, domain, can be seen in the accounts of his testimony before the Mazet Committee hearings dealing with Tammany corruption. See *New York Press*, April 22, 1899; *New York Daily Tribune*, April 22, 1899; *New York Times*, April 22, 1899.

7. *New York Daily Tribune* August 19, 1895; Seymour, *Baseball: The Early Years*, vol. I, p. 296.

8. *New York Daily Tribune*, April 17, 1896.

9. *New York Daily Tribune*, April 21, 1896.

10. Seymour, *Baseball: The Early Years*, vol. I, p. 297; *New York Daily Tribune*, April 26, 1896; *The Baseball Encyclopedia...*, p. 1278.

11. *The Press* (New York), April 23, 1896; *New York Daily Tribune*, April 23, 1896; The *New York Times*, a Democratic paper, did not mention this contretemps of a Tammany leader.

12. *New York Daily Tribune*, April 23, 1896.

13. See, for example, *The Press* (New York), April 27, 1896, for a long article quoting several New York businessmen in support of Freedman. Although *The Press* was a

staunchly Republican paper, and Freedman was a Tammany democrat, ideology overcame party in this instance. The values of upholding the superiority of management over labor were paramount. See also succeeding articles in *The Press* echoing this line and quoting other papers that did, too. *The Press* (New York), April 29, May 3, 4, 18, September 14, 1896.

14. *New York Daily Tribune*, April 17, 22, 1896; *The Press* (New York), April 17, 22, 1896. Estimates of the attendance varied. The *New York Times* placed it at 16,000, the anti-Freedman *Tribune* guessed 12,000, and noted that the usual crowd behind the ropes in the outfield was missing. *The Press*, rather pro-Freedman, put the attendance at 20,000, probably a bit on the high side.

15. See the *New York Daily Tribune*, August 9, 1896, for the announcement of the new manager. For the team's performance under Joyce in 1896, see *The Baseball Encyclopedia...*, p. 1395. For comments on the growing problem of rowdiness and "kicking," see *Spalding's Official Base Ball Guide: 1893*, pp. 106–107; 1895, p. 42.

16. For the final standings of 1896 see *New York Daily Tribune*, September 27, 1896; *Spalding's Official Base Ball Guide: 1897*, p. 12; *The Baseball Encyclopedia...*, p. 79.

17. *New York Daily Tribune*, June 30, 1896.

18. *The New York Press*, April 15, 1897.

19. *The New York Press*, April 21, 1897.

20. *New York Daily Tribune*, April 13, 14, 1897; *New York Times*, April 13, 18, 21, 22, 1897; *The New York Press*, April 13, 14, 15, 21, 22, 23, 1897.

21. *The New York Press*, April 19, 1897.

22. For the final standings of the 1897 season, see *Spalding's Official Base Ball Guide: 1898*, p. 33; *New York Daily Tribune*, October 3, 1897; *The Baseball Encyclopedia...*, p. 79. For an example of the general satisfaction in New York with the Giants' performance in 1897, see *The New York Press*, October 4, 1897.

23. *Spalding's Official Base Ball Guide: 1899*, pp. 12, 41; *New York Times*, October 16, 1897; *The Baseball Encyclopedia...*, p. 80.

24. *The New York Press*, September 30, 1898; *New York Times*, June 19, July 1, September 18, October 2, 1898. The official verdict that the war was the culprit was obviously preposterous. The war did not similarly affect other sports, and there was no discernible reason why baseball alone should have suffered, unless one looked at the management problems and the lack of competition within the game itself.

25. See *Reach's Official Base Ball Guide: 1899*, pp. 48–49 for a chronology of the Ducky Holmes affair; *New York Times*, July 26, 1898; *New York Daily Tribune*, July 26, 1898; *The New York Press*, July 26, 1898. By the nineties, "lobster" had replaced "muffin" as the ultimate term of contempt for a weak player.

26. See *The New York Press*, August 16, 1898, for a complete story on the board meeting and decision. See also the *New York Times*, August 16, 1898 and the *New York Daily Tribune*, August 16, 1898.

27. *The New York Press*, August 17, 1898; *New York Times*, August 17, 1898.

28. *The New York Press*, August 20, 1898.

29. *The New York Press*, August 25, 26, 1898; *New York Times*, August 25, 26, 1898; *New York Daily Tribune*, August 25, 26, 1898. The magnates who agreed with Cleveland owner Frank Robison were: Arthur Soden (Boston), John Brush (Cincinnati), James Hart and the Spaldings (Chicago), Ferdinand Abell, Harry von der Horst, and Ned Hanlon (Baltimore), Al Reach and Col. John Rogers (Philadelphia), Muckenfuss (receiver of the bankrupt St. Louis franchise), Barney Dreyfuss (Pittsburgh) and J. Earl Wagner (Washington).

30. *The New York Press*, August 30, 1898; *New York Times*, August 26, 28, 30, 1898.

31. *Sporting Life*, vol. 33, #4, April 15, 1899, p. 10. For details about the Rusie negotiations see *Sporting Life*, vol. 33, #3, April 8, 1899, p. 5. Rusie was to be reduced from $3,000 to $2,000 and forced to agree to a $100 fine for each drink and a clause providing no pay unless he was in shape. Obviously, Rusie could not sign on these terms, and their tender by Freedman was a deliberate attempt to force Rusie out of baseball. It succeeded. For Seymour's signing, see the *New York Times*, May 12, 1899.

32. For the final standings of the 1899 season, see *Spalding's Official Base Ball Guide: 1900*, p. 18; *Sporting Life*, vol. 34, #5, October 21, 1899; *The Baseball Encyclopedia...*, p. 81.

33. For estimates of the New York attendance in 1898 and 1899, see *Sporting Life*, vol. 34, #6, October 28, 1899, p. 3.

34. *Sporting Life*, vol. 34, #2, September 30, 1899, p. 6.

35. *Sporting Life*, vol. 33, #8, May 13, 1899, p. 5; vol. 33, #23, August 26, 1899, p. 6.

36. *Sporting Life*, vol. 33, #3, April 8, 1899, p. 9; vol. 33, #8, May 13, 1899, p. 5.

37. *Reach's Official Base Ball Guide: 1900*, p. 6; *Sporting Life*, vol. 33, #13, June 17, 1899, pp. 1, 4; vol. 33, #17, July 15, 1899, p. 1; vol. 33, #19, July 29, 1899, p. 5; vol. 34, #3, October 7, 1899, p. 4.

38. *Sporting Life*, vol. 33, #8, May 13, 1899, p. 4; see vol. 33, #11, June 3, 1899, p. 4, for a comment by Washington owner J. Earl Wagner that the league will be reduced to eight clubs after the season and a new major league will emerge. This was a totally accurate prediction. See also *Sporting Life*, vol. 33, #13, June 17, 1899, p. 4, for comments by Ban Johnson, president of the Western League, about a reduction in the National League. See *Sporting Life*, vol. 33, #15, July 1, 1899, p. 7; vol. 33, #16, July 8, 1899, p. 4; vol. 33, #18, July 22, 1899, p. 4; vol. 33, #20, August 5, 1899, p. 4; vol. 33, #26, September 9, 1899, p. 1, for stories and rumors about a reduction in the National League to eight clubs. See *Sporting Life*, vol. 34, #1, September 23, 1899, for Brooklyn president Charles Ebbets' prediction that Baltimore, Washington, Cleveland, and Louisville would be dropped from the National League.

39. *Reach's Official Base Ball Guide: 1900*, p. 48.

40. *Sporting Life*, vol. 34, #4, October 14, 1899, p. 4; *Reach's Official Base Ball Guide: 1900*, p. 48.

41. *Reach's Official Base Ball Guide: 1900*, pp. 48–50; Seymour, *Baseball: The Early Years*, vol. I, pp. 304–306; Voigt, *American Baseball...*, vol. I, pp. 270–72.

42. *Reach's Official Base Ball Guide: 1901*, pp. 26–28; *The Baseball Encyclopedia...*, p. 82; S. C. Thompson, *All-Time Rosters of Major League Baseball Clubs*, pp. 234–35.

43. *Reach's Official Base Ball Guide: 1901*, p. 6.

44. See *Spalding's Official Base Ball Guide: 1902*, pp. 42-50, for details of the 1901 pennant race, p. 58 for the final standings in 1901, p. 83 for the Giants' pitching records in 1901. See also S. C. Thompson, *All-Time Rosters of Major League Baseball Clubs*, p. 235; *The Baseball Encyclopedia...*, p. 83.

45. On the rise of the American League and the role played by the Protective Association of Professional Baseball Players, see Seymour, *Baseball: The Early Years*, vol. I, pp. 308–17; and Voigt, *American Baseball...*, vol. I, pp. 303–309.

Chapter Eight

1. *Spalding's Official Base Ball Guide: 1895*, p. 123. This is an interview with Spalding by editor Harry Chadwick.

2. Seymour, *Baseball: The Early Years*, I, pp. 300–303; Voigt, *American Baseball...*,

I, pp. 239, 265–68. Voigt maintains that the financial losses of the 1898 season were at the root of the sudden flowering of syndicate baseball and I find this interpretation persuasive and compelling.

3. Voigt, *American Baseball...*, I, pp. 238–39, 267–70; Seymour, *Baseball: The Early Years*, I, p. 302.

4. *Sporting Life*, vol. 33, #2, April 1, 1899, p. 5.

5. *Sporting Life*, vol. 33, #22, August 19, 1899, p. 5.

6. *Sporting Life*, vol. 33, #21, August 12, 1899, p. 5.

7. *Reach's Official American League Base Ball Guide: 1902*, pp. 117–18; Seymour, *Baseball: The Early Years*, I, p. 317; See *The New York Press*, January 13, 1902, and the *New York Times*, January 13, 1902, for publication of a letter of July 15, 1901, sent by John Brush to Frank Robison, owner of the St. Louis club, describing the Spalding scheme. Brush was Spalding's enemy, and he was trying to dissuade Robison from throwing his lot in with Spalding, so the description of Spalding's plans was caustic and emphasized its negative aspects. Spalding, of course, had a history of monopolistic practices as Robison well knew. Spalding had built a sporting goods conglomerate which operated to stifle competition, and he had always favored a single major league with a monopoly control over professional baseball. He was the author of the Spalding Classification Plan, which envisioned a ranking of the minor leagues, all under the control of a single major league which would dictate both rules of play and business practices. Thus, a charge of monopoly, or a trust scheme, made against Spalding was, at the very least, plausible and likely to be believed. See also *The New York Press*, December 14, 15, 1901.

8. *New York Sun*, December 11, 1901; *Albert Spalding, America's National Game...*, pp. 305–306; see *The New York Press*, December 14, 1901, for a letter from Brush to Freedman of February 8, 1901, in which Brush outlined his trust plan.

9. In fact, the Syndicate did lose, admitting defeat on April 6, 1909, when Charles Frohman sent Mrs. Fiske a telegram opening the Syndicate theaters to her. For two views of this episode in the management of American theater, see Isaac Marcosson and Daniel Frohman, *Charles Frohman: Manager and Man* (New York, 1916), pp. 185–190. This book, put together as a memorial to Charles Frohman, who had gone down with the Lusitania, discreetly glossed over the attempt at theater monopoly. See also Frank Carlos Griffith, *Mrs. Fiske* (New York, 1912), pp. 59–73, for an account by a former manager that stresses Mrs. Fiske's heroism. See also Archie Binns, *Mrs. Fiske and the American Theater* (New York, 1955), pp. 77–258. This book is also strongly hostile to the Theater Trust.

10. *Reach's Official American League Base Ball Guide: 1902*, p. 118.

11. *The Sporting News*, vol. 32, #14, December 14, 1901, p. 1; *New York Daily Tribune*, December 13, 1901; *New York Times*, December 12, 1901.

12. Spalding's speech, appropriately puffed up and smoothed out for publication in the grand tradition of Cicero, may be found in *Spalding, America's National Game...*, pp. 308–314; *New York Times*, December 12, 1901; *The Sporting News*, vol. 32, #14, December 14, 1901, p. 1. In justice to Spalding, the contemporary newspaper descriptions of his speech match pretty closely the text Spalding gave in his memoirs. A general account of Spalding's activities with regard to the baseball trust may be found in Levine, *A. G. Spalding and the Rise of Baseball*, pp. 66–70.

13. *The New York Press*, December 14, 1901.

14. *Reach's Official American League Base Ball Guide: 1902*, p. 119; Spalding, *America's National Game...*, p. 315; *New York Daily Tribune*, December 13, 1901; *The New York Press*, December 14, 1901; *New York Times*, December 14, 1901.

15. *New York Daily Tribune*, December 14, 1901; *New York Times*, December 14, 1901.

16. *New York Daily Tribune*, December 14, 1901.

17. *Reach's Official American League Base Ball Guide: 1902*, pp. 119–20; Spalding, *America's National Game...*, p. 316; *The New York Press*, December 14, 1901; *New York Times*, December 14, 1901.

18. *The Sporting News*, vol. 32, #15, December 21, 1901, p.5; *The New York Press*, December 14, 1901; *New York Times*, December 14, 1901; *Reach's Official American League Base Ball Guide: 1902*, pp. 120–21.

19. *The Sporting News*, vol. 32, #15, December 21, 1901, p. 5; Spalding, *America's National Game...*, pp. 317–19; *Reach's Official American League Base Ball Guide: 1902*, pp. 120–21.

20. *The New York Press*, December 15, 1901; *Spalding's Official Base Ball Guide: 1902*, p. 210; *The Sporting News*, vol. 32, #15, December 21, 1901, p. 5.

21. *Spalding's Official Base Ball Guide: 1902*, p. 210; *Reach's Official American League Base Ball Guide: 1902*, p. 121; Spalding, *America's National Game...*, pp. 320–21; *The New York Press*, December 15, 1901; *New York Times*, December 15, 1901; *New York Daily Tribune*, December 15, 1901; *The Sporting News*, vol. 32, #15, December 21, 1901, p. 5.

22. *The New York Press*, December 15, 1901; *New York Times*, December 15, 1901.

23. *New York Times*, December 16, 1901.

24. Freedman's statement is given in extract in the *New York Times*, December 15, 1901, and is given in extenso in *The New York Press*, December 15, 1901, along with the Spalding correspondence and contracts.

25. *New York Times*, December 17, 1901; See *The New York Press*, December 17, 1901, for an exultantly pro-Freedman account; *New York Daily Tribune*, December 17, 1901; *Reach's Official American League Base Ball Guide: 1902*, pp. 121–22; *Spalding's Official Base Ball Guide: 1902*, p. 210; Spalding, *America's National Game...*, p. 322.

26. *New York Daily Tribune*, December 17, 1901.

27. *The Sporting News*, vol. 32, #16, December 28, 1901, pp. 3–4; Spalding, *America's National Game...*, pp. 322–24; *New York Times*, December 21, 1901; *The New York Press*, December 21, 1901; *Reach's Official American League Base Ball Guide: 1902*, p. 122.

28. *The New York Press*, December 24, 1901.

29. *New York Times*, December 18, 20, 1901; *The New York Press*, December 18, 19, 1901; on the sale of the two clubs, see the *New York Times*, January 5, 1902, for a letter from Spalding to the eight club owners describing his conversations with Talcott. See also *The New York Press*, January 3, 4, 6, 1902.

30. Letter printed in *New York Times*, December 23, 1901.

31. *The Sporting News*, vol. 32, #14, December 14, 1901, p. 4; #16, December 28, 1901, p. 1; see #17, January 4, 1902, p. 1, for an editorial urging Brush to leave baseball; see #18, January 11, 1902, p. 2, for an article stating that Spalding will free baseball from its evils. Support for Spalding was a complete reversal of the previous policy of *The Sporting News*. See also the *New York Times*, December 26, 27, 1901.

32. Spalding's letter was printed in *The New York Press*, January 8, 1902, and the *New York Times*, January 8, 1902.

33. *The New York Press*, January 6, 1902.

34. Letter printed in *The New York Press*, January 13, 1902, and the *New York Times*, January 13, 1902. See also *The New York Press*, January 9, 1902, for an earlier statement that Spalding was responsible for the trust plan.

35. *New York Times*, January 14, 1902. For a more extensive statement of the Brush position, see *The New York Press*, January 14, 1902.

36. *New York Times*, January 15, 1902.
37. *New York Times*, February 7, 1902.
38. *Reach's Official American League Base Ball Guide: 1902*, p. 122; *The New York Press*, January 18, 19, February 11, 1902.
39. Letter printed in *The Sporting News*, vol. 32, #18, January 11, 1902, p. 3; *New York Times*, January 5, 1902.
40. Letters printed in *The New York Press*, January 8, 1902.
41. *The New York Press*, January 11, 1902; *New York Times*, January 11, 1902.
42. *The Sporting News*, vol. 32, #19, January 18, 1902, p. 1; the entire file of correspondence between Spalding and the Boston owners can be found in *The New York Press*, January 11, 1902.
43. *The New York Press*, February 7, 1902.
44. *The Sporting News*, vol. 32, #19, January 18, 1902, p. 3; #22, February 8, 1902, pp. 3, 4; *The New York Press*, January 8, 10, 24, 27, February 10, 1902.
45. *Spalding's Official Base Ball Guide: 1902*, p. 210; *The New York Press*, January 28, March 12, 1902.
46. *The Sporting News*, vol. 33, #1, March 15, 1902, p. 4; *The New York Press*, March 11, 12, 1902; *Spalding's Official Base Ball Guide: 1902*, p. 210.
47. *New York Daily Tribune*, March 30, 1902; *New York Times*, March 30, 1902; *The New York Press*, March 30, 1902.
48. The text of Spalding's letter may be found in *Spalding's Official Base Ball Guide: 1902*, p. 210; *New York Daily Tribune*, April 3, 1902; *New York Times*, April 3, 1902.
49. *New York Times*, April 1–4, 1902; *New York Daily Tribune*, April 1–3, 1902; for a Freedmanite view, *The New York Press*, March 31, April 1–5, 1902. See also *The Sporting News*, vol. 33, #4, April 5, 1902, p. 1.
50. Quoted in Mark Sullivan, *Our Times: America Finding Herself* (New York, 1927), p. 253.
51. Again, see Mark Sullivan, *Our Times: America Finding Herself*, p. 253. There are hundreds of books on the trusts, many more detailed and scholarly than Sullivan's examination of the America he lived in. But Sullivan's books, partly personal reminiscences, partly a history of popular opinion, partly an examination of the fabric of American life and experience in the years after 1896, give the flavor of the era that escapes many historians.
52. A good example of the old style of patrician reform is the Rev. Charles H. Parkhurst, an eminent divine who was the president of the City Vigilance League (1892) and a member of the New York Society for the Prevention of Crime (1878). The Rev. Dr. Parkhurst created a sufficient stir with his forays to gather evidence of police corruption that he more or less launched the Lexow Committee investigation (1894), which led to rapid and thorough strengthening of Tammany by demonstrating how much money was involved in graft and how loosely it was controlled. I am currently working on a book on the rationalization of graft and politics. On the Lexow Committee, see the *Report of the Special Committee Appointed to Investigate the Police Department of the City of New York*, 5 vols. (Albany, 1895); see also, on reform, William Howe Tolman, *Municipal Reform Movements in the United States* (New York, 1895), a sort of directory of late patrician urban reform groups. See also Rev. Charles H. Parkhurst, *Our Fight with Tammany* (New York, 1895).
53. Augustus Cerillo Jr., "The Impact of Reform Ideology: Early Twentieth Century Municipal Government in New York City," in Michael H. Ebner and Eugene M. Tobin, eds., *The Age of Urban Reform. New Perspectives on the Progressive Era* (Port Washington, New York, 1977), p. 68.

54. See Jane S. Dahlberg, *The New York Bureau of Municipal Research* (New York, 1966).

55. On tenement reform see Robert W. DeForest and Lawrence Veiller, eds., *The Tenement House Problem*, 2 vols. (New York, 1903), particularly vol. 1. See Roy Lubove, *The Progressives and the Slums: Tenement House Reform in New York City 1890–1917* (Pittsburgh, 1962), particularly chapters 5 and 6; see also G. Wallace Chessman, *Governor Theodore Roosevelt: The Albany Apprenticeship. 1898–1900* (Cambridge, 1965), pp. 231–33; See also the important article by Richard Skolnik, "Civic Group Progressivism in New York City," *New York History*, vol. LI, #4, June, 1970, pp. 411–39; see also Augustus Cerillo, Jr., "The Impact of Reform Ideology...," pp. 68–73.

56. On the work of progressive era urban reformers see two extremely important books: Martin J. Shiesl, *The Politics of Efficiency...*, previously cited, and Robert H. Wiebe, *The Search for Order* (New York, 1967). These are essential for seeing the progressive reform as a whole. Specifically for New York, see three exceptionally significant articles: Richard Skolnik, "Civic Progressivism in New York City," Augustus Cerillo Jr., "The Impact of Reform Ideology...," both previously cited, and Augustus Cerillo Jr., "The Reform of Municipal Government in New York City: From Seth Low to John Purroy Mitchell," *The New York Historical Society Quarterly*, vol. LVII, #1, January, 1973. These articles are essential for understanding New York reform in the new century.

57. On the consolidation of power within Tammany by Richard Croker and Charles Murphy see Martin Shefter, "The Electoral Foundations of Political Machine: New York City, 1884–1897," in Joel H. Sibley, Allan Bogue, and William H. Flanigan, eds., *The History of American Electoral Behavior* (Princeton, 1978), pp. 263–98; see also Jacob A. Friedman, *The Impeachment of Governor William Sulzer* (New York, 1939).

Chapter Nine

1. Mrs. John H. McGraw, *The Real McGraw*, ed. Arthur Mann (New York, 1953), p. 12. This book is a combination of a formal biography and personal reminiscences. It has the great advantage of being written with access to McGraw's personal papers, and it contains interpretations of the man and his activities not found in other accounts. Naturally enough, the basic interpretations found in this book tend to place John McGraw's actions and motivations in the best possible light. For that reason, the views advanced by Mrs. McGraw have often been ignored by historians. This is, I feel, a dangerous practice in view of the documentary material she possessed. Moreover, John McGraw possessed an extremely strong sense of personal honor, and considered his word his bond, and it is not unreasonable to assume that he acted with at least as much probity as Ban Johnson, who was a notorious politician with an immense ability to justify his actions.

2. Mrs. John McGraw, *The Real McGraw*, pp. 9–128; John J. McGraw, *My Thirty Years in Baseball* (New York, 1923) pp. 31–87, 107–34; for McGraw's playing record, see *The Baseball Encyclopedia...*, pp. 639, 1400.

3. Mrs. John McGraw, *The Real McGraw*, pp. 158–63. The interpretation here is simple: John McGraw kept his word and never jumped a contract.

4. *New York Clipper*, vol. L, #20, July 12, 1902, p. 436; #21, July 19, 1902, p. 456; #22, July 26, 1902, p. 475; *The Sporting News*, vol. 33, #18, July 12, 1902, p. 1; #19, July 19, 1902, pp. 1, 4, 6; #20, July 26, 1902, pp. 1, 3; *New York Daily Tribune*, July 8, 9, 18, 20, 21, 1902; *New York Times*, July 8, 10, 17, 18, 20, 1902.

5. See, for example, the novel by Eric Rolfe Greenberg, *The Celebrant* (New York, 1986).

6. On the general subject of play as ritual see J. Huizinga, *Home Ludens. A Study of the Play Element in Culture*, tr. R. F. C. Hull (London, 1949), particularly chapter 1; see also, for a general introduction to Christian liturgy, Bard Thompson, *Liturgies of the Western Church* (New York, 1962), particularly chapters II and III. See also Gregory Dix, ed., *The Treatise on the Apostolic Tradition of St. Hippolytus of Rome* (London, 1937). See also the more general treatise of Gregory Dix, *The Shape of the Liturgy* (Westminster, 1947). Both will make clear the nature and meaning of liturgy and ritual.

7. For an introduction to the theology and political thought of Spanish Jesuit theologians of the Golden Age, see Guenter Lewy, *Constitutionalism and Statecraft during the Golden Age of Spain. A Study of the Political Philosophy of Juan de Mariana. S.J.* (Geneva, 1960). See also Luis Molina, S.J., *Concordia liberi arbitrii cum gratiae e donis divina praescientia. providentia, praedestinatione et reprobatione* (Paris, 1876). This issue (salvation), essentially Augustinian in origin, was given new currency during the Reformation by the pamphlets of Erasmus, *De Libero Artitrio* (1524), and Luther, *De Servo Arbitrio* (1525). Molina's contribution to this discussion of grace and free will was to add beautifully argued complexities, which did not solve the problem. The infield fly rule was the more successful. For the infield fly rule see *Spalding's Official Base Ball Guide: 1910*, p. 368 (Rule 51, section 8).

8. Plato, *Laws*, ed. A. E. Taylor (London, 1934), vii, 796, 803.

9. The perfection of the various elements of baseball, such as 90 feet between bases, has been often noted and is not dependent on the observer being caught up in the ritual elements of play.

10. Rolfe Humphries, "Polo Grounds." In the first note in the first chapter there appeared George Will, *Men At Work*, a book advertised to be about the craft of baseball. It is about that all right, but it is also about much more. Will captures, as only he, Bernard Malamud and Rolfe Humphries can, the sense of time, of lost youth and innocence, of elegy, of nostalgia, of morality that inform baseball. Baseball is a game of excellence within rules, though the management of baseball is not. The "natural" is a player, not an owner. America likes to think of itself as a society devoted to excellence within the rules of liberty and equality (and sometimes is), so baseball is, therefore, on existential grounds, the national game. It holds a mirror up, not to our nature, but to our best hopes and our better days.

INDEX

Abell, Ferdinand 127, 135, 168, 172–73, 179
Addison, John 126, 127
A.G. Spalding and Bros. 104–06
Ahe, Chris von der 6, 63, 82, 83, 123, 128, 171, 172
A.J. Reach and Co. 104–05
Albee, Edward F. 59
Alexander, Walter 18
American Association 15, 31–34, 46–47, 62–63, 82–83, 90, 94, 102, 107, 109–10, 123, 125, 127–29, 135, 140–42, 145, 152
American Bicycle Company 105
American League 136–37, 169–70, 174, 176–77, 181, 184, 187, 192, 194
American Red Cross 86
Anson, Adrian C. "Cap" 7–10, 28–30, 38–40, 46, 81, 106–08, 114, 138, 193, 197
Arthur, Chester A. 37
Atlanta Crackers 2
Augustine, St. 21

Bacon, Henry 115, 119
Baltimore American 18
Baltimore Orioles Base Ball Club (American League) 169, 192, 194–95
Baltimore Orioles Base Ball Club (National League) 8, 27, 30, 39, 134–35, 137, 141, 150, 151–54, 160, 162–68, 172–74, 194, 196
Baltimore Sun 18
Balzac, Honore de 21
Baring Brothers and Company 132
Barnie, William 123, 126, 128

Barondess, Joseph 18
Barton, Clara 86
Baseball: as American national game 1–5, 10, 195–97; club and team 30–31; compared to theater 25–26; lawsuits in 96, 102, 113–20, 128–29, 181–82, 186; liquor and 5–10, 13, 31–32, 36, 103; luck in 28; racism and 2; reserve system 30–31, 92, 95–96, 101, 116–20, 136, 169; rules 3, 60, 69–70, 75, 95–96, 134, 196; skill 26–29; statistics 134; styles of play 39, 196; on Sunday 31, 37; syndicate schemes in 170–91; time 29, 197; umpires 40–42
Baudelaire, Charles 21
Begley, Edward 60–61
Bell, Digby 64, 81, 150
Berlin, Irving 26
Bevens, Floyd 26
Billings, Josh 23–24
Boldt, Fred 80
Boston Base Ball Club (American Association) 128
Boston Base Ball Club (American League) 169
Boston Base Ball Club (Players' League) 106–07, 127–28
Boston Braves Base Ball Club (National League) 15, 110
Boston Red Stockings Base Ball Club (National League) 13, 27, 30, 36, 43–44, 63, 67, 69, 74, 77, 80, 85, 87–90, 93, 95, 108, 110, 121, 126, 132, 135, 137–38, 140–41, 149, 152, 162, 167, 171, 173, 175, 177, 179, 181, 185
Bowery B'hoys 49–50
Boyle, Henry 108

236 INDEX

Boyle, Jack 142
Bresnahan, Roger 195
Brodie, Steve 151
Brooklyn 2, 16, 56, 83
Brooklyn Base Ball Club (American Association) 90–91
Brooklyn Base Ball Club (National League) 2, 16, 102, 110, 114, 122, 127, 135, 143, 149–51, 157–58, 163, 166–68, 171–75, 177–79, 194
Brooklyn Base Ball Club (Players' League) 106–07, 126–27
Brooklyn Bridge 37–38, 48
Brotherhood of Professional Base Ball Players 15, 85, 91–94, 96–97, 99–103, 106–16, 118–19, 122, 124–26, 129, 131–36, 138, 140, 143, 152, 169–70
Brouthers, Dennis J. "Big Dan" 67, 151
Brown, Willard "Big Bill" 107
Brunell, Frank H. 130
Brush, John T. 96, 110, 164, 167–68, 171, 175–79, 181, 183–85, 187–88, 191, 195
Brush Classification Plan 96–97, 102, 132, 136, 146
Bryan, William Jennings 24, 188
Buckley, Dick 121
Buffalo Base Ball Club (National League) 39–40, 44, 63, 67
Buffalo Base Ball Club (Players' League) 106
Bureau of Municipal Research 190
Burkett, Jesse "Crab" 110, 121, 172
Burns, George 25
Burns, Tom 107, 158
Byrne, Charles H. 114, 123, 127, 171–72

Cahan, Abraham 18, 21, 23, 25–26
Capital National Bank of Indianapolis 147
Capone, Alphonse 26
"Casey at the Bat" 77
Caskin, Ed 33, 45
Casualty Company of America 155
Cather, Willa 23
Central Pacific Rail Road 148
Chadwick, Henry 129
Chamberlain, Elton 83
Charity Organization Society 190
Chemical National Bank of Chicago 147

Chicago Base Ball Club (American Association) 128
Chicago Base Ball Club (American League) 169
Chicago Base Ball Club (Players' League) 106, 107, 126
Chicago Burlington and Quincy Rail Road 146
Chicago White Stockings Base Ball Club (National League) 6, 8, 11, 13, 27–29, 38–40, 60, 63–69, 72, 74, 77, 79–82, 89, 93, 104, 106, 110, 113–14, 122, 127, 132, 135, 138, 140–41, 175, 177–79, 193
Choate, Joseph A. 115–17, 119
Cincinnati Base Ball Club (American Association) 140–41
Cincinnati Base Ball Club (National League) 31, 102, 110, 121–23, 140–41, 149, 162, 164, 166–67, 169, 175, 179, 181–82, 195
Cincinnati Enquirer 112
Cincinnati Red Stockings Base Ball Club 8, 72
Clapp, John 32–33, 36, 43–45, 59
Clarkson, John 74, 81, 90, 108, 110
Cleveland, Elmer 75, 79
Cleveland Base Ball Club (American League) 169
Cleveland Base Ball Club (National League) 39, 62, 89–90, 110, 123, 135, 138, 152, 163–64, 166–67, 172–74
Cleveland Base Ball Club (Players' League) 106, 127–28
Cleveland Leader 112
Cobb, Tyrus Raymond "Ty" 2, 195, 197
Cody, William "Buffalo Bill" 59
Columbia National Bank of Chicago 147
Columbus Base Ball Club (American Association) 33, 123
Comiskey, Charles A. "The Old Roman" 107
Commercial and Financial Chronicle 148
Comstock, Anthony 50
Connor, Roger 10, 11, 33, 36, 45, 67–68, 78, 81, 92–93, 107, 110, 118–19, 121, 136, 138–40, 149
Coogan's Bluff 87
Cooperation 101

INDEX 237

Cooper, Peter 38
Cooperstown, New York 10
Corcoran, Larry 28, 39–40
Crane, Ned "Cannonball" 75, 78–80, 84, 87–91, 107
Crane, Sam 157–60
Croker, Richard 41, 50, 154, 156, 158, 190
Cummings, Amos 81

Dalrymple, Abner 69, 81
Davis, George 150, 157, 168–69
Davis, Richard Harding 19
Day, Clyde "Pea Ridge" 10
Day, John B. 7, 32–33, 35, 39, 44–46, 59, 62–63, 67, 71, 73, 75, 77, 82, 84–87, 91, 100, 102, 108, 110, 112, 114–16, 118–20, 122–24, 126, 136–37, 139–40, 143–45, 149, 171
Dead Rabbit Riot (1857) 41, 49–50
Deasley, Thomas 63, 67
Delahanty, Ed 136
DeMontreville, Gene 173
Denny, Jerry 108, 110
Depew, Chauncy 5
Detroit Base Ball Club (National League) 33, 39–40, 44, 67–68, 74, 79–80
DiMaggio, Joe 2, 26
Distilling and Cattle Feeding (Whiskey Trust) 146–47
Dorgan, Mike 7, 11, 36, 43, 61, 92
Doubleday, Abner 10
Doyle, Jack "Dirty" 144, 157, 168
Doyle, Joseph 127
Draft Riot (1863) 41, 49
The Dramatic Mirror 176
Dreiser, Theodore 20
Dreyfuss, Barney 135, 166, 177, 186
Duffy, Hugh 81
Dunne, Finlay Peter (Mr. Dooley) 20
du Pont, Bidermann 97–98

Eastern League 69, 142–44
Ebbets, Charles 168, 173
Edison, Thomas 58
Engel, Nick 46, 91, 129, 136, 149
Erie Railroad 148
Erlanger, A.L. 175

Esterbrook, Tom "Dude" 11, 62, 72
The Evening World 159–60
Ewing, William "Buck" 28, 32, 36, 39–40, 43–45, 60–61, 64, 67–68, 70–72, 77–81, 87–88, 91, 93, 107–08, 110, 114, 118–21, 123, 136, 138, 140, 150, 162, 168, 197

Farrar, Geraldine 72
Farrar, Sid 72
Farrell, Duke 151
Fields, W.C. 62, 193
Financial Panics (1890, 1893) 131–32
Fiske, Harrison 176
Fiske, Minnie Maddern 176
Five Points 49
Fleishmann, Julius 195
Fleishmann, Max 195
Foster, Elmer 75, 78–79
Fourth Avenue Tunnel Gang 41, 50
Freedman, Andrew 6, 154–88, 191, 194–95
Frohman, Charles 175
Fuller, William B. "Shorty" 142
Furillo, Carl 2

Ganzel, Charles 108
George, Henry 54
George, William 72
George Bernard and Co. 105
Gerhardt, Joseph "Move-up Joe" 63, 67, 72, 92
Gillespie, Pat 11, 33, 36, 43
Glasscock, John "Pebbly Jack" 108–10, 121
Godkin, E.L. 57
Gogol, Nicolai 21
Goldsmith, Fred 39
Goodwin, Wendell 123–24, 127
Gordon, Joseph 32–33
Gore, George "Piano Legs" 11, 69, 79, 81, 139, 143
Grant, Ulysses S. 35

Hallman, Bill 118–19
Hamilton, William R. "Sliding Billy" 110
Hankinson, Frank 11, 33, 43

Hanlon, Ned 30, 98, 100, 125, 150–51, 168, 172–74
Hanna, Mark 98, 112
Harris, W.I. 112
Hart, James A. 140–41, 187
Hatfield, Gil 87, 108, 110, 136
Hayman, Al 175
Hearst, William Randolph 19
Hewitt, Abram S. 37–38, 54, 81
Holmes, James W. "Ducky" 163–64, 166–68, 170
Home Plate Saloon 46, 91, 129, 136
Hop Bitters Nine 46
Hopper, DeWolf 64, 77, 81, 91, 143, 149–50, 153–54
Horst, Harry von der 150, 152, 163–64, 168, 172
Howland, Henry 115–16
Hoyt, Wayland 56
Hulbert, William 29–32, 45, 103–04, 175, 178
Humphries, John 33, 43, 45, 59, 61, 139
Hurst, Edward 159–60
Hutchison, William F. "Wild Bill" 107

Indianapolis Base Ball Club (National League) 96, 102, 106, 108, 110, 171
I.R.T. (Interborough Rapid Transit) 155
Irwin, Arthur 125, 160

Jansen, Larry 2
Jefferson, Joseph 77, 176
Jennings, Hugh 150, 173
Jewish Daily Forward 24, 26
Johnson, Albert 97–99, 123–29, 132
Johnson, Byron Bancroft "Ban" 169, 184, 194
Johnson, Tom 97–98, 189
Johnson, Will 98
Johnstown Flood 86, 98
Joyce, William "Scrappy Bill" 160–62

Kalbfleisch, Martin 56
Kansas City Base Ball Club (American Association) 110
Kansas City Base Ball Club (National League) 95
Kansas City Grain Company 147

Keefe, Tim 10–11, 33, 47, 62, 67–68, 70–72, 74, 79–81, 83–85, 87, 90, 92–93, 97, 100, 106–08, 110, 121, 130, 138–39, 142, 162, 197
Keeler, "Wee Willie" 144, 150–51, 169, 173
Keeshan, Bob 77
Keith, B.F. 59
Kelley, Joseph 150, 173
Kelly, "Honest John" (Tammany Sachem) 8, 54, 154, 190
Kelly, Michael Joseph "King" 11, 16, 27, 39, 46, 60, 69, 81, 89, 93, 95, 107, 126, 140–41, 150
Kent, Frank 18
Ketchem, V.S. 128
King, Charles "Silver" 83, 142
Klaw, Marc 175
"Know Nothings" 10, 16, 49
Knowles, Fred 180
Koslo, David 2

Lavagetto, Harold "Cookie" 2
Lexow, Clarence 155
Lexow Commitee (1894) 52, 155
Lindsay, Vachel 24
Linton, Edward 127
Lockman, Carroll "Whitey" 2
Loman, Willy 174
Louisville Base Ball Club (National League) 31, 135–36, 141, 163, 166–67
Low, Seth 22, 56–58, 155, 189
Lucas, Henry V. 62, 132
Luciano, Charles "Lucky" 26
Lyons, Denny 142

McAlphin, E.A. 124, 139, 171
McCall, Edward 164
McCormick, James 69
McGinnity, Joe "Iron Man" 174, 195
McGraw, Blanche Sindall 192
McGraw, John 3, 15, 28, 137, 152–53, 160, 173–74, 192–95
Mack, Connie 70
McKinley, William 189
McKinnon, Alexander 60
McLaughlin, Hugh 56
Maglie, Sal 2
Mandelbaum, Frederika "Marm" 50–52

INDEX 239

Mansfield, Richard 176
Marshalltown, Iowa 8
Maryland Fidelity Guarantee Company 155
Mathewson, Christy 169, 195, 197
Mayer, Louis B. 26
Mays, Willie 2
Meekin, Jouett 151, 153, 173
Mencken, H.L. 4, 18
Menotti Gian Carlo 26
Mills, Abraham G. 5, 32, 37, 62, 77, 178
Missouri Pacific Rail Road 146
Mize, John 2
Morgan, J.P. 58–59
Mungo, Van Lingle 2
Municipal Tenement House Department 190
Murphy, Charles 190
Murphy, Pat 107–08, 110
Mutrie, "Truthful James" 7, 8, 46–47, 62–69, 72, 75, 77–80, 88, 90–91, 122, 136–40, 142–43, 157

National Association 29, 32, 103
National Cordage Trust 146–47
National League 13, 15, 29–32, 35, 37–39, 45–46, 60–63, 74, 81–82, 87, 93–118, 122–25, 127–31, 133, 135, 140–42, 152, 157, 159, 161, 163–64, 166–78, 180–88
Nativism 10–11, 15–18, 23
New York Base Ball Club (Players' League) 106–07, 119–20, 123, 126
New York City 5, 11, 15–16, 18–19, 22, 24, 27, 29, 32, 35–39, 41–42, 44–46, 48–55, 58–59, 64–66, 74–75, 81, 104, 118, 121, 123, 125–27, 132, 137, 143, 145, 154, 159, 165, 171, 176, 189–90
New York Clearing House 132, 148
New York Clipper 95, 107, 112–13
New York Commercial Advertizer 21, 24–25
New York Daily Tribune 66–67, 77, 112
New York Giants Base Ball Club (National League) 2–3, 5–8, 10–11, 15–16, 27–28, 31–48, 59–93, 100, 106–08, 110, 115–22, 126–27, 132, 135–45, 149–54, 157–69, 171, 173, 175, 179–81, 185, 191, 194–95
New York Journal 19

New York Metropolitans Base Ball Club (American Association) 32–34, 44, 46–47, 62
New York Mutuals Base Ball Club (National League) 45
New York Press 107, 112, 157, 159, 191
New York Society for the Suppression of Vice 50
New York Sun 112
New York Times 66, 95, 107, 112, 148
New York World 19
Niblo's Theatre 77
Nichols, Charles A. "Kid" 110, 121
Nicoll, De Lancey 155, 182, 186
Nimich, W.A. 106
Nops, Jerry 173
Northern Pacific Rail Road 148

O' Brian, Morgan J. 115–17, 119–20
O'Day, Hank 91, 97, 107
O'Neill, James "Tip" 33, 43–44, 59–61, 69
O'Rourke, James "Orator" 10, 11, 63, 65, 67–68, 72, 79–80, 92–93, 100, 107, 121, 138–39, 142–44
Ott, Mel 2

Page, Thomas Nelson 20
Parkhurst, Charles Dr. 155
Pearce, Grayson 33, 45
Peck and Snyder 105
Pennsylvania Rail Road 146
Pennsylvania Steel Company 147
Pfeffer, Fred 111, 136
Philadelphia Base Ball Club (American Association) 127–28
Philadelphia Base Ball Club (American League) 169
Philadelphia Base Ball Club (National League) 7, 30–32, 42–45, 70, 72, 74, 77, 79–80, 109, 119–21, 142, 149, 160, 162, 165–66, 171, 175, 177–79, 195
Philadelphia Base Ball Club (Players' League) 106, 111, 127
Pingree, Hazen 20, 189
Pittsburgh Base Ball Club (National League) 69, 71–72, 74, 79, 87–90, 106, 110, 122–23, 135, 150–51, 163, 166, 168, 175, 177–79, 186

Pittsburgh Base Ball Club (Players' League) 106, 126
Pittsburgh Post 112
Players' League (1890) 8, 13, 15–16, 99–103, 106–08, 110–14, 116–19, 121–34, 136, 141, 145
Plunkitt, George Washington 16
Polo Grounds 7, 33, 35–37, 40, 42, 44, 59–60, 64, 70, 72, 74, 77, 79–80, 84, 86–87, 89, 120–21 137–38, 142–43, 148–49, 157, 159–60, 163, 165
Populists 10
Powers, Patrick Thomas 142–44
Price, James L. 60–61
Prince, Charles A. 127–28
Protective Association of Professional Baseball Players 169, 176
Providence Base Ball Club (National League) 15, 33, 37, 61, 67, 132
Pulitzer, Joseph 19

Radbourne, Charles "Old Hoss" 37, 43, 61
Raines Excise Law 156
Reach, Albert 166, 171
Reading Rail Road 146–47
Reed, Thomas 182
Reitz, Henry 151
Restell, Madame "Ann Trow Lohman" 50
Richardson, Abram Harding "Hardy" 67
Richardson, Danny 60, 72, 92, 107, 118–19, 140, 142
Richter, Francis 113
Ripley, William Z. 17
Roberts, Robin 2
Robinson, T.B. 124
Robinson, Wilbert 137, 173
Robison, Frank 135, 164, 166–67, 172, 174–75, 177, 179, 183–84
Robison, Stanley 135, 174
Rochester Base Ball Club (American Association) 128
Rogers, John Col. 102, 114, 118, 166, 179–80
Roosevelt, Theodore 5, 20, 42, 54, 189–90
Rowe, Jack 67
Rusie, Amos 110, 121–22, 138–40, 142, 145, 151, 153, 157, 159–62, 165
Ruth, George "Babe" 33

St. Lawrence River Skiff, Canoe, and Stern Company 105
St. Louis Base Ball Club (National League) 31, 64, 95, 141, 143, 151, 163, 166, 171–72, 174–75, 177, 179, 181
St. Louis Browns Base Ball Club (American Association) 6, 27, 59, 63, 69, 82–84, 90, 107, 132
Sandberg, Ryne 2
Selee, Frank 110
Seymour, James B. "Cy" 165, 169
Sharrott, John 28
Sherman Silver Purchase Act (1890) 147–48
Shindle, Bill 151
Slattery, Michael J. 11, 75, 78–79, 91
Slaughter, Enos 2
Soden, Arthur 167, 171, 173, 175, 179–80, 185–87
Spahn, Warren 2
Spalding, Albert G. 6–10, 13, 69, 81–82, 85, 93–97, 99, 102–06, 108, 112–14, 123–28, 130, 132, 164, 171, 174–75, 178–88
Spalding, Walter 104
Spalding Guides 104, 129
Spanish-American War 19–22, 163
Spink, A.H. 83
Sporting Life 99, 112–13, 176, 183–84
The Sporting News 99, 112–13, 176, 183
Stallings, George 110
Star Theatre 81
Steffins, Linoln 21
Stern, Aaron 122
Strong, Willliam 155, 157, 160
Sunday, Billy 6, 8–10, 13, 69, 81, 106
Syracuse Base Ball Club (American Association) 128

Talcolt, E.B. 123–24, 126–27, 132, 139, 149, 154, 171, 182, 185
Tammany Hall 16, 22, 24, 41, 49–54, 58, 84, 154–56, 158, 161, 165, 189–91
Tarbell, Ida M. 189
Tarkington, Booth 23
Taylor, Luther H. "Dummy" 169
Temple, William C. 152, 187
Temple Cup 153–54, 157, 162, 168
Thompson, Samuel L. "Big Sam" 109–10

Thomson, Bobby 2
Thurman, Allan W. 123, 125, 128
Tiernan, Michal "Silent Mike" 11, 69, 78–79, 83, 107–08, 110, 121, 138, 145
Titcomb, Ledell 73, 76, 79, 87
Tocqueville, Alexis de 113
Toledo Base Ball Club (American Association) 128
Treadway, George 151
Troy, John "Dasher" 11, 33, 36, 45
Troy Base Ball Club (National League) 31–33
Twain, Mark ix, 5, 48
Tweed, William M. "Boss" 37–38, 50, 54

Union Association 62, 75
United States Immigration Commission 18, 21
United States Industrial Commission 17–18, 189

Valentino, Rudolph 25
Van Cott, Cornelius 124, 139
Vanderbilt, Cornelius 53
Van Haltren, George 151, 168
Veiller, Lawrence 190–91

Wagner, George 127–28
Wagner, Honus 2, 166, 195
Wagner, J. Earle 127–28
Wald, Lillian 18
Wall Street 146–47, 151
Wallack's Theatre 77
Ward, John Montgomery 5–6, 10–11, 15–16, 27–28, 33, 36, 39, 43, 45–46, 60, 64–65, 67–72, 74, 77–80, 84–85, 90, 92–97, 99–103, 106–08, 110–21, 124–27, 129–32, 136, 149–54, 159, 162, 186–87
Washington Base Ball Club (American Association) 7, 59
Washington Base Ball Club (American League) 169
Washington Base Ball Club (National League) 70, 76, 85, 89, 102, 110, 141–43, 149, 151, 160, 163, 166–67
Watkins, Harvey 157
Welch, Michael "Smiling Mickey" 11, 32–33, 39–40, 43, 45, 60–61, 63–65, 67, 72, 77, 79, 83–84, 87, 91–92, 107–08, 110, 121–22, 136, 138–39, 143
Westervelt, Huyler 151
White, James "Deacon" 67
Whitney, Arthur 79, 81
Will, George 199, 233
Whyos 50
Williams, Alexander S. "Clubber" 52–53, 155
Wood, Fernando 48–49, 53–54
Worcester Base Ball Club (National League) 31–32
Wright, Harry 8, 37, 72, 151
Wright and Ditson 105
Wrigley Field (Chicago) 2

Yale University 107
Yekl 21, 23–26
Young, Denton True "Cy" 169, 172
Young, Nicholas 62, 94, 99, 142, 145, 162, 164, 166, 179–82, 184–86

www.ingramcontent.com/pod-product-compliance
Ingram Content Group UK Ltd.
Pitfield, Milton Keynes, MK11 3LW, UK
UKHW041939140426
5217IPUK00014B/566